Regime and Religion

Shrewsbury 1400–1700

Regime and Religion

Shrewsbury 1400–1700

by

Barbara Coulton

LOGASTON PRESS
Little Logaston Woonton Almeley
Herefordshire HR3 6QH
logastonpress.co.uk

First published by Logaston Press 2010

ISBN 978 1 906663 47 6

Typeset in Garamond by Logaston Press
and printed in Malta by
Gutenberg Press

Contents

Acknowledgments

My thanks are due to all staff, past and present, of Shropshire Archives, Shrewsbury; Lancaster University, History Department and Library; Lichfield Record Office, Staffordshire; Hereford Cathedral and Diocesan Archives; John Rylands Library, Deansgate, Manchester; British Library, London; Dr Williams's Library, London; Friends' House Archives, London; Chester Archives and Grosvenor Museum, Chester; Queens' College, St John's College and Emmanuel College, Cambridge; and Weston Park, Shropshire. I would also like to thanks the editors of academic journals which have published my work and the organisers of university conferences and seminars who have invited me to speak on the neglected subject of Reformation and post-Reformation Shropshire.

Introduction

From 1539 the antiquarian and traveller John Leland spent six years recording journeys he made in England and Wales. An early journey brought him out of Wales and into Shropshire. Between Alberbury and Shrewsbury he travelled through six miles of fertile arable, woodland and pasture, and from Shrewsbury he rode to the Augustinian abbey at Haughmond. It was on a later journey that he described Shrewsbury itself, and we can do no better than follow him. He entered 'Shrobbesshire' from Herefordshire, stopping first at the well-walled town of Ludlow, then going twenty miles on to 'Shrobbesbyri'. On his right hand he passed the woods of Wenlock Edge and the Long Forest, stocked with roe deer, then through the Strettons and Leebotwood.

> Then for four miles I crossed flat country which grew some corn, and a further two miles of better arable soil, which brought me to Shrewsbury ... As I entered Shrewsbury close to the abbey there was a three-arched stone bridge over the Meole; just below this bridge is the confluence of the Rivers Meole and Severn ... There are two large and important bridges at Shrewsbury which cross the Severn in its entirety. The greater and more attractive is the Welsh Bridge, which lies upstream of the other ... towards Wales. It stands on the western side of Shrewsbury, and at the one end of it is a large gate which allows access to the town; at the other end, facing Wales, is a mighty strong tower which prevents enemies from getting on to the bridge ... The town of Shrewsbury stands on a rocky outcrop of stiff red earth, and the River Severn encircles it to such an extent that were it not for a little neck of land it would be an island ... Shrewsbury has a strong wall of more than a mile in circuit, and is well defended by water, which may be regarded as taking the place of a town ditch. There are three gates in the town. The castle, which stands in the northern part of the town, has been a strong building, but is now largely in ruins. The town has four parish churches.[1]

The abbey lay outside the town, the churches in close proximity to each other within the walls. The main church was St Chad's, a collegiate church with a dean and ten prebendaries, under the patronage of the bishop of Lichfield. St Mary's was also a collegiate church, with a dean and nine canons, under the patronage of the king. 'St Alkmund's parish church was appropriated by Lilleshall Priory, and close to St Alkmund's is St Julian's parish church; this was appropriated by Battlefield Chapel, one mile north of Shrewsbury.' These appropriations, or use of endowments, will be explained later. Leland also noted the presence of the Franciscans (Grey Friars) and Dominicans (Black Friars). 'The Austin Friars, founded by the Stafford family, stood a little below Welsh Bridge.' The Austin Canons, as they are more properly called, open our story.

By taking Leland as our initial guide we are entering sixteenth-century Shrewsbury, some half-way through our narrative. Leland's description emphasised the defensive nature of the town, and the threat from Wales. Shrewsbury's situation, on the Severn and on the route to Coventry and London, and near the Welsh border, was of strategic importance throughout the middle ages and the period of our study, *c.*1400 to 1700. The town was a local centre of royal or government authority, so was not cut off from wider events. In any case, local history is shallow if it is not rooted in the larger scene.

With the larger scene in view, therefore, we begin with the deposition of one monarch and end with that of another. The case of Richard II in 1399 was in the minds of many connected with that of James II in 1689. Changes of regime mark the history of those times, while religion fired the conflicts and dominated the lives of the people. Shrewsbury was directly involved in many of the rebellions and wars of these centuries, while the history of an established church along with a tradition of reform proved to be of overwhelming importance. The twin themes of regime and religion are therefore the subject of this study in which we will trace changing patterns of orthodoxy and a constant undercurrent of dissent. As far as the documentary evidence allows we will be trying to enter the lives of local people and setting the history of the town in the national context.

Chapter 1
Rebellion and Religion

Our narrative begins with regime change; it will end in the same way. We begin with the political situation at the end of the fourteenth century, for which we have an eyewitness in Adam (of)Usk, a doctor of laws with patrons among families such as the Fitzalans, earls of Arundel. They were powerful in the Welsh Marches but had suffered under Richard II. Thomas Arundel, archbishop of Canterbury, was exiled and his nephew Thomas Fitzalan was deprived of his inheritance and imprisoned. The king also undermined the family that had the best claim to succeed to the throne: John duke of Lancaster and his son Henry, who was also exiled. The parliament of 1397 was resumed in January 1398 at Shrewsbury. Adam Usk writes that the king was 'hastening to his fall', keeping in his following 400 supernumeraries from the county of Cheshire, 'men of the utmost depravity who went about doing as they wished, assaulting, beating, and plundering his subjects with impunity'. These were the formidable Cheshire archers. Richard was at this time preparing to take his army to Ireland. Of the two grandsons of the great king Edward III, Richard and Henry, cousins of the same age, it was Henry who had all the kingly attributes. Richard had always proved to be an unfit king. In July 1399 Henry returned from exile as duke of Lancaster, his father John of Gaunt having died. Richard's tyranny had left him no alternative but 'to return and start a revolution'. On 2 August 1399 Lancaster came with his forces to Hereford (of which he was earl then duke), lodging at the bishop's palace. The next night he spent at the priory of Leominster, that following at the king's castle of Ludlow, before moving on to Shrewsbury. Adam Usk relates how he himself interceded with Lancaster for the release of Thomas Prestbury, 'a monk of Shrewsbury and a contemporary of his at Oxford'. Prestbury was made abbot of Shrewsbury that year, remaining there until his death in 1426.

King Richard's reluctant abdication was made on the feast of Michaelmas, 29 September 1399. He was then placed in captivity, first at Chester and finally at Pontefract, where he was murdered. Henry IV was now king and his son Henry was created Prince of Wales.[1] In September 1400 Owain Glyndwr, soon proclaimed the Welsh Prince of Wales, began his nationalist rising; his ally was subsequently to be the disaffected earl of Northumberland, Henry Percy VI. This brought Shrewsbury into prominence. On 19 September 1400 Henry IV sent a mandate to the bailiffs and good men of Shrewsbury 'to take security from all Welshmen residing within the town that they will be faithful to the king ... and to keep the town safely against the invasion of the rebels'. From Shrewsbury itself Henry sent the quartered remains of the rebel 'Grenowe ap Tuder' (Goronwy Tudor) to the sheriffs of Bristol, Ludlow, Hereford and Chester, to be displayed.[2]

Corporation seal 1425 (ID SA-IMG24344)

On 12 February 1402 letters patent approved by the king confirmed the ruling of 1389 that Shrewsbury should have two bailiffs and two chamberlains to be elected by a majority of burgesses and commonalty. Expenditure of the town's money was to be supervised by the bailiffs and six assessors to whom accounts were to be rendered along with six other persons to be elected by the commonalty. This ruling was made for the tranquillity of the town, while Robert Thornes and Nicholas Gerard 'who were the cause of the dissension of the town' were to be bound to keep the peace under the penalty of £1,000 each and final expulsion from the town. Some of the expenditure was on the upkeep of walls and bridges, murage and pontage. The common seal of the town was to be placed in a common chest with the treasure and account books, under eight locks.[3] In 1377 the inhabitants of Shrewsbury aged 14 years or more, 'including 100 persons discovered moving from street to street to evade the collectors of the poll tax', numbered 2,083, 'indicating a probable total population of more than 3,000 and a town comparable in size with Gloucester and larger than any other strictly within the Welsh march'. It had three annual fairs and was 'probably the most important trading centre along the river [Severn].' The town, a royal borough, sent two representatives to parliament; some of them were in royal service as administrators. We have, therefore, a picture of a busy town, burgesses acting as borough officials and a developing system of local government, with two bailiffs elected annually. In July 1403 Shrewsbury was at the centre of events: the king trapped the rebel Hotspur, the son of the earl of Northumberland, outside the town, an advance troop holding the gates and bridges, while he led the main army (Plate 1). At the site of the battle on 21 July the king later founded the collegiate church of Battlefield, one of his three religious foundations.[4]

Religion permeated secular life. Once again we have a local guide, writing *circa* 1400: John Mirk, a canon of Lilleshall. This abbey, lying east of Shrewsbury, was closely connected to the town since it was founded from endowments of St Alkmund's, a church then in decay and without priests. The Augustinian or Austin canons, while semi-monastic, were particularly concerned with parochial and pastoral duties. (The houses of the Augustinians were mostly ranked as abbeys even if they were insignificant in size.) There was also the house noted by Leland, lying near Welsh Bridge. Of course, the town had the preaching friars, but the Austin canons are of special interest. They were part of the diocese to which they belonged as much as secular priests. Lilleshall was founded between 1145 and 1148, a decade after the sister house at Haughmond, also near Shrewsbury.[5] Shrewsbury was the centre of the westernmost archdeaconry of what was at this time the third largest English diocese (after York and Lincoln): the diocese of

Coventry and Lichfield. To the north and east of the archdeaconry of Shrewsbury were those of Chester, Stafford, Derby and Coventry. Lilleshall Abbey lay in Shropshire where it owned several granges (farming demesnes) including Atcham, near Shrewsbury; there it had the grant of a three-day fair. The lands of St Alkmund's brought in additional income.[6] It is probable therefore that Mirk visited Shrewsbury where a provincial chapter was held at the Augustinian house in 1400. Two of Mirk's works were popular and much copied: his *Festial*, a collection of homilies in the vernacular (in West Midland dialect) and his *Instructions for Parish Priests,* also in the vernacular, in lively octosyllabic couplets.[7] These works take us within the religion of the time. Two of the homilies were apt for Shrewsbury: those for the feasts of St Alkmund and St Winifred. Each short homily is followed by one or more stories. For the latter feast these tell of the beheading of the Welsh virgin and her restoration to life by her uncle, and of how her bones were brought to the new abbey of Shrewsbury where a great multitude came when her miracles began. Another story tells how three Shrewsbury men were bitten by 'an adyrcope that some call a vryn' – a spider. Two men died but the third prayed to the saint and was saved. Mirk's homily exhorts the congregation to 'do worschip to this holy maydyn and martyr'. These English homilies 'set out to give the common people that simple instruction in points of ritual and religious duties ... everything that the Church deemed needful for the ordinary man and woman to know'.[8]

The Fourth Lateran Council (held in Rome in 1215) promoted efforts to provide a better-educated clergy to help the laity understand the essentials of Christian belief and practice. Bishops were to teach regularly; parish priests should reside in their parishes with a reasonable income and security; the laity should be married in church and at least once a year make confession and receive holy communion. There were various fourteenth-century Latin manuals for priests, notably the *Oculis Sacerdotis* by the Berkshire parish priest William of Pagula. John Mirk drew in part on this work, but his *Instructions* were in English – in the dialect used in Shropshire and neighbouring parts. It has been described as 'the best-known 15th-century manual of religious instruction in English'.[9] Mirk's work begins with a familiar adage (the blind leading the blind):

> God seyth hym-self, as wryten we fynde,
> That whenne the blynde ledeth the blynde,
> Into the ditch they fallen both,
> For they ne sen where-by to go.

The parish priest is instructed how to guide his parishioners through the creed and other articles of faith, and how to teach them about the seven sacraments, the seven deadly sins, the seven virtues, and so on. The priest is himself instructed as to his behaviour and dress. He is not to be greedy, not to frequent taverns, not to engage in trade, not to take part in sports such as wrestling and shooting, or leisure pursuits such as hawking, hunting and dancing. Nor must the priest wear 'cuttede clothes and pykede schone'. Whether any priests did wear fashionable slashed garments or tapering shoes we cannot say. They are enjoined to wear 'honeste clothes' and to shave beard and crown. They must be hospitable to all, but must forsake 'wymmones service'. They must despise earthly vanity. Their care must be for their parishioners: women in childbirth are especially mentioned. Husbands as well as wives must be corrected if they have sinned. Instructions are given for administering baptism and hearing confession, and for preparing a child for confirmation by the bishop. Then there is the matter of weddings and forbidden degrees; objections may be raised openly at the church door.

The parishioners are also to be instructed in how to behave at mass and at the taking of the sacrament, both host and wine. There is their posture, for instance:

No man in chyrch stonde schal,
Ne lene to pillar ny to wall,
But fayre on knees they schule hem sette,
Knelyng doun up-on the flette [floor]
And pray to god wyth herte meke
To give hem grace and mercy eke.

They are to stand for the reading of the gospel but when that is done

Teche hem again to knele doun sone;
And whenne they hear the belle rynge
To that holy sakerynge [consecration]
Teche hem knele downe, both young and olde,
And bothe here hondes up to holde ...

When they see a priest pass in the street carrying the host they are also to kneel, to worship the God who made all things. When the priest took the host to the sick it was to be placed in a pyx (a closed box) and carried solemnly, accompanied by candles and bells. Lying behind these strictures is the doctrine that the bread and wine were actually changed into the body and blood of Christ, in essence, by the words of consecration. This doctrine was defended by the Norman archbishop of Canterbury Lanfranc and was further defined (as 'transubstantiation') at the Fourth Lateran Council.[10] The feast of Corpus Christi was instituted in the early fourteenth century: it was held in late May or June on the Thursday after Trinity Sunday and became an occasion for community celebration. The borough assembly minute book for 1389-90 includes an 'Order for the procession of craftsmen of the town of Shrewsbury on the feast of Corpus Christi. Millers Bakers Fishermen Cooks Butchers Tanners Shoemakers Smiths Saddlers Carpenters Fletchers Coopers and Bowers [bowyers] Weavers Shearmen together with Barbers [and] Apothecaries'.[11] These celebrations were developed in some cities, such as Coventry and Chester, into a whole cycle of plays on the fall of man, and his redemption by Christ's death. One of Mirk's homilies, for the feast of Corpus Christi, tells the story of Holy Week:

> For right as each cristen man and woman that wol be saved must nede have perfite charite in the Trinite, right so must he have fayth and beleve in the sacrament of Christ's body that is made in the altar by vertu of the holy wordys that the prest sayed there, and by working of the Holy Gost.

The efficacy of holy images is expounded:

> For as Saynt Austyn sayde: 'The memory of Christ's passion is the best defence against temptations of the fiend.' And therfor roodes and othyr ymages ben necessary in holy chirch, whatever these Lollardes sayn.

So we come to the pre-Reformation dissenters, followers of the Oxford theologian John Wycliffe. Their enemies called them Lollards.[12] The term was a borrowing from the Low Countries where it denoted a heretic. The eucharist became a central feature of Lollard thought. 'If it was not a movement with a coherent system of belief ... still Lollardy has an important place in cultural and religious history for its significance in bringing theology into the English language.'[13] Mirk's homily directly addressed Lollard teaching.

The people of Shrewsbury had experience of this heterodox teaching, 'heretical' in the Church's terms, when William Thorpe was allowed use of the pulpit of St Chad's. Thorpe and his Shropshire associate John Pollyrbach (Pulverbatch?) were described as chaplains.

They did not have the bishop's permission to preach and the dean was an absentee; perhaps a minor canon gave permission. It was on Sunday 17 April 1407, three weeks after Easter. They were treading on dangerous ground: by a statute of 1401 (*De Haeretico Comburendo*) heretics risked death by burning, and there was other legislation against unlicensed preaching, suspect books, and unauthorised schools or 'conventicles'.[14] Mass was being celebrated in one of the side chapels of St Chad's as Thorpe ascended the pulpit, facing a standing congregation.

> As I stood there in the pulpitte, busying me to teach the commands of God, someone rang a sacring bell and therefore much people turned away roughly and with great noise ran from me. And I, seeing this, said to them thus 'Good men you were better to stand here still and to hear God's word! For certes, the virtue and the value of the most holy sacrament of the altar standeth much more in the belief thereof that ye ought to have in your souls than it doith in the outward sight thereof. And therefore you were better to stand still quietly and to hear God's worde, since through hearinge thereof men come to true belief.'[15]

Popular belief may be illustrated from Mirk's Corpus Christi homily: those who had been shriven and were repentant and who attended both evensongs of the feast and mass and matins would gain a hundred days pardon (from the pains of purgatory) for each attendance, and forty days more for every hour spent in worship. During that time a worshipper would suffer no loss of sight nor sudden death, 'and longe as the masse lesteth he schal not waxe olde; and his angele telleth each pass that he goeth to the chirch in gret worschip to hym' (as recorded in Mirk's *Festial*, 169-70). Even gazing on the host was believed to bring benefits, which is why many of the congregation left the sermon for the mass. Thorpe admonished his audience on other points of orthodox teaching: he condemned the veneration of images and relics, and going on pilgrimages. With a shrine to St Winifred and, it was believed, her bones at the abbey, and the town on the route to Holywell, this must have dismayed many. Here is Thorpe on pilgrimages (lines 1296-331):

> As I said in Schrousberie, though they ... spend much money to seek and visit the bones or the image of that saint or of that, such pilgrimage is neither praiseable nor thankful to God neither to any saint of God, since in effect all such pilgrims despise God and all his saints ... seeing that such people waste blamefully God's goods in their vain pilgrimage ... upon vicious hostelries and upon tapsters, which be often

> unclean women of their bodies, and at the last those goods, of which they should do the works of mercy after God's command to poor needy men and women ... these runners about offer to rich priests which have much more livelihood than they need ... I know well that when divers men and women will go thus after their own wills and devices out on pilgrimage, they will ordain beforehand to have with them both men and women that can well sing roaring songs, and also some of these pilgrims will have with them bagpipes so that in each town that they come through, what with the noise of their singing, and with the sound of their piping, and with the jingling of their harness bells, and with the barking out of dogs after them, these maken more noise than if the king came with his trumpeters and many other minstrels. And ... many of them a half year after shall be great boasters, tale tellers and liars.

The last statement is close to that of the West Midlands poet William Langland in his great work *The Vision of Piers Plowman* (written at a date before 1385): pilgrims and palmers 'had licence to lie for the rest of their lives ... Whatever tale they told, their tongues were attuned to lying'. The reference to offerings given to priests to say masses would not have gone down well in the collegiate church of St Chad's with its chantries, altars where a priest said masses and prayers for a donor and his family, or for their souls after death. Lollards did not believe in the efficacy of prayers for the dead, nor in a place of punishment and purgation in the afterlife (purgatory). Thorpe also insisted that true pilgrimage was a spiritual journey and that the true priest's duty was to preach the word of God. This was why Wycliffites produced the Bible in English, so that everyone could have access to scripture. In the 1390s the distribution of these was speedy and widespread.[16]

Thorpe was arrested on the order of bailiffs John Perle and John Scryven. The next day, questioned at the abbey by Abbot Prestbury, he affirmed his Lollard beliefs. The abbot and the bailiffs wrote to Archbishop Thomas Arundel, the chancellor. The bailiffs had the advice of a burgess, David Holbache, who had represented Shropshire in the 1406 parliament. In December a statute had been passed against Lollards, and this the bailiffs cited in their letter. In response Arundel issued a writ in Chancery (*Habeas Corpus Cum Causa),* to be returned with a schedule attached giving the reason for Thorpe's detention. (According to his own account he was in the town gaol for at least a month.) The writ, issued on 16 June 1407, ordered the transfer of Thorpe and Pollyrbache to Westminster.[17] These events must have caused a stir in Shrewsbury. During this period the feast of Corpus Christi fell on 26 May: perhaps Mirk's sermon was preached then, against 'these

Lollards'. His sermon for the previous Sunday, Trinity Sunday, also attacked Lollards for their smooth and pleasing words that led people away from the faith of the holy Church

The Abbey Church (interior) (SA-IMG24337)

(*Festial*, 164). The rest of the story is told by Thorpe himself in his *Testimony*, a skilfully presented dialogue between the preacher, reasonable and calm, and an increasingly irate Archbishop Arundel; the victor of this contest is of course Thorpe. There is no record that he was ever put on trial and he may have escaped to the continent. His *Testimony* survived to provide reading for Lollards and excellent Protestant propaganda. 'Possession of or familiarity with the text appears to have been one of the certain signs by which the "known man" was betrayed to the church authorities.' (Wycliffe himself used the term *secta*, sect, for the 'known men'.) Circulated first in manuscript, the work was later printed in Antwerp in 1530. Three early Protestant luminaries – William Tyndale, John Bale, and John Foxe – all participated in the editing, translating, or printing of Thorpe's narrative.[18] In Shrewsbury in 1407 orthodoxy prevailed: Holbache was appointed to the Shropshire peace commission; a kinsman, Hugh Holbache, a doctor of canon law, was appointed dean of the king's free chapel of St Mary's, the other collegiate church in the town. The bailiffs' accounts record the payment to entertainers at the betrothal of another of Holbache's kinsmen, 'for the honour of the town'.[19]

Thomas Arundel, archbishop and chancellor, was a determined opponent of Wycliffism or Lollardy. In this, according to its leading scholar, 'is found a sequence unusual in medieval times, of a heresy that began as a product of academic speculation but that moved out of the academic world to become a popular movement'. The collaboration between Wycliffe's academic disciples and Lollard gentry helped the movement's rise during the early phase, between 1381 and 1413,[20] but it is not clear if they saw themselves as a 'church'. Their views on the eucharist (opposed to the doctrine of transubstantiation), the sacraments, images, pilgrimages and prayers to saints were 'heretical'. They saw Christ as the only mediator between God and man, and priesthood as belonging to all believers. The Bible was the prime source of religious knowledge, *sola scriptura.* They questioned the status of priests and the power of the hierarchy. The papacy was untrustworthy – the outbreak of the papal schism in 1378 reinforced Wycliffe's view. (On the death of Gregory XI in March 1378 the cardinals elected Urban VI (1378-89), a violent and overbearing pontiff, soon repudiated by some of the cardinals, who elected instead the Cardinal Bishop of Geneva as Clement VII – this faction established itself at Avignon. The Church was divided: two popes, rival colleges of cardinals, rival bishops and abbots.) As for church buildings, Wycliffe held ornamentation to be undesirable – it would be more meritorious to give money to the poor. There were others of like mind. The layman Walter Brut of Herefordshire wrote his testimony on the eucharist in Latin, for Bishop John Trefnant. The bishop's registers for 1395-7 mention 'libros Anglicos' of those 'quondam Lollardos vulgariter nominatos'.[21] This phrase echoes through the commissions issued during the early years of the fifteenth century, to arrest and imprison 'persons vulgarly called Lollards'. Commissions were sent in April 1407 to Coventry and in May to Shropshire: to Thomas abbot of Shrewsbury, Thomas earl of Arundel, Edward lord of Powys, Hugh lord of Burnell, Thomas le Yonge, John Burley, David Holbech, Thomas Lee and the bailiffs in the towns of Shrewsbury, Bridgnorth and Ludlow. Later commissions extended the scope from East Anglia through the Midlands to the West Country. At Oxford in 1410 Arundel enacted thirteen 'constitutions' against Lollards, the first four dealing with preaching.[22]

When newly king, Henry IV had made an oath to uphold orthodox religion. He was pious, had made the pilgrimage to the Holy Sepulchre at Jerusalem, and saw Lollardy as a serious threat to the Church (as indeed it was). Henry's biographer asks how 'a would-be merciful king enacted *de heretico comburendo*', of the burning of heretics. He answers:

> It was meant to be the ultimate threat [twice used in his reign] ... but it was also meant to show that Henry was as firmly committed to stamping out religious dissent as he was to eradicating its political equivalent, treason. Mercy was all very well in theory, but ... there were limits to how merciful a king could be.[23]

In 1410 we find heresy and potential rebellion coming together: Archbishop Thomas Arundel instituted an enquiry into a priest maintained in the house in Kent of Sir John Oldcastle of Herefordshire. John Thomson suggests, although it cannot be proved, that Oldcastle 'may have been attracted to heresy when still young, as the area in which he grew up had seen manifestations of religious radicalism during these years'. Oldcastle served Henry IV as a military leader in the Welsh wars; he also served as sheriff of Herefordshire. In 1410 Oldcastle was in touch with Jan Hus of Bohemia, which led the English authorities to suspect him of unorthodoxy.[24]

Henry V was likewise faced by the problem of disorder, in particular on the Welsh Marches. The revolt of Sir John Oldcastle at the end of 1413 resulted in persecution of the Lollards, whose leader Oldcastle aspired to be. Lollardy itself was made a felony, punishable by death. The second parliament of the reign, held at Leicester in May 1414, passed a statute empowering all royal officials to investigate and co-operate with the ecclesiastical authorities in persecuting Lollards. 'But the acts of parliament were not as significant as the despatch of the court of King's Bench', on a circuit through Staffordshire and Shropshire.' Nearly 1,800 indictments were received.[25] The court of king's bench never left Westminster during the previous reign. 'It is all the more striking therefore, that Henry V chose to revive the superior eyre [circuit] as the centrepiece of his campaign for law enforcement in 1414.' It sat in Shrewsbury from 15 to 30 June, presided over by Edward duke of York, the king's cousin. Just over a hundred of those summoned in Shropshire were Welshmen, all but three of whom failed to appear: living in Wales or the Marches, they were beyond the jurisdiction of the sheriff, Sir Robert Corbet. The king's real objective was, it seems, to separate the warring factions of the Welsh and English and to restore observance of the peace. Having escaped from the Tower of London, Oldcastle was at large during 1415 and 1416 but the following year returned to his Herefordshire manor of Almeley, and was finally captured near Welshpool in November. Taken to Westminster where parliament was in session, he was condemned as a heretic and traitor on 14 December and was immediately burned.[26]

One assessment of Henry V sees him as the dominant leader of church and state, persecuting the Lollards because he saw them as traitors as well as heretics. He also tried unsuccessfully to enforce reform on the English Benedictine monasteries, 'and at the same time [he] rigidly excluded the pope from the exercise of any practical power in the English church'.[27] The question at that time was, which pope? The Council of Pisa in 1409 tried to deal with the matter of the rival popes, Gregory XII of Rome and Benedict XIII of Avignon, by deposing them and electing Alexander V: since neither Rome nor Avignon accepted this, there were now three popes. In 1415 the Council of Constance deposed John XXIII, the 'anti-pope', and Benedict XIII, the Avignon pope, and allowed the Roman pope Gregory XII to abdicate, electing instead Martin V (1417-31). 'The high papal prestige and unchallenged papalist theory of the era of Innocent III [1198-1216], however, was gone for ever.' The Council of Constance decreed that even the pope was answerable to the Church in council.[28] It was Martin V who made Henry Beaufort, bishop of Winchester and the king's uncle, a cardinal, without Henry's assent. The elevation was quashed by the king, 'an impressive reflection of Henry's will to be master in his own house, in church as well as in state'.'[29] In 1416, Adam Usk records, 'the king most devoutly made a pilgrimage on foot from Shrewsbury to St Winefride's well in north Wales'. The shrine was in the vicinity of the ambushing of Richard II in 1399. Owain Glyndwr had by this time died and been buried secretly. The Welsh revolt was over, and 'the Welsh people would henceforth have to cultivate their identity as a people within the experience of conquest, not in protest against it'.[30]

Henry was in Shrewsbury again in early March 1421 when he received and answered many petitions. This was a programme of reconciliation, 'lovedays' (*dies amoris)* when wine was provided by the borough. One of those who now accepted a pardon was Meredudd, son of Glendower: this stated that although Owen had rebelled against the crown his son had lived peaceably, coming into the king's presence in the spirit of humility. Holy writ is cited (Ezekiel, 18, 20): 'The son shall not bear the iniquity of the father.'[31] This seems a revealing quotation in view of the nature of Henry IV's succession. Henry V returned to France to pursue his claim to that throne; he died there in 1422, leaving a nine-month-old son and a council to take over the government. Henry's forceful actions combined with his piety foreshadowed another King Henry – but he was cut short by death.

As orthodoxy prevailed over heterodoxy in religion Wycliffism went underground: those holding such dissident views would not necessarily cast them aside, but nor would they seek martyrdom. There is little to fill in the gap between early Lollards and later dissenter groups, between the 1430s and the 1480s, so this topic must for the moment be laid aside. For an insight into churchgoing of the orthodox kind we can return to Mirk's *Festial* which takes us through the liturgical year. On Advent Sunday the preacher (whether Mirk or some other) addresses the congregation:

> Good men and woymen, thys day, as ye known well, ys cleped [called] Sunday in the Advent; that ys, the Sunday of Cristys comyng. Wherfor thys day holy chyrch makyth mention of the two comings of Crist, Godys son, yn to thys world, forto buy mankind out of the devil's bondage, and to bryng hym and welldoers to the bliss that ever schall last. And his other comyng, that schall be at the day of doom, forto deme [judge] all wykitdoers ynto the pyt of hell for evermore. But the former comyng of Cryst ynto thys world broght joy and blysse with hym; therfor holy chyrch useth some songs of melody, as Alleluja and other.

As it happens there is a rare survival of music written to be sung at this time in the Lichfield diocese, perhaps in the cathedral: it occurs in fragments of ecclesiastical plays, English and Latin verses spoken or sung in polyphony by characters in 'The Angels and the Shepherds', 'The Three Maries at the Sepulchre', and 'The Two Disciples going to Emmaus'. These survivals were until recently known (misleadingly) as 'The Shrewsbury Fragments' but have been re-labelled the 'Lichfield Processional'.[32] Mirk also refers to melodies for the second coming of Christ, in judgement, in those days of dread. The damned soul will face Christ, 'his domes-man so wroth, that no tongue can tell', while on the other side fiends will claim him as theirs: 'under hym hell yawning, and gaping, and spyttyng fyre and stench forto swallow hym unyo the payne that never schall have ende'. In his fine study of medieval preaching, commenting on a similar scene in the sermon for Saint Bartholomew's day, G.R. Owst suggests that Mirk 'seems to be actually reading off to us from the walls of some ancient Shropshire church where he is preaching'.[33]

We have added to our insider's view of church-going: not just sermons and stories but also music and wall-paintings. We also learn incidentally of customs, as in the Easter sermon. The hall 'schall thys day be arrayed with green rushes, and sweet flowers strewed all aboute, showing an high example to all men and woymen that, ryght as they maken clene the howse all wythyn, bearing out the fyre and strewing flowers, ryght so ye schall cleanse the howse of your soule'. On the eve of Whitsun they must fast and cleanse their souls, to receive the Holy Ghost and his various graces. For the high feast of the Assumption of Mary on 15 August Mirk visualises the (non-scriptural) scene, reminding people to come to church 'and worschip our holy lady wyth all your might and conyng [knowledge]'. A verse litany with responses is included in this homily. We may single out from the numerous saints' days that of St Alkmund, as being especially relevant to Shrewsbury: as patron of the churches dedicated to him he is their defender – the role of saints in heaven. Mirk tells the history of St Alkmund, in pre-Norman times, an anachronistic 'duke of the Marche and Wales, and was a cursed liver', but gives no details of his sins. Alkmund died in battle, fighting for God's people, an apt patron for Shrewsbury.

There were also the ceremonies outside the church, such as the Corpus Christi procession, when the consecrated host, carried by a priest in a pyx or a monstrance, was the centrepiece. The various crafts, mentioned earlier, proceeded to a stone cross some two miles south-east of the town where the people bewailed their sins and prayed for a plentiful harvest. The procession returned in the same order to the church of St Chad, where each group was assigned a place in the choir. There is no suggestion that the procession in Shrewsbury resembled that in Coventry, for instance, where ten pageants or stages were paraded through the city with enactments of scenes from the lives of Christ and his mother. The mercers there, with their trade in luxury goods like silks, performed the Assumption of Mary. The text of the Coventry Shearmen and Taylors' play survives: it tells in verse of the annunciation, the nativity, Herod and the three kings (great potential for display and drama), and the killing of the Holy Innocents. It ends with the song 'Lully, lulla' (the 'Coventry Carol'). Later the mercers of Shrewsbury would be fined for absconding to Coventry on Corpus Christi day – one can understand the temptation. The Mercers' Company at Shrewsbury maintained a priest at St Chad's to officiate daily at the altar of their patron, St Michael. Likewise, the Drapers, originally the gild of the Blessed Trinity, had the Trinity chapel in St Mary's church. The Shearmen had a chantry in St Julian's.[34]

Processions such as that at Corpus Christi and other feasts were official and communal. 'In most English towns the unit for organisation became the craft gild, and the regulating body, by necessity, the town council, whose function in all town business was to arbitrate and mediate between disparate bodies.'[35] The borough of Shrewsbury also developed its system of local government, with a new 'composition' in 1433. In many respects it was a repetition of that of 1389, but election day was altered to the Friday, instead of the Sunday, after the feast of St Giles (1 September). The official formerly called the 'common clerk' was now termed the 'town clerk'. In 1444 the burgesses petitioned the House of Commons that the composition be perpetuated: the council of twelve burgesses assisting the bailiffs were now called 'aldermen'. Among those named were Roger Eyton, Thomas Thornes (son of Robert), Thomas Ottley and Richard Stury – members of families which will recur through the town's history. The assemblies of the common council (representing the whole body of burgesses) were to be held in the Guildhall. Elections were now fixed for the Friday after the feast of St Michael (29 September).[36] Sessions of justices of the peace were held in the town early in 1438 when expenses were incurred for 'wine to the great town inquest at the session of the justices of the peace held on Tuesday the morrow of St Hilary in the sixteenth year [of the reign of Henry VI, i.e. 14 January 1438] and for the earl of Stafford's minstrels being at Shrewsbury at the same time'.

During 1444 to 1446 there are payments relating to processions held on the eve of the nativity of St John (the feast was on 24 June), the eve of the feast of the apostles Peter and Paul (29 June), and expenses 'of Lady Talbot, the wife of Master John Talbot, at her breakfast and on wine dispensed for the said lady in her structure [presumably a platform and seating constructed for her] at a play outside the walls in Whitsun week for two days of the said week'. (There is clearer evidence later of Whitsun plays performed at Shrewsbury, outside the walls, but we do not know when they began.) The sum spent on Lady Talbot was large: 76s 6d. This lady must have been Elizabeth Butler, who married John Talbot, heir of the military hero Sir John Talbot, before March 1445. The Talbots were from Shropshire, the elder Sir John serving with Henry V in Wales and later in France; he continued the latter service under Henry VI, who created him earl of Shrewsbury in 1442. The earl and a younger son were killed at Castillon in 1453. 'The nobility had by far the largest stake in the Hundred Years' War which fittingly ended with the slaying of two members of the ancient house of Talbot.' The second earl would die fighting for Henry VI at Northampton in 1460.[37]

It is clear from the items noted in the borough accounts that May and June were busy with festive occasions. To take 1450 as an example: Whit Sunday fell on May 24, Corpus Christi on 4 June (these were movable feasts), with the feasts of St John and Saints Peter and Paul, as usual, on 24 and 29 June. Prominent in the processions were minstrels who preceded the bailiffs and 'other honourable and legal men'. The records of fifteenth-century boroughs show that royal and magnate entertainers made regular tours of provincial towns, a custom continued in Tudor times with players and interluders in addition. In 1450 the minstrel of the lord earl of Shrewsbury was in Shrewsbury, as were the 'entertainers' (also referred to as minstrels, a term which originally might mean only servants or 'minstrelli') of the lord duke of York. We find another feast celebrated in 1452: 'for the breakfast of the bailiffs and other legal men at the second great court, held on the Thursday immediately before the feast of St George the Martyr this year [i.e. 20 April] ... for four minstrels of the lord duke of York in the presence of the bailiffs and other honourable men for the honour of the town'. Wine was dispensed to these minstrels, who may have been seen as representing their lords or may simply have been availing themselves of the immunity from prosecution afforded by wearing a lord's livery while they earned a living, for otherwise they might have been treated as vagabonds or beggars.[38]

In 1452 'The Early Chronicles of Shrewsbury' record 'a commocion by the Duke of Yorke and other noble men commynge out of the marches of Wales'. Richard duke of York had a good claim at that time to be treated as the heir of the childless Henry VI: all four sons of Henry IV were dead and Richard was of the blood royal, descended on both sides of his family from Edward III, but he was excluded from the king's government. Instead, the house of Beaufort, the illegitimate but legitimised descendants of John of Gaunt and Katherine Swynford, were in favour. 'Having failed to take control of the government by constitutional means for any length of time in 1450-51, York resorted to force in 1452.' This attempt failed and York 'had no choice but to humble himself before the king and retire in disgrace to Ludlow',[39] the administrative centre of the huge Mortimer estates which York had inherited. Relations between York and in particular the queen, Margaret of Anjou, were now all but irreconcilable and that autumn York sailed for Ireland where he continued to plot.[40]

The Yorkist lords returned to England in 1460, taking control of London and the south while the Lancastrians retreated further north. On 30 December York and his younger son Edmund earl of Rutland were killed at the battle of Wakefield, but York's heir, Edward earl of March, had remained at Ludlow to act against Jasper Tudor, earl of Pembroke, and the Welsh Lancastrians. The town of Shrewsbury sent 51 men in answer to the royal summons to provide soldiers.[41] Edward, now duke of York, defeated Pembroke at Mortimer's Cross on 2 February and Jasper retreated to Pembroke. It was at this time that a Shropshire gentleman, Richard Corbet of Moreton Corbet, helped save Pembroke's nephew Henry, both having been in the Herbert household at Raglan. He took Henry Tudor to his uncle Jasper and the Tudors went into exile.[42]

Edward of York took possession of the crown on 1 March 1461 in right of his title recognised at the last parliament. The first reign of Edward IV had begun, to be punctuated by various battles, the bloodiest at Towton in Yorkshire on 29 March that year. The action was now well away from the Welsh Marches. It was in 1461 that Edward IV granted the Drapers' Company of Shrewsbury their charter; Degory Waters seems to have been the emissary to London to obtain it, at a fee of forty marks. The 'lord king' who now sent his minstrels to the town was Edward. In the summer of 1464 he married Elizabeth Woodville, a widow four years his senior (Plate 6).[43] The reign was interrupted by the 'Re-adeption' of Henry VI in 1470. Yorkist victories at Barnet and Tewkesbury, and Henry's murder in the Tower, settled the issue. The second, peaceful, reign of Edward IV began in 1471. His heir, Edward, born in November 1470 in sanctuary at Westminster Abbey, was set up with his own household at Ludlow. He was probably escorted by his parents when he first moved there in 1473. The queen was certainly in Shropshire because her second son by Edward, Richard, was born at Shrewsbury. 'This yeare', wrote the unknown chronicler, 'the Duke of Yorke was born in the Black Friars within the towne of Shrewsbery the which ... standethe under Sainct Mary's churche in the sayde towne.' Thomas Mytton and John Trentan were the bailiffs. The two young princes appear in the bailiffs' accounts over the next few years, sending minstrels or, in the case of Edward, visiting the town with his gentlemen. He stayed at the abbey: 'money paid for bread ... given to the Lord Prince with two carts at the abbey'. His uncle, Richard of Gloucester, sent a minstrel called a taborer and the king sent six minstrels.[44]

At this point, in the late 1470s, we can zoom in from the national scene to the town itself, indeed to one particular man, Degory Waters. He epitomises the upright, community-minded citizen, as opposed to the less worthy (we have already come across embezzlers). On 28 July 1477 he made his will, bequeathing his soul to Almighty God, our blessed Lady, and all the saints. Worldly and spiritual matters are combined. To the new building of St Mary's he left 13s 4d; he also left money to the three orders of friars in the town, Dominicans, Franciscans, and Austin Canons. He devised all his lands in the town and fields and pastures outside it to Richard Watur of Salop, Draper, 'to hold as in a certain Deede thereof made more plaine appeareth.' The town properties were a shop under the Guildhall, a tenement in the High Street, a cottage in Shoppelegge, rent from a tenement in Mardull which his brother John had lately inhabited, and rent from a tenement in Frankville. He left money for the building of a certain chimney in the Drapers' Hall. To the Wardens of the Craft of Drapers he left money for lights (candles in the church) on Corpus Christi day. He gave the wardens and their successors the lands and tenements listed so that they could find 'an honest and vertuous Prieste to Cellybrate in the said Churche in a certain chappell called Leybourne Chappell for the salvation of my soul my Parents & Benefactors Soules'. He also willed that the rents should sustain the poor people in St Mary's almshouses, next to the church. Waters died that same day and was buried 'in Sainct Mary's churche in Salop, in Trynytie Chappel he in hys lyffe tyme buyldyd all the Almshowses in St Marys churche yarde and dwellyd in the Almshowses hall there amongst them and wold also kneele amongst them in the same churche in a fayre longe pewe made for them and hym selfe'.[45]

In fact, Degory Waters seems a remarkable man: a successful businessman content to live in the almshouses he had built, sharing the lives and worship of the poor men there. We might be reminded of Anthony Trollope's Warden, but Septimus Harding would not have made a successful businessman. Degory's spiritual concerns are rooted in the orthodox religion of the time, with its veneration of saints and belief in purgatory and in the efficacy of masses for one's soul. Richard Watur (presumably a kinsman) appears in the bailiffs' accounts as providing livery for the three town waits at five shillings each. We learn too that Prince Edward visited the town in 1480: on 11 May, in the name of his 'most drede lorde and fader Edward the fourth', he confirmed the composition of the mercers, ironmongers and goldsmiths.[46] The prince, not yet ten at this time, was already being trained for his future role by his governor, his maternal uncle Anthony Lord Rivers, 'that he may be virtuously, cunningly and knightly brought up'. But Edward was only twelve when his father the king died in April 1483.[47]

News of the death of Edward IV did not reach Ludlow until 14 April, five days after it occurred. Ten days later Rivers and the young king set out for London for the coronation, fixed for 4 May. On 29 April, at Stony Stratford in Northamptonshire, they met up with Richard of Gloucester. The late king's brother was resentful and suspicious of the influence of the queen's family, the Woodvilles. The outcome was tragic. Installed in the royal apartments at the Tower, Edward V was joined by his brother Richard, reluctantly given up from sanctuary by his mother. The coronation was postponed and Gloucester was proclaimed king instead. We began our story with the deposition of a king. Nearly a century later we have a usurpation, and a terrible crime. Some modern historians try to exonerate Richard III, but it will not wash. The most recent Yorkist study gives the most balanced account. Edward's uncle declared him a bastard, but the prince had been acknowledged as his father's heir from his birth and had been declared king on his father's death. 'He was too intelligent and too well educated not to be aware of the fate of dethroned kings and his state of mind is painful to imagine as all his attendants were withdrawn, he and his brother were removed from the royal apartments to inner rooms and allowed less and less freedom within the Tower, until finally they were fully prisoners.' They were never seen again in public.[48]

Richard's main support was in the north but in the south and in Wales there were attempted rebellions. One was organised from Brecon by Henry Stafford earl of Buckingham, one of only three surviving adult males of the blood royal. He was found in Shropshire, taken to Shrewsbury, then to the king at Salisbury where he was beheaded on 2 November; his six-year-old son Edward was hidden in Shropshire. There were now two adult claimants: Richard already occupied the throne but was stained by his crimes; Henry Tudor was in exile (his claim was through his mother, Margaret Beaufort). The reign of the last Yorkist king was to last only two years. By summer 1485 preparations were being made at Harfleur for the voyage of French mercenaries and English exiles to Wales. Very few letters survive of those sent to his followers by Henry Tudor but one is worth quoting, sent to the Shropshire knight Sir Roger Kynaston, steward of the estates of his brother-in-law Lord Powys, who had known Tudor at the French court and promised his support. It is headed 'By the Kyng' and refers to the promise of his 'trusty and welbelovyd cosin the lord Powys'. The letter was written at Machynlleth on 14 August 1485.[49] Kynaston, sheriff of Merioneth, was also constable of Harlech, and men from Gwynedd did join Tudor's army on the way to Shrewsbury. The town's chronicler relates that the senior bailiff, Thomas Mytton, refused Tudor entry because of his oath to Richard III. This difficulty was overcome, with Henry promising that his army would march quietly through Shrewsbury.[50] It must have been

Welsh Bridge (see also Plate 4)

a worrying sight, all those armed men, mostly foreigners, going through the narrow streets from Welsh Bridge to English Bridge. Relief ensued, both for the town and for Tudor, who was joined by troops from Shropshire: Sir Gilbert Talbot with five hundred men and Sir Richard Corbet with eight hundred. (Corbet had been Tudor's saviour after the battle at Mortimer's Cross.) The march continued through Stafford to Atherstone, reaching this rendezvous on 21 August. The battle took place near Market Bosworth next day, hanging in the balance until the Stanleys at last committed themselves and their troops. Thomas Lord Stanley, third husband of Margaret Beaufort, was Tudor's step-father; his brother Sir William was step-father to Richard Corbet. Richard III was killed and Henry hailed as king – he dated his reign from the day before Bosworth. His magnificent coronation preceded his marriage to Elizabeth of York, the rightful Yorkist heir. Authority in Wales and the Welsh Marches was given to his uncle Jasper Tudor, now created duke of Bedford.[51]

During the last decades of the fifteenth century Shrewsbury continued as a busy trading centre: a common market was probably held weekly and there were two fairs a year, one at the beginning of June, the other towards the end of September, around the feast of St Matthew (21 September). The fairs were occasions of some note. There were official breakfasts for the bailiffs, and guards were appointed to escort these officials and to watch the lanes and – especially – Welsh Gate. The Welsh were still objects of suspicion, not just as rebels and horse thieves but as traders also. The makers of Welsh cloth were finding it more convenient to dispose of their products at Oswestry and Welshpool, the cause perhaps of the apparent decline in Shrewsbury's trade and income from tolls. The men of Shrewsbury were themselves participating in this trade, which made matters worse. Of the eighteen craft gilds in the town in the fifteenth century no fewer than six dealt with wool and cloth: shepherds, weavers, shearmen, tailors, drapers and mercers. The last two were powerful companies with trade links extending through London to the continent. They also played an important role in town government: not democratic but oligarchic. We have already noted their patronage of chantries in the churches in the town. There are no figures for the population of Shrewsbury during this century so we cannot say whether it rose or fell. Despite the problems the wealthy families flourished as a small elite who ruled the town: 'within such a small ruling clique, each man would have been well known to the others'. Disputes were settled among the group and this plus the apparent lack of faction suggests 'that the ruling classes of Shrewsbury were well content with their commanding position'.[52]

This was the situation at the beginning of the Tudor period, when church and state, and the border town of Shrewsbury, were under strict and integrated rule. In the country as a whole the Catholic Church was accepted as an essential part of society, and there were royal contributions to the building and foundation of churches and religious houses. But there was also a resurgence of heresy, 'Lollardy', though not all those accused may have been 'Lollards'. The views of later Protestant groups were, however, similar to those of the early Lollards. Anne Hudson comments: 'Whatever the truth about the numbers of Lollards after the 1430s, it remains ... important to draw attention to the different nature of the evidence for heterodoxy in the second half of the "Lollard era" ... Much remains to be done in the

Henry Tudor's House, Wyle Cop, where Henry is reputed to have stayed in 1485 (SA-IMG24725)

investigation of this period.'[53] A more recent study of religious tolerance and intolerance in the period 1500 to 1700 notes: 'It is clear that on the eve of the Reformation, the term [Lollard] was applied loosely and imprecisely to men and women who boldly criticised Catholic doctrines and ceremonies ... and who revered Scripture as the source of all spiritual authority and sustenance.'[54] Apart from a continuation of dissent there was criticism within the Church and demands for reform, particularly from better-educated laymen and clergy, at the time when the orthodox Tudors established a new dynasty. The mother of Henry VII, Margaret Beaufort (Plate 5), an influential lady, noted for her piety, was a visitor to Shrewsbury, staying at its abbey: a reminder perhaps of the continuing religious regime under the early Tudors.[55]

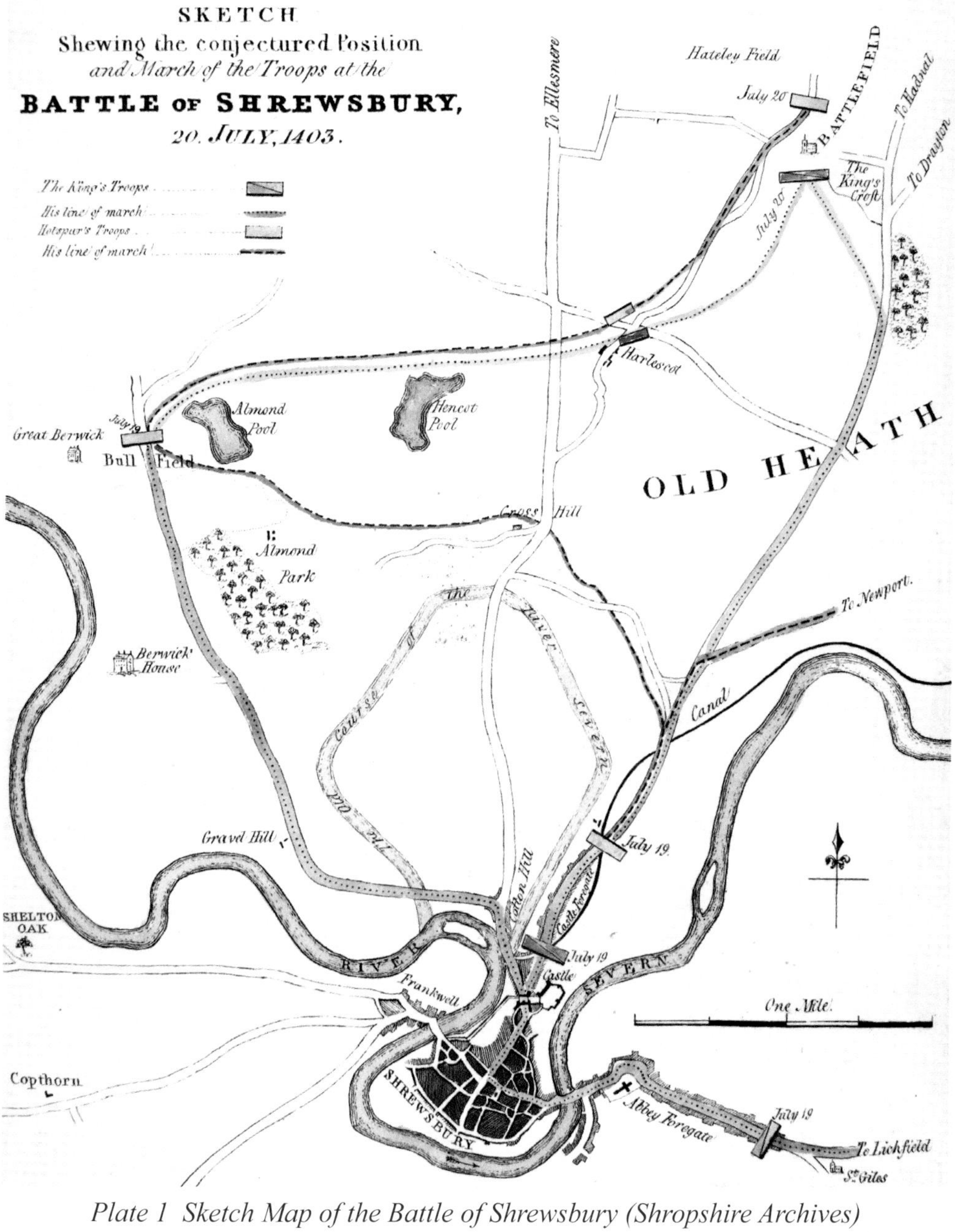

Plate 1 Sketch Map of the Battle of Shrewsbury (Shropshire Archives)

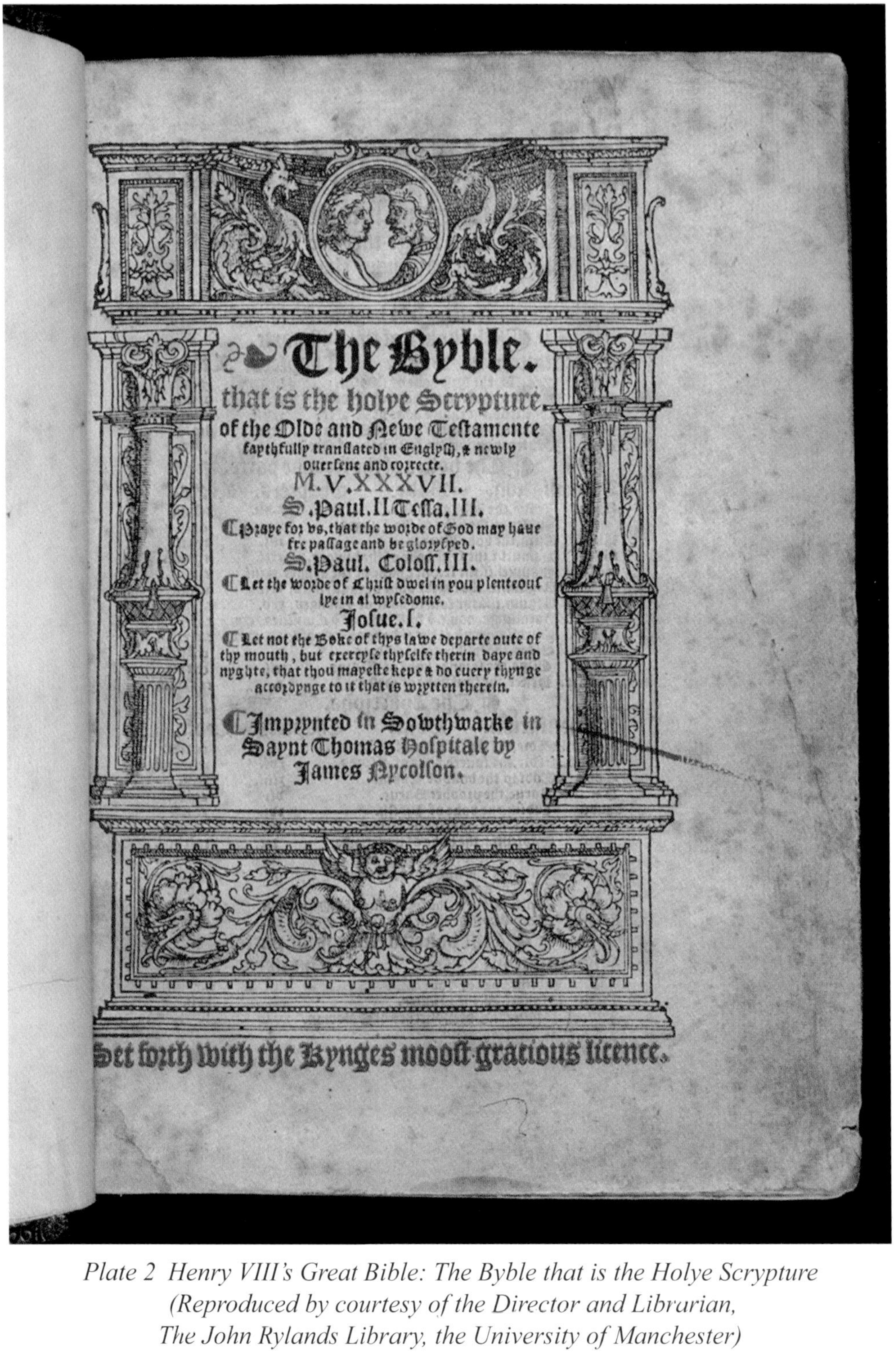
The Byble.
that is the holye Scrypture,
of the Olde and Newe Testamente
faythfully translated in Englysh, & newly
ouersene and correcte.
M.V.XXXVII.
S.Paul.II Tessa.III.
Praye for vs, that the worde of God may haue
fre passage and be gloryfyed.
S.Paul. Coloss.III.
Let the worde of Christ dwel in you plenteous
lye in al wysedome.
Josue.I.
Let not the Boke of thys lawe departe oute of
thy mouth, but exercyse thyselfe therin daye and
nyghte, that thou mayeste kepe & do euery thynge
accordynge to it that is wrytten therein.
Imprynted in Sowthwarke in
Saynt Thomas Hospitale by
James Nycolson.
Set forth with the Kynges moost gracious licence.

Plate 2 Henry VIII's Great Bible: The Byble that is the Holye Scrypture
(Reproduced by courtesy of the Director and Librarian,
The John Rylands Library, the University of Manchester)

Plate 3 Shrewsbury Castle (Shropshire Archives)

Plate 4 The Welsh Bridge (Shropshire Archives)

Plate 5 Right: Lady Margaret Beaufort (By permission of the Master and Fellows of St John's College)

Plate 6 Lower left: Elizabeth Woodville (By permission of the President and Fellows of Queens' College, Cambridge)

Plate 7 Lower right: Francis, Lord Newport (1619-1708), created earl of Bradford 1694, painted by Sir Godfrey Kneller (Courtesy of the Trustees of the Weston Park Foundation)

Chapter 2
The Tudor Re-Forming of Religion

In the early years of the new reign two events in Shrewsbury epitomised aspects of religion that we have already traced. In March 1486 the archdeacon of Shrewsbury, Edmund Hale, and Hugh Lehe, a canon of St Chad's, were required to attend at Coventry, at St Michael's church, the trial of eight men for heresy. Bishop John Hales presided. One of the eight was John Blumston, physician, described as a 'true heretic'. All eight men were persuaded to sign a form of abjuration and made to walk at the head of a religious procession, barefoot and bareheaded, wearing only a linen garment and bearing on their shoulders faggots of wood as a reminder of the fate heretics might suffer. In contrast to these men were some of the leading townspeople of Shrewsbury who joined the monks of the abbey in a new fraternity, the gild of St Winifred. The Coventry eight denied the authority of the pope, the benefit of prayers for the dead, making pilgrimages and venerating images of saints. All these beliefs and practices were essential to the idea of the fraternity. Both groups in the same diocese suggest continuity from the preceding century, a point which has been debated in the case of 'heresy' but which is not controversial as far as orthodoxy is concerned.

The abbey had had a special devotion to St Winifred since it acquired her relics in *c.*1138. Her cult grew in importance in the fourteenth century when a new shrine was built in the abbey. There were links between Shrewsbury and Holywell near Flint. Henry V, we may recall, walked from Shrewsbury to Holywell where the saint had died and been restored to life; he also intended establishing a chantry in the abbey church for one chaplain. He died before he could implement his plan and it was not until 1463 that Abbot Thomas Mynde secured the appropriation of the church of Great Ness to provide the stipend for a chaplain to celebrate Mass at the altar of St Winifred for the souls of King Henry and his heirs. Those were Yorkist times, however, so it was not until 9 February 1487 that a royal license was granted to Thomas Mynde, abbot of St Peter's, Shrewsbury, 'to found a perpetual fraternity in honour of St Winifred, in the parish church of Holy Cross [within the abbey] ... to the intent that one or two priests may be supported to celebrate divine service at the altar of St Winifred, for the good estate of the king, Elizabeth his consort and the said abbot, and for their souls when they are departed this life'. Leading townspeople were to join the fraternity, one of the first being Thomas Mytton, bailiff of Shrewsbury in 1485. The gild brought monks and burgesses together; there were not more than eighteen monks at Shrewsbury at any one time.[1]

Seal of St Winifred's Gild (SA-IMG24320)

With this sketch of relations between abbey and town to add to what we know of the churches within the walls, the worship, the preaching, and the processions, we have quite a good idea of parish life in Shrewsbury at the end of the fifteenth century. This approach accords with a recent scholarly dictum that religion should be seen in its parochial setting, a blend of local and universal belief and practice: the phrase 'the Christianity or religion of the parishes' better captures 'the organic nature of the lived religion in the locality' than does the term 'popular religion'.[2] One aspect of religion at that time seems to have had no scope in the tightly-controlled town of Shrewsbury: dissent, such as was found at Coventry. Some scholars find in certain places a survival-revival of Lollardy which had gone underground, but this metaphor may be misleading. Geoffrey Blyth, bishop of Coventry and Lichfield from 1503 to 1531, pursued his investigations into heresy but, writes Anne Hudson, not all those detected may have been 'Lollards'. Yet groups of dissenters were found to be holding household meetings and sharing books, English versions of the Bible. According to John Foxe seven Coventry dissenters were arrested in the spring of 1520 and were burned to death.[3]

When we return to the records of Shrewsbury we find reminders of its status as an important border town, of its civic pride, and of its support of the Tudor regime. The first son of Henry VII and Elizabeth of York was born at Winchester on 20 September 1486. He was named Arthur after the mythical British hero associated with both Winchester and Wales. The king adopted the Yorkist method of controlling the region by establishing a council at Ludlow with the prince as its nominal head. From 1493 until his death Prince Arthur's principal residence was at Ludlow but he also used the royal manor house at Tickenhill near Bewdley and spent short periods at other places in the borders, especially Chester and Shrewsbury. His visit to Shrewsbury in 1493 is attested by the borough accounts: payments for bread, wine and beer 'as a gift to the Lord Prince Arthur at his coming to the town of Shrewsbury this year'. The royal party stayed, as was usual, at the abbey. The king and queen provided entertainers, as did Lord Powys and the earl of Arundel – the earl's men were musicians as we see from the phrase 'hearing their melody'. Painters painted 'various things necessary for the interlude to meet the said lord prince'. Thomas Skinner was paid 'for the mending of the beards' for the use of the players for whom there was some kind of 'structure'. Others in attendance included men-at-arms, serjeants of arms, heralds and footmen, and also the king's lion-keeper. It is difficult to know what kind of entertainment might have been put on. Cities like London and York could stage elaborate pageants, while a royal progress 'was an important and traditional instrument of royal propaganda'. On the first of the Tudor progresses the city of Worcester presented the king with the keys of the city while a herald likened him to a series of famous and ancient personages. In Hereford that same May crowds lined the streets while dignitaries welcomed the king, a pageant of George and the Dragon being played at the main gate. At Gloucester there were no pageants as it was Trinity Sunday and ceremonies were confined to religious observances. Wales produced prophetic verse dwelling on British themes and the red dragon was sported as a device. When Prince Arthur became the focal point of court spectacle suitable scenes were played, as at Coventry where 'King Arthur' greeted the prince in verse.[4] We can only wonder who the bearded actors represented at Shrewsbury and what was staged there.

The visit of the prince two years later was recorded in Shrewsbury's 'Early Chronicles': in 1495, when John Gittins and Lawrence Hosier were bailiffs, the Exchequer was painted within with antique work and the arms of England and Wales along with the arms of the town. 'This yeare the Kynge and the queene of England with prynce Arthur came to Shrosbury' and a new franchise was granted. 'The king's lady mother' Margaret Beaufort was also present, a particularly esteemed guest. One attraction for this pious lady may have been the shrine of St Winifred at the abbey where she was staying. Lady Margaret was one of the benefactors of the shrine at Holywell where her emblem appears in the well chapel.[5] The chief reason for the royal visit to Shropshire was to escort Prince Arthur to Ludlow Castle, from which, only twelve years before, the queen's young brother, Edward V, had made his fateful and fatal journey. For anyone prescient or prophetic there may have been a sense of doom: in December 1501 Arthur, newly married at the age of just fifteen, took his bride to Ludlow, where he died the following April; he was buried in Worcester Cathedral. Presumably Shrewsbury, like other towns, tolled its bells and had masses said for the dead prince, the more so since the altar of St Winifred at the abbey was dedicated for the royal family. Arthur's death left the younger prince, Henry, as heir to the throne. The betrothal of the king's daughter Mary to the young Archduke Charles in 1507 was celebrated: 'Shrewsbury and Dover were physically further away from London than many other towns, yet it was they, used to seeing themselves as local centres of royal authority, and not others, that mounted triumphs to celebrate the betrothal.'[6]

Shrewsbury's sense of itself as a local centre of royal power is important and may help to explain its seeming acceptance of the various changes of regime. A similar habit of obedience may explain its conservatism in a religion which was a compound of theology, devotion and superstition. Attacks on such beliefs were seen as heretical. Some of the dissenters were prepared to die for their beliefs, as at Coventry. There were many such communities throughout southern England and the Midlands, though they seem not to have reached the Welsh border. 'English Lollards in the fifteenth and early sixteenth centuries remained aware of their indebtedness to Wyclif, of course ... [but] Lollardy seems to have become something of a broad church in the decades after Wyclif's death, with his doctrines acquiring a penumbra of other beliefs and practices.' There was, however, no Wycliffite canon 'and no equivalent to the Lutheran doctrine of justification by faith alone'.[7] It may be that the label 'Lollard' is inappropriate for these late groups. In Shrewsbury the borough authorities and the religious houses had certain disputes, some concerning property and privileges within the town.

In May and June 1507 the town and abbey took a dispute to the law courts at Westminster. Shrewsbury Abbey was in some disorder at this time, with many buildings becoming dilapidated. The friaries were also in decline and some friars were accused of affray, including tavern brawls, trespass and debt.[8] Despite these problems there is no sign of disaffection with the Church in Shrewsbury's official records during the early years of the reign of Henry VIII, who ascended the throne in April 1509. The abbey played its part in the life of the town. In 1516, for instance, money was spent on wine, apples, wafers and delicacies given to the abbot and monks 'at the play and show of the martyrdoms of Feliciana and Sabina, the martyrs, in the quarry behind the walls of the town for the honour of the said town in Whitsun week this year'. A location outside the walls has been noted earlier, when Lady Talbot was an honoured guest. The entertainers in May 1516 were rewarded and given livery, while the abbot and his company joined the bailiffs in the general procession on the feast of Corpus Christi (22 May). In 1519 money was spent 'for the three kings of Cologne riding in the interlude for the recreation of the town of Shrewsbury on the feast of Pentecost', which fell on 12 June. There are occasional references to entertainers from Chester – in 1510 five shillings was given to three entertainers. That city included two plays about the kings, the Magi, in its mystery cycle, put on by the Vintners and the Mercers; perhaps the visitors performed their play in Shrewsbury. (Maybe a local hopeful was found to play Mary: 'You royal kings in rich array ...'.) In 1521, among many entertainers, there is a new feature: a reward of a penny was given to the common bellman for going about the town 'to make proclamation for attending upon the Abbot of Marham at May-time this year'.[9]

The abbot was not a visiting dignitary but a mock abbot, a lord of misrule. For an earlier reference we have to go to the adjoining county of Staffordshire. In 1498 a case came to court of assaults and conflict in the small towns of Wednesbury, Walsall and Wolverhampton. Mummers from these places toured local fairs with morris dancers and a pipe and tabor player to perform a Robin Hood play. This year there was violence and two men were locked up at Walsall. Their friends, with many armed followers, tried to release them. The magistrates ordered the mob to back down and the inhabitants of various towns not to attend the fair at Willenhall. This order was ignored and two hundred people wearing armour were led by William Milner, 'styling himself the Abbot of Marham'. Here we have an association between the abbot and the well-known character Robin Hood. In Shrewsbury, however, the mock abbot's performance was better controlled and officially funded. In 1521 the borough paid 6s 9d 'for a new painted robe, sandals, and other necessary rewards and expenses done upon Richard Glasier, Abbot of Marham, for the honour and pleasure of the town'. In 1532 expenses of 6s 7d were paid for 'garnishments, liveries, and a minstrel for the Lord Abbot of Marham, in time of the month of May this year, for the honour of the town'. During these years the abbot of Shrewsbury also attended the Corpus Christi processions, 1535 and 1537 being two such occasions. We have therefore to question Ronald Hutton's observation that the abbot of Marham's procession was 'an opportunity to poke fun at the former religion': England's religion was not yet altered at these dates. Chris Humphrey writes: 'In the end, however, the full extent to which misrule was accompanied by subtle allusions or more overt references to topical events in medieval England is something which can only be guessed at.' It is difficult also to guess at what lay behind an incident reported in Shrewsbury upon Twelfth Day 1534, 6 January, the feast of Epiphany:

> the dyvyll apearyd in Sainct Alkmonds churche there when the preest was at highe masse with great tempest and darknes so that as he passyd throughe the churche he mountyd up the steeple ... and put the prynt of hys clawes upon the iiijth bell and toocke one of the pynnacles awaye with hym ...[10]

The devil with his claws and feathers was familiar to people, not just from wall paintings and books but also from pageants and plays. What happened or was thought to have happened lies in the mists of a medieval mind-set. But new ideas were emerging.

One March in the 1520s the town clerk of Shrewsbury, Thomas Cowper, received a letter from his son George in London. The young man was deferential, thanking his father for the expense he put him to, and giving news of relations living in London. His letter ended: 'Ser, as for newes ther ys none, but of late ther was heretyks here, which dyd take Luters openyons.'[11] (So Luther was not news?). It may be instructive to consider the experience of George Cowper: as the son of a leading Shrewsbury official he would have been brought up in the traditional faith, attending masses and the processions which marked feasts during the liturgical year; as a traveller through Coventry he would have known of heretics and their fate; and as a sojourner in London, in the city or at the inns of court, he would have learned about Lutherans. Martin Luther, born in 1483, entered the Augustinian house at Erfurt in 1505; in 1511 he transferred to Wittenberg where he was made professor of theology; in 1513 he began his lectures on the Psalms and Paul's Epistle to the Romans. This course of study brought him relief 'from his spiritual grief and depression' at his sense of alienation from God and of his own sinfulness. The other great influence on Luther was Augustine of Hippo, as Michael Mullett explains in his illuminating biography of the reformer: 'Luther cited Augustine with the highest approval on such subjects as the realisation that in the face of God we "are nothing at all" and the fact that the gospel makes it known to us that we are children of wrath, helpless without the mercy of God.' During these years Luther had made 'his breakthrough into the essential doctrine of justification by faith' (instead of salvation earned by good works). In 1517 he drew up his famous 95 Theses, 'intended by their author to highlight what he saw as an ecclesiastical abuse harming the laity', namely the selling of indulgences. The theses are theologically conservative, 'including an unquestioning acceptance of the doctrine of purgatory'. They caused a sensation, however, and the sequel was Luther's excommunication by the papacy in 1520: 'Luther's role altered irretrievably from that of a would-be reformer of the Catholic Church to a declared foe of that institution, as it refused to heed his call to bring its beliefs and practice into line with the doctrines he had been uncovering in his lectures on the Psalms and the Epistle to the Romans.'[12]

Of importance at this point was the presence in London, especially in the leading merchant companies, of cells of dissenters in the Lollard tradition, a situation examined by Susan Brigden who also notes the influx of forbidden books containing 'Lutheran errors'. London may be seen as 'the centre of interchange between residual Lollards and innovative Lutherans'. Despite the new ideas, the English Church 'was functioning as effectively as at most periods of its history'. We must turn to Henry VIII's matrimonial problems and financial needs as the specific cause of the Reformation in England.[13] A picture of late medieval English piety has been drawn by Eamon Duffy, a picture which has its critics. Patrick Collinson has written: 'Eamon Duffy's justly celebrated *The Stripping of the Altars* restores the vital juice of a living faith to our late medieval Catholic ancestors. But we need to acknowledge, as Duffy does not, the religious vitality of those subjects of Henry VII and Henry VIII who stood somewhat apart from the Church of the social majority.' Robert Lutton contrasts the community of Tenterden in Kent, with its Lollard tradition, with that of Duffy's Morebath whose piety 'is portrayed as the collective piety of the parish as a whole'. Lutton advocates a reassessment of the thesis 'that pre-Reformation religious culture was intellectually and culturally coherent across the social spectrum, universal and largely homogenous and that most people in most places did not welcome reform'.[14] In Shrewsbury orthodox piety included Corpus Christi processions, like that of 1522 which was attended by Bishop Blyth of Coventry and Lichfield, 'president of the Council of the lord king in the Marches of Wales'. That council was holding its last meeting under its prevailing arrangements, in Shrewsbury. The abbot of Marham also paraded in May-time in his new embroidered gown and shoes.[15] We cannot surmise from such public displays that the whole town was pious, or that no-one wanted reform.

In the spring of 1523 a young Gloucestershire man arrived in London hoping to print the New Testament in English: William Tyndale (*c.*1494-1536). He hoped for the patronage of the bishop of London, Cuthbert Tunstall, but was snubbed. Despite this Tyndale was able to stay in London for nearly a year supported by merchants in the cloth trade, especially Humphrey Monmouth. Realising that he would not be able to work in England Tyndale went to Cologne where the printer Peter Quentell produced some of his work, until the print shop was raided. Tyndale moved, probably in 1525, to the Lutheran city of Worms where Peter Schoeffer undertook the printing of an English New Testament and a tract on Paul's Epistle to the Romans. Tyndale's work was circulated in England, one of his chief agents being his fellow preacher George Constantine. In May 1528 Richard Cotton, curate of Atcham near Shrewsbury, was accused of reading Lutheran books and holding frequent disputations and conversations with the disciples of the Lutheran sect 'and mainly with a certain George Constantine in the towns of Whitchurch and Atcham'. Cotton was made to abjure his heresies at Lichfield Cathedral.[16] If there were Lutherans in towns so close to Shrewsbury one wonders about that town too. In the borough accounts for 1526-7 there is the item: 'Reward and wine given to a messenger of our Lord the King bearing commissions touching ... the books of Martin Luther'. These books were banned in England. It was in 1526 that Thomas Wolsey authorised a raid on the Hanseatic community in the London Steelyard, a move followed by more book-burning; he also tried, without success, to have Tyndale extradited from the Low Countries.[17] Although Shrewsbury considered itself a centre of royal authority there were merchants with links to London, and eventually members of that class would emerge as committed Protestants (a word not in use until after 1529), so we must keep an open mind on the question of pious orthodoxy in the town. We need also to trace the progress of the king's move away from Rome.

The year 1525 brought another phase: a new Council in the Marches was established for the king's heir, nine-year-old Princess Mary. Bishop Veysey of Exeter was president, the councillors included the Shropshire lawyer George Bromley, and the princess's lady governess was Margaret Pole, countess of Salisbury. At the same time the king created his illegitimate son, Henry Fitzroy duke of Richmond and Somerset. Shrewsbury entertained the lady princess's interluders and the lord king's camel-keeper who 'showed the bailiffs and their fellows the tricks of that camel'. More seriously, the bailiffs and the abbot of Shrewsbury took part in the Corpus Christi procession. The significance of the new royal provisions reached beyond the Marches: the princess, the king's heir apparent, would gain valuable experience of ceremonial duties, but recognition of his son was occasioned by 'the precariousness of leaving the succession to the throne dependent on the survival of a young girl'. The princess returned to court in 1527: 'The decisive factor in that respect was the king's reconsideration of his options in regard to remarriage and the succession, which prompted reservations about the princess's status.'[18]

That reconsideration involved lengthy negotiations with the papacy to have the marriage to Catherine of Aragon annulled, on the grounds that she had previously been married to Henry's brother Arthur and that a dispensation should not have been given. The chancellor Thomas Wolsey was much involved, and eventually brought down by the business. There were also the complications of disputes between the papal forces and those of the Emperor Charles, nephew of Queen Catherine, and the fact that the king fell in love with Anne Boleyn. These entanglements can be traced in the letters between all the parties from 1526 to 1529 by which time Thomas Cromwell had taken over the king's 'great matter'. 'Oh, the slippery turns of this world!' wrote Erasmus in a letter of December 1529. Wolsey died the following year. 'Within two years, Henry VIII declared himself supreme head of the Church in England, and thus split the English Church from the Church of Rome.'[19] In August 1529 writs were sent out to assemble the first parliament for six years; the member for Much Wenlock, Edward Hall, wrote of events during the next few years in his famous *Chronicle.*

After the parliament of November 1529 the king kept Christmas at Greenwich with the queen, 'with great plentie of viaunds, and divers disguisynges and Enterludes, to the great rejoicing of his people'. At the end of 1530, Hall records, after the death of Cardinal Wolsey (on 30 November at Leicester Abbey), the king and queen again kept Christmas at Greenwich, with interludes, masks, disports and a great banquet.[20] During this time, however, the business of the annulment of the marriage continued. According to George Bernard's reading of events Henry had from early on in the proceedings threatened a break from Rome. In July 1530 he assembled nobles, bishops and abbots to sign a letter to Pope Clement VII (Giulio de' Medici) pointing out the evils of delaying the king's divorce. In February 1531 Henry demanded that English churchmen acknowledge him as their supreme head. On 31 May 1532 Queen Catherine was told that she and Henry must separate. After her trial at Blackfriars she was sent to Kimbolton Castle in Huntingdonshire. In October that year the king took Anne Boleyn on a state visit to France. Hall wrote: 'This yere the Kynge kept his Christemas at Grenewyche wyth great solempnitie, but all men sayde that there was no myrthe in that Christmas because the Queene and the Ladies were absent.'[21]

Henry wanted the divorce so that he could remarry and produce a legitimate male heir, and he wanted to govern his own national church, neither of which aims is difficult to understand. The supremacy of Rome was not a feature of the earliest centuries of the Church. In 1527-8 Henry wrote to Erasmus: 'we have felt for several years, and now feel [that] our breat, incited without doubt by The Holy Spirit, is kindled and inflamed with passion that we should restore the faith and religion of Christ to its pristine dignity'. Bernard comments that Henry was 'in significant respects reformist; and Erasmian is by no means an unhelpful description of that reforming thrust.' A clique around the dukes of Norfolk and Suffolk were prepared in 1529 to give the king 'the power to reform abuses in the church, drastically pruning the church's wealth and even considering the dissolution of all English monasteries.'[22] Thomas Cromwell, a London lawyer skilled in conveyancing, joined the privy council in 1530; he also managed affairs in the Reformation Parliament. The Convocation of Canterbury sat concurrently at Westminster, alternating its sittings with those of parliament. The king drove events. In 1532 Convocation agreed to make no more church canons without royal licence and the Submission of the Clergy was subscribed in May 1532. In the next year the bill for ending the royal marriage was drafted, Cromwell submitting the draft to leading clerics and canon lawyers. Thomas Cranmer archbishop of Canterbury was among them as was Rowland Lee, soon-to-be bishop of Coventry and Lichfield. By the time the bill was finalised the king was married to the already pregnant Anne – Elizabeth was born in September. The Act of Supremacy and that to secure the Succession followed. In 1534 the king ordered preachers to denounce the pope in their Easter sermons. In August convents of Observant Friars (who had opposed the divorce) were dissolved. During that year Cromwell worked at enforcing the recent legislation, all subjects being required to swear to the legitimacy of the new marriage, thus acknowledging the king's new powers. In January 1535 he was made the king's vice-gerent or vicar general, with a commission to organise visitations of the two provinces of the English Church – Canterbury and York. There were some martyrs, notably the London Carthusians and Bishop John Fisher and Sir Thomas More. Henry's religious instincts were conservative but he was determined to take a leading role in reform.[23]

The Shrewsbury chronicler recorded for the year 1534-5: 'This yeare also all the abbeys and priories with nooneries in all England were vysyted by one Doctor Lee being auctorisyd by the king's majestie.' The royal visitors, commissioned by Cromwell, were Richard Layton, Thomas Legh (Doctor Lee), John ap Rice and John Tregonwell. Layton, from Cumberland, asked that he and Legh (from Cheshire) might serve as commissioners in the north country where he feared that monasteries might be centres of disaffection. Both men had 'familiar acquaintance within 10 or 12 miles of every religious house, so that no knavery can be hid from them, nor can they suffer any injury'. They would discover 'all cloaked sanctity, superstitious rules of pretended religious and other detestable abuses', including the selling off of jewels and plate. In their report they noted pilgrimage shrines and relics, and alleged sexual immorality among monks and nuns. Their remit included Shrewsbury but the report on this abbey was not salacious, merely adverse. The abbot, Thomas Butler, could supply no inventory and kept no accounts; there was no infirmary; the dormitory was unlit and in bad repair; the roof above the high altar was collapsing and the monks in choir got wet when it rained; masses were neglected. The abbot was accused of taking glass for his own chamber and of pulling down houses and selling off timber and tiles. The valuations and visitations were not necessarily steps towards dissolution: in 1535 the king may have intended to reform 'the great and honourable monasteries of religion', not to destroy them, but reports on smaller houses showed that they would not be susceptible to reform. Richard Layton's fears about monasteries in the north were borne out by the unsuccessful Pilgrimage of Grace of 1536. There was no such trouble in Shrewsbury, where the abbey was not surrendered until 1540.[24]

At this point we must turn to the problem of Wales and the difficulty of imposing law and order on the native lordships. Henry VIII visited Shrewsbury in June 1534 to hold an important conference with the Marcher lords, following complaints made in parliament about outrages in Shropshire, Herefordshire and Gloucestershire. Agreement was reached as to various reforms. The man capable of dealing with the situation had already been appointed: Rowland Lee, consecrated bishop of Coventry and Lichfield by Archbishop Cranmer on 19 April 1534. Lee visited his diocese in July and by 10 August was at Shrewsbury as lord president of the council in the Marches, in succession to Veysey.[25] We have seen how councils had been set up as an extension to the establishment of the heir to the throne since the second reign of Edward IV, but something more permanent and clearly defined was needed. The formal preamble to the Act of Union between England and Wales of 1536 spells this out, not without some (possibly deliberate) obscurity:

> Albeit the Dominion, Principality and Country of Wales, justly is and ever hath been, incorporated and annexed, united and subject to and under the Imperial Crown of the Realm as a very member of the same, wherefore the King's most royal Majesty is very head, king, lord and ruler; yet notwithstanding, because in the same country divers rights, usages, lawes and customs be far discrepant from the laws and customs of the realm and also because the people do daily use a speech nothing like nor consonant to the mother tongue used within this realm [of England],

some rude and ignorant people have made distinction between the King's subjects of this realm and his kingdom of Wales ... His Highness, therefore ... hath, by the advice of the Lords Spiritual and Temporal, and by the Commons in this present Parliament, ordained that the country or dominion of Wales shall for ever, from henceforth, be united and annexed to and with his realm of England.

Rowland Lee was bishop of the third largest diocese in England but he delegated most diocesan work to his senior ecclesiastics, devoting himself to the work of the Council in the Marches in a peripatetic programme, visiting Wigmore, Bishops Castle, Ludlow, Hereford, Worcester, Chester, Bewdley, Newport in Shropshire and Shrewsbury (as shown by his letters). Even when he was resident in his diocese he was usually at Shrewsbury. (Ludlow was not in his diocese but in that of Hereford.) The status of Shrewsbury as a centre of royal authority was thus enhanced. By 1541 Bishop Lee was able to appoint his brother George as dean of the collegiate church of St Chad in Shrewsbury, and it was there that Rowland Lee was buried in January 1543. Michael Jones describes Lee as 'a true Henrician who promoted his master's cause and believed in what he was doing'.[26] Lee, we may recall, had been one of the first bishops to swear the oath of supremacy.

Early Chronicles record that three dukes visited Shrewsbury in 1535-6, a time when there were only three dukes in England. Charles Brandon duke of Suffolk had been associated with north Wales and with Shropshire and would have been known in

Old St Chad's (SA-IMG24343)

Shrewsbury, but his connection with the area was over by 1525. Of the other two dukes, the duke of Richmond and Somerset was Henry Fitzroy, beloved but illegitimate son of the king, and the other was Thomas Howard duke of Norfolk, uncle of Anne Boleyn. Fitzroy was brought up in Norfolk's household and Norfolk's son Henry, earl of Surrey, was his companion and friend.[27] They were on their way to Holt Castle in north Wales. As dukes, Richmond and Norfolk would have had large retinues and they evidently gave little notice of their arrival. The parliament of 1536 passed a statute which indicates that Shrewsbury, Ludlow, Bridgnorth and towns elsewhere needed improvements. Many houses were 'in great ruin and decay', especially in the principal streets where in times past there had been beautiful dwellings, now replaced by 'desolate and void grounds'. Uncovered pits and cellars and vaults lying open were dangerous for travellers. Such decay was 'to the impoverishment and hinderance of the same towns'. We do not know quite how bad Shrewsbury was but there was some cleaning up of the bridges and streets to be done before the dukes' imminent arrival. Despite 'the shortness of time' the borough was able to lay on wine, swans, capons, oxen, calves, conies (rabbits), dainties, wafers, hippocras [spiced wine], spices, comfits 'and divers other things for the honour of the town of Salop'.[28]

The month of May 1536 brought a severe blow to the king with the fall from grace of Anne Boleyn, in a disastrous weekend of folly, flirtation and vicious court gossip. As Edward Hall recorded, the king had held jousts at Greenwich but had suddenly departed for Westminster; the queen was arrested and taken from Greenwich to the Tower of London, accused of incest, adultery and high treason. She and her friends paid the ultimate price, although probably innocent. The borough council of Shrewsbury paid forty pence 'to Richard E. riding to the commissioners touching new rumours concerning the lady Anne, late queen'. In July 1536 the king's son Henry Fitzroy died in London.[29]

In 1538 the bailiffs and abbot of Shrewsbury were together in the Corpus Christi procession, but another entry for that year suggests a process of reform: 22 shillings 'spent on players of the lord prince, the lord privy seal, the lord visitor and on the servants of the lord president and the sheriff of Shropshire and on the Council and for other gentlemen for the honour of the town'. The lord president, Rowland Lee, represented reform; the Council is that of the Marches. The lord prince, Edward, had been born on 12 October 1537, his mother Jane Seymour dying soon afterwards. The mention of players and of the lord privy seal is of interest, especially as Thomas Cromwell, lord privy seal, was patron of

John Bale and his troupe who were touring in the Midlands. One of the plays at that date was *King Johan*, which treated the papacy as a foreign power trying to gain dominion over England. But in November 1538 the king condemned those who were too hasty in breaking rites not yet abrogated and causing contention. The practices at issue were 'the ceremonies of holy bread, holy water, procession, kneeling and creeping on Good Friday to the Cross, and Easter Day, setting up of lights before the Christi, bearing of candles upon the day of Purification of Our Lady' and other 'laudable ceremonies'. The king charged his subjects that these customs were to be observed 'without superstition'. He referred to 'the great and manifold superstitions and abuses which have crept into the hearts and stomachs of many of his true, simple, and unlearned loving subjects for lack of the sincere and true explication' and understanding of Scripture. Bernard finds these aims 'not incompatible': the king was 'neither conservative nor Lutheran' – he wanted an end to contention. The Injunctions to the Clergy of 1536, an extension of the Ten Articles of Religion drawn up by Cranmer earlier that year, forbade preachers to 'set forth or extol any images relics or miracles for any superstition or lucre nor allure the people by any enticements to the pilgrimage of any saint'. There was also an order that by 1 August 1537 every parish church should have a copy of the Bible in Latin and English, an impractical order since the only complete English Bible had been published less than a year before without official approval.[30]

There might be confusion in the minds of parishioners as to which way reform was heading but the chronicler of Shrewsbury (with the benefit of hindsight) grasped the main points which had been at issue in 1538:

> This yeare all the notable Imagys in England unto the which people usyd to goe in pylgremage weare utterly taken awaye with all shrynes ... This yeare lord Croomwell beinge Lord Pryvey seale and vicegerent to the king's majestie sent furthe Iniunctions to all byshopps and curats throughe the realme charginge them to see that in every parryshe church the byble of the largest volume printyd in English [Plate 2] weare placedd for all men to reede on and that a boocke of regester were also provydid and kept in every parishe churche wherein shallbe wrytten every weddinge christeninge & burieinge within the same paryshe for ever.

The first comment refers to Cromwell's campaign in January 1538 against idolatry. In February Cranmer's suffragan, Richard Ingworth, bishop of Dover, was commissioned to visit all houses of friars. At Shrewsbury the Greyfriars surrendered as part of the

Council House Gateway (SA-IMG24332)

dissolution programme – friars and prechers were suspect, as they did at Stafford and Bridgnorth. The bishop left one of the friaries in Shrewsbury, Blackfriars, but he later argued that it should be suppressed, along with that of Austin Friars, 'two naughty friars' houses'. On 24 June 1537 Cranmer had consecrated Lewis Thomas, late abbot of Cwmhir in Radnorshire, as suffragan bishop of Shrewsbury, to assist Lee. The idea of creating a new bishopric in Shropshire had been abandoned, but the archdeaconry of Chester was detached from Lichfield diocese to create the new see of Chester. There was also a suggestion that 'Mr Newton's house ... be bought for the Lord President': this may refer to what came to be called the Council House, between the castle and St Mary's church.[31] A first version of a Great Bible, compiled mainly from translations by Tyndale (executed as a heretic at Antwerp in October 1536), John Rogers and Miles Coverdale, was published in 1539 under the pseudonym 'Thomas Matthew'. This was the English Bible 'of largest size' ordered to be used in the parish churches. 'For the first time English men and women could consult the whole Bible for themselves with the consent of Church and State.' The Great Bible was revised and reprinted seven times between 1539 and 1541.[32]

Richard Rex concludes from his study of Henry's Reformation that the Protestants of late Henrician England 'were an articulate, committed, and conspicuous minority'. John Sommerville remarks: 'It is astonishing to think that a single individual could be responsible for changing the character of English culture, but Henry VIII exercised that power.' The dissolution of the monasteries was the most obvious and dramatic aspect of secularisation.[33] The case of Shrewsbury exemplifies these assessments. The dissolution of Shrewsbury abbey followed its surrender by Abbot Thomas Butler in 1540. On 9 January 1541 the borough council agreed to make suit to the king 'that the Abbey may stand and remayne, to receyve the prince's grace or any other nobilitie of the realme that shall resort to this towne'. An alternative suggestion was to turn it into a college or free school. Neither plan was implemented. In April 1542 the borough was granted a new charter and the abbey lands. Richard Mytton, a lawyer of the Inner Temple and MP for Shrewsbury, and Reginald Corbet of the Middle Temple, MP for Much Wenlock, were among those who subsequently took leases of ex-monastic properties.

The work of reconstructing the government of Wales was completed by the Act of Union of 1542, with the establishment of the Council in the Marches as the instrument of the Privy Council. It had under its supervision the twelve Welsh counties, Monmouthshire, and the counties of Shropshire, Hereford, Worcester and Gloucester. The centres were at Ludlow and Shrewsbury. It may be that religious changes are reflected too in the traditional May procession when the lord of misrule, still played by Richard Glasier, is called the Abbot of Mar-all – indicating perhaps a more openly satirical performance, with real abbots now removed.[34]

Prince Edward, Henry's son by Jane Seymour, was clearly being brought up in a court where reform was being advanced, and one minor member of the prince's household is of relevance to our story being a member of the Corbet family which helped shaped Protestantism. Richard Corbet, elder brother of the lawyer Reignald, was the king's carver, a humble-sounding but in fact treasured position. In 1539 Richard had been given the wardship of his nephew Andrew, heir to Moreton Corbet. The boy's grandfather Lord Windsor (after whom he was named) continued as keeper of the king's wardrobe until his death in 1543. Through his mother's family Andrew Corbet was also related to the Dudleys. In November 1543 Andrew came of age; in 1547 he was in the retinue of Sir John Dudley, viscount Lisle and earl of Warwick, in the Anglo-Scots war and was knighted. As Bishop Rowland Lee discovered when he first went to Shropshire in 1534, in the absence of a resident aristocracy power and authority were in the hands of the gentry. The Shropshire gentry also had influence in the borough of Shrewsbury, forming part of an urban elite with lawyers and merchants. Among these we find convinced Protestants, like John Mynton, a wealthy draper. In his will of 1549 he wrote: 'The ground of my belief is that there is but one mediator between God and man, which man, as Paul saith, is Christ Jesus.' At his funeral he wanted no mass or *dirige* (the Catholic office for the dead), only the English Te Deum, and godly psalms, for the comfort and edifying of the people. He condemned the mass as something to be 'abhorred of all those that professeth Christ. For as Paul saith, Christ hath offered himself once for all ...'. Mynton's brother Edward was an officer in the Drapers' Company and a parishioner of

St Chad's, but John may have spent most of his life in London. John wanted only the ministers of St Chad's to be at his funeral, with three sermons preached 'asson as myn executors can get a godly learned man'.[35] This very individual testament shows what one man believed; there were others like him.

Edward's reign began on 28 January 1547, in his tenth year. The evangelical group surrounding him worked for a thorough reformation in religion. In July Cranmer issued his book of homilies (to remedy the shortage of preachers) along with royal articles and injunctions; in August visitors went out to oversee the removal of images. Processions were to end: the last Corpus Christi procession had already taken place in Shrewsbury. Parliament and Convocation opened in November, the main part of the mass being said in English on this occasion. Convocation was to consider the setting up of 'true religion' and the abolition of 'popish abuses'. At the end of January 1548 came the banning of Candlemas candles, Ash Wednesday ashes and Palm Sunday palms. The first general modification of the mass used the term the Order of the Communion, its use to begin on Easter Day, 1 April 1548. In Shrewsbury holy images were publicly burned:

> the pycture of our Lady owt of St Mary's ... and the picture of Mary Mawdelen and the pycture of St Chadde owt of Sainct Chaddes churche ... were all three burnyd in the market place there commonly callyd the corn market.

During the following year the book 'made for the unyformities of common prayer and the admynystracion of Sacraments in Englyshe' was acquired, and 'the masse was cleane abolyshed.'[36] One of the two MPs for Shrewsbury in the 1547 parliament was Reignald Corbet, who was also made recorder of the town. The other member, John Evans, was clerk of the Council in the Marches. An entry in the borough accounts for Michaelmas 3 Edward VI (1549) shows the town's wish for a school: 'Paid Reginald Corbett, the recorder, for a supplication exhibited to the lord chancellor [Richard Rich] to obtain a free school. 10s.' Ten shillings was also paid to 'a servant of the lord chancellor'. This petition was not successful but school buildings were purchased that year (near St Mary's church). A further petition was presented in 1550: one of the town's sponsors was Hugh Edwards, a mercer who had been resident in London. Another Shropshire-man in London was Sir Rowland Hill, four times master of the Mercers' Company (which administered the affairs of Colet's school, St Paul's); in 1550 he founded a grammar school at Market Drayton in Shropshire. There was a close tie between the London Mercers and reforming clergy in the city. Hill died in 1550, in the same year as the John

Mynton we have already noted. Mynton was described by the Shrewsbury Chronicler as a 'true constant protestant'. There were other true Protestants such as the wealthy mercers Thomas and Robert Ireland, executors of Mynton's will. Thomas Ireland left a Protestant will in 1554, one of his executors being Sir Thomas Bromley, Shrewsbury's chief law officer (its recorder) and chief justice of the King's Bench. Bromley, another Protestant, died in 1555. These men all left generous legacies to the poor of Shrewsbury.[37]

Shrewsbury's other reformist enterprise, the establishment of a school to advance the youth of the town 'in good lerninge and godly education', began during Edward's reign, a charter being granted in 1552.[38] That same year saw the publication of Cranmer's second Prayer Book. Cranmer's achievement has been summed up by noting the changes in the liturgy from the beginning of Henry's reign, from the Latin Breviary and Books of Hours to the single service book, in English, for national use. The rubrics were pruned, the Scripture readings reformed and the congregation given a greater part in the service. Traditional doctrines and practices such as the sacrifice of the Mass, underpinned by belief in transubstantiation, confession, invocation of saints and petitions for the departed, were reformed or removed. This second Prayer Book received only minor revisions in 1559, 1604 and 1662. The six years of Edward's reign, writes Diarmaid MacCulloch, 're-shaped the culture which the union of the English, Scots and Irish crowns later exported to the rest of the world'.[39] There are, however, indications that some valuable church goods were removed secretly, in Shrewsbury as elsewhere, either out of reverence or to keep them out of official hands. Church property was also passing into the hands of local merchants and gentry.[40] This too may have been a sensible measure, to retain local control over such property. What cannot be calculated is the extent of adherence to the old religion. There must have been a retention of Catholicism in the country at large, more in some places than others, but until recusancy laws were in operation later in the century we do not have numbers. As the young king lay dying the Protestant faction at court was concerned about who would succeed Edward, his Catholic half-sister, or his Protestant cousin, Jane Grey, daughter-in-law of John Dudley duke of Northumberland, who hoped to make this pawn a queen.

Chapter 3
The Daughters of Henry VIII

Mary Tudor, daughter of Queen Catherine, was born on 18 February 1516; Elizabeth, daughter of Catherine's supplanter, Anne Boleyn, was born at Greenwich on 7 September 1533. Both sisters attended the christening of their half-brother Edward, born 12 October 1537. In 1543 the king married Katherine Parr: relations between the new queen and the princesses were good. For Elizabeth, writes David Starkey, 'the last two years of her father's reign were to be the happiest and most secure of her life'. She also shared with her brother the prince a remarkable education, with gifted Cambridge scholars as tutors. This continued when Edward was king and Elizabeth settled at Hatfield – her household was a veritable 'university extension college' (Starkey again).[1] In 1543 the sisters' place in the succession was settled: in default of heirs from Edward, Mary was to succeed; in default of heirs from Mary, Elizabeth was to succeed; if she had no heirs the succession would pass to the line of Margaret Tudor/Stuart, sister of Henry VIII. In order to resume her position at court Mary had to acknowledge her father's supremacy in the Church but, she said later, she remained true to Rome *interiormente.* Outwardly it seems she 'fitted quite comfortably into the circle around her father's last queen ... the core of her piety was the Mass, and in that she resembled Henry himself'.'[2]

Elizabeth saw her brother less frequently when he became king in 1547 until 1550 when she was welcomed at court, but she was excluded when the Protector John Dudley, created duke of Northumberland in 1551, attempted to divert the succession from both Mary and Elizabeth. This plan failed, as did his attempt on the death of Edward VI to seize power through his daughter-in-law Jane Grey. Mary proclaimed herself queen on 10 July 1553, gaining popular support. However, the unpopularity of Northumberland, and the popularity of the rightful heir, did not mean a rejection of the whole reforming programme. At Mary's entry into London Elizabeth rode just behind her but after the coronation relations between the sisters soured and Elizabeth retired to her own household in Hertfordshire for Christmas. After the abortive risings planned by Sir Thomas Wyatt that winter, Elizabeth was kept in the Tower from March to May, when she was sent to Woodstock to live under surveillance for nearly a year; she did not receive permission to return to Hatfield until October 1555. On 25 July 1554 Mary married Philip of Spain, an alliance that was not popular in England. Her phantom pregnancy had to be acknowledged as such by the following summer. Elizabeth's 'sufferings' at the start of her sister's reign became part of the Protestant mythology.[3]

Mary Tudor was deeply committed to the Catholic faith, above all to the mass: this central Catholic rite was immediately restored in the chapel royal. Within weeks a proclamation authorised its use and before Christmas the Book of Common Prayer was outlawed. The Edwardian statutes were repealed from 20 December 1553. The royal Articles of March 1554 included the command that bishops should 'deprive or declare deprived ... all such persons from their benefices or ecclesiastical promotions, who contrary to the state of this order, and the laudable custom of the church, have married and used women as their wives'. Priests, as agents of the miracle of transubstantiation, should be celibate. This is the background to a brief entry in the *Early Chronicles* of Shrewsbury: Edward Stephens, curate of St Chad's, was married and had to be deprived 'when all the olde religion was wholy restoryd agayne'.[4]

From the autumn of 1553 Mary also set about purging the bench of bishops. Archbishop Cranmer stood his ground but obeyed the summons to appear in Star Chamber: he was sent straight to the Tower to join Hugh Latimer and Nicholas Ridley. His establishment was dissolved in the following weeks, Mrs Cranmer being given certain domestic furnishings, enough 'to keep her in modest comfort'.[5] By June 1554 thirteen Edwardian bishops were excluded and six Catholic bishops restored. Four Protestant bishops escaped into exile: Barlow, Scory, Coverdale and Ponet. Cranmer, Ridley, Hooper and Farrer were later burned for heresy. No fewer than ten bishops conformed: one was Richard Sampson of Coventry and Lichfield, a civil lawyer who also served a term as president of the Council in the Marches. Sampson died in September 1554 and was replaced by Ralph Baynes, a Cambridge scholar of strongly conservative views.[6] The central figure in the full restoration of Catholicism was Cardinal Reginald Pole, the English aristocrat who had gone to Rome in 1530 and achieved high office in the papal state. He was one of three cardinals at the Council of Trent established to counteract Lutheranism in the winter of 1545-6 and had sympathy with the moderate reformers. Back in England as papal legate, or ambassador, he presided on 30 November 1554, the feast of St Andrew, at a ceremony reconciling England to Rome. Pole was well aware of the number of Protestants in England and of the challenges confronting the Marian church: he praised Bishop Edmund Bonner of London for his work.[7]

Among the church's and Bonner's enemies was John Bale, author of the play *King Johan*. Bale, a former Carmelite, had converted to the new learning and the gospel of reform, becoming a follower of Luther and Tyndale. He edited for publication in Antwerp William Thorpe's *Testimony* or *Examination*, Thorpe's own account of the sermon he preached at Shrewsbury in 1407 and of his subsequent examination by Archbishop Arundel. Bale typically set dramatic discourses (such as Thorpe's) against Catholic 'dumb show', contrasting the true religion with the false. He attacked Bonner in two pamphlets: *Yet a course at the Romyshe foxe* (Zurich, 1543) and *A declaration of Edmonde Bonners articles.* In the second attack Bale casts the bishop as the grand Vice who presides over 'that prodigious apes play of antichrist', the eucharist, but abhors Christian plays 'because they have opened so plainly the knaveries of his Romish sect'. Bale's last appointment under Edward VI was to be made bishop of Ossory, from the end of which period he recounted that two of his own plays were performed at the market cross in Kilkenny. Young men played *The Chief Promises of God* (under the old law), and the plays of *John the Baptist* and the *Temptation of Christ:* works which presented divine promises or covenants as precursors of the Protestant Reformation. These performances coincided with the coronation of Mary Tudor, a display of what Bale called the 'mad masteries' of the Catholic church, 'the madam of mischief and proud synagogue of Satan, with gold, silver, pearl, precious stone, velvets, silks, mitres, copes, crosses, cruets, ceremonies, censings, blessings, babblings, bawlings, processions, puppets ... to provoke the carnal idiots to her whoredom in the spirit'. Bale anticipated John Foxe in his presentation of a native English church defiled by the various Roman intrusions, from Augustine of Canterbury on. (Wales had its own myth of foundation by Joseph of Arimathea, thus trumping the English story; it was also different in its tradition of married priests at all levels of society.) In Bale's historiography it was not until the break from Rome by Henry VIII that Christian liberty was restored to an England which was once again God's favourite nation.[8] Little wonder that Pole tried to control the press in an attempt to keep out heretical books, a policy that never worked. Writers as lively as Bale were popular and influential, and Bale advocated the reading of his plays when they could no longer be performed. After Mary's accession he moved to Frankfurt and Basle along with other exiles where he produced polemical works, smuggling the pamphlets into England.[9]

The restoration of traditional ceremony was 'probably one of the regime's strongest popular cards', write Eamon Duffy and David Loades, but not everything could be restored. The monasteries had been dissolved and their properties and goods widely redistributed, a fact recognised by Rome's renunciation of any claims to these properties in the bull *Praeclara* of 20 June 1555: all English religious houses became canonically defunct. Mary established some half-dozen new foundations, in the south of England.[10] Some care was taken over men who had lost by the dissolution of chantries and colleges: at St Mary's in Shrewsbury sums of between £1 and £5 were paid to ten former prebendaries or vicars choral, though it is not known what became of these men. The name of the priest serving in 1554 is given in one document: John Lane had a wage of £4 a year.[11] Pole attributed the evils of recent years to the slackness of priests and had plans for reform, but what is better remembered is the campaign against so-called heresy – the dreadful burnings at Smithfield and elsewhere. Between February 1555 and November 1558 almost 300 people were burned, and many others died in prison. It is estimated that 85% of the burnings were carried out in the south-east.[12]

Of particular interest to the story of Shrewsbury is Bishop Baynes' campaign in his diocese of Coventry and Lichfield. Robert Glover was examined at both Lichfield and Coventry and was burned at the latter place on 19 September 1555. He was one of a group who denied the real presence of Christ in the Eucharist and acknowledged only two sacraments, baptism and holy communion. His wife's uncle, Hugh Latimer, one of the famous Oxford martyrs, was burned in October. When Robert Glover's brother William died at Wem in Shropshire the bishop refused him burial in consecrated ground. Robert's wife Mary was one of the unsung women who gave support to the preachers. 'The Glovers,' writes Susan Wabuda, 'were part of a reforming network ... in which women were active.' After her husband's death Mary Glover sheltered one of the Nowell brothers, well-known Protestants, probably Laurence (later dean of Lichfield).[13] The third Glover brother, John, was spiritual adviser to a leading figure in the evangelical circle centred upon Lichfield, a gentlewoman named Joyce (Jocasta) Lewis who was burned at Lichfield in September 1557: one of the 'more spectacular episodes' cited by A.G. Dickens. She spent her last night in prayer, readings and discussions with her friends. The Swiss preacher Augustine Bernher accompanied her to the stake, where she drank to her fellow evangelicals, who joined in drinking with her. 'There and then her numerous backers joined in open prayers for the abolition of the mass and "papistry". Even the officiating sheriff Nicholas Bird cried "Amen" with the rest, while an unsympathetic priest compiled a list of the main demonstrators, many of whom (including Bird) were afterwards arrested and forced to do public penance.'[14] Another unsympathetic clergyman was the priest at St Chad's in Shrewsbury, John Marshall, who refused a Protestant burial to Edward Burton of Longner just as Elizabeth came to the throne. Instead, his friends buried him in his own grounds, as bringing him closer to God than the churchyard.[15]

Cardinal Pole's more positive agenda for the Marian church has been studied by Eamon Duffy.[16] Preaching and teaching were given high priority in the decrees of his legatine synod. 'The first decree indeed invented a ground-breaking propagandist technique, normally associated with the Protestant regimes which succeeded Mary. The decree provided for an annual procession and thanksgiving Mass on St Andrew's Day (30 November), the anniversary of the reconciliation of England with the papacy', in the course of which a sermon should be preached to explain to the people the significance of the occasion. Such a day 'of extraordinary Catholic triumphalism' was held in London in 1557: the procession, mass and a sermon in the morning; a chivalric display in the afternoon, attended by all the bishops, during a solemn mass at Westminster Abbey; and in the evening after dinner another sermon, preached by Pole, to lawyers, city governors, lords and knights, ladies and gentlemen. He did not advocate the rebuilding of the monasteries but said that his hearers should help rebuild their parish churches. Those who bought up church property were like greedy children and should turn instead to charity and poor relief. (In this respect, as it happens, Pole's sermon resembles those given by the great Protestant preacher Thomas Lever in 1550, before court and city.) 'Having thus neatly stolen the reformers' clothes on the question of poor-relief, Pole pressed home his argument.' He condemned contempt for the clergy, the undermining of morality and godly order, and the rejection of the sacraments. 'Heresy was a calamity in society', a treason which overthrew the foundation of the commonwealth.

London was the centre of the campaign against heresy, with many burnings taking place there. Pole was preaching an emphatically London sermon, but the synodal decrees applied to the whole church stressing the need for orthodox teaching and discipline in the parishes where provision should be made for the public reservation of the Blessed Sacrament on the high altar of every church. Clerical residence should be enforced, and the bishop should preach often in person. For priests who were not capable preachers, homilies were to be prepared. 'All this ... was Pole's own agenda.' At this time Mary and Pole had an enemy at Rome: the aged Giovanni Caraffa, elected pope as Paul IV in May 1555, would be pontiff throughout the rest of Mary's reign. He had denounced Pole as a heretic (as he had Ignatius Loyola) and now the 'terrifying old man', as Eamon Duffy describes him, 'undermined the Catholic restoration in England by withdrawing Pole's legatine authority'. Pole ignored the summons back to Rome while Mary sided with her husband and Spain against Paul IV and Rome. She was not excommunicated but, writes David Loades, 'relations with Rome were not at all cordial in the last 18 months of her life'. After Philip left England in the summer of 1555 the burning of Protestants continued, 'clearly driven by the queen, dragging a reluctant Pole behind her'. The policy was 'a catastrophic mistake'.[17]

The underground Protestant church in London had links to other regions such as the Midlands and to the exiles abroad. Augustine Bernher, the preacher associated with the Lichfield group, is known to have ministered in London. Early in 1558 a clergyman exile, Thomas Bentham, returned as pastor to the London congregation. A continental model of worship and discipline was followed in London – there was even an ordination, as Brett Usher has discovered. Bentham acted as chief pastor among equals, not as a quasi-bishop: 'the London congregation continued to be a "team ministry" which ... chose its ministers by common consent'. While in exile Bentham, as a scholar of Hebrew, was invited to join the group working at Geneva on the translation of the Bible into English; before that he had been at Frankfurt and at Basel where it seems he lived in the Claraklοster with John Bale and other exiles. At Geneva, during the winter of 1557-8, he married a fellow exile, Maud Fawcon, who returned to England with him. In July 1558 he wrote to Thomas Lever, pastor at Aarau: before the exile Lever had been master of St John's College, Cambridge; early in Mary's reign he went with others from Cambridge to Strasbourg, then to Zurich, Geneva and Frankfurt; in 1557 he settled at Aarau where Miles Coverdale and his family were members of the congregation. Bentham told his 'dere brother and lovyng freynde' of various burnings at Smithfield, asking for prayers from Lever's 'godly company'. John Strype records that Bentham himself comforted the sufferers at Smithfield. Within two years or so the friends would play a great part in Shrewsbury's Reformation history, Bentham as bishop of Coventry and Lichfield and Lever as archdeacon of Coventry.[18]

A third man, even more important to Shrewsbury, cannot be located at this time: Thomas Ashton had been a fellow and bursar at St John's, Cambridge, in Lever's time, but he is not listed among exiles in German or Swiss cities. There was another exile centre, rather neglected by historians, at Emden, where an English congregation was established as well as a printing press. One of the books produced there in 1557 was Cranmer's *Defensio*, a Latin translation of his *Defence of the True and Catholic Doctrine of the Lord's Supper* of 1550, one of the most important of his doctrinal works. A copy of the *Defensio* was owned by Ashton and taken to Shrewsbury but whether this means a connection with the Emden congregation is not known. [19]

The martyrs and exiles (numbered at about 400 and 800 respectively) were only minorities, though powerful ones. The majority of the population conformed, whether from Catholic conviction or pragmatic convenience. There was another possibility in that some may have lain low and bided their time, waiting for the Protestant reformation to be resumed. John Calvin condemned such conformers, labelling them Nicodemites, after the pharisee who went to Jesus by night (John, chapter 3 and 19: 39). As Andrew Pettegree argues, there were various factors leading to reluctant conformity, even the hope of preparing for the fullness of reformation: such people could take practical steps, forming networks and lending their skills, as did William Cecil, another alumnus of St John's, Cambridge. He had been secretary of state under Edward VI and a leading lay promoter of religious reform. After Edward's death he gave up high office but was used on certain missions, such as escorting Pole back to England. In 1550 Princess Elizabeth had appointed him surveyor of her estates, a service which continued to bring the two into contact, building a mutual trust which was to be very important when she was queen.[20] Another who did not retire abroad was Matthew Parker, future archbishop of Canterbury, but, as Nicholas Tyacke reminds us, he had been one of the early evangelicals at Cambridge, master of Corpus Christi, vice-chancellor, and an intimate of the great German reformer Martin Bucer. A Dominican priest, Bucer had been converted by Luther and had been leading pastor at Strasbourg, but he was exiled in 1550. Cranmer made him regius professor at Cambridge where he must have been in contact with many English reformers in addition to Parker, Thomas Lever for one. Bucer's last book, *On the Kingdom of Christ,* was a programme of reform for England, dedicated to King Edward. Ian Hazlett refers to Bucer's 'theological diplomacy', and his encouragement to 'Nicodemites' in Cologne not to secede from the old church.[21] Matthew Parker was fully attuned to events without going abroad. Perhaps the same was true for the elusive Thomas Ashton, who must also have known Bucer at Cambridge, as well as Lever and others at the university.

By the last months of Mary's reign Protestants, not least Princess Elizabeth, were quietly preparing for a change of regime, though its exact nature was not then clear. Some of the ruling elite were clearly marked for a prominent role, but other groups were also present in local society. 'These local elites have received less attention in studies of the Elizabethan settlement, but they would play a vital role in ensuring the success of the new religious policy in 1559.'[22] This was so in the case of Shrewsbury, with what we might call a 'Cambridge connection' assisting the local Protestants who were to take the initiative in engaging in a programme of religious reform. First, however, there was the change of regime. Mary died in the morning of 17 November 1558; Pole died that evening. Parliament was already in session so the death of Mary and accession of Elizabeth were proclaimed. Elizabeth received news of Mary's death at Hatfield: Cecil was already there ready to take up his duties as secretary of state and private secretary to the new queen. Mary's Catholic funeral was being planned before Elizabeth left Hatfield for London; she was buried at the restored Westminster Abbey on 13 December. There was curiosity about what Elizabeth's choice of religion would be, since she had ostensibly conformed under Mary. On Christmas Day she processed to the public service in her chapel royal where she remained in her closet overlooking the chapel as Bishop Owen Oglethorpe of Carlisle said mass; she left after the reading of the gospel. Oglethorpe officiated again at the coronation mass: the epistle and gospel were read twice, in Latin and English, but when the bishop elevated the host at the consecration Elizabeth withdrew to her closet in the traverse behind the altar in St Edward's chapel; she would not have taken communion. 'The action spoke louder than words.'[23]

There was still the question of what sort of reformed religion Elizabeth wanted – that of her father or her brother? A study by Roger Bowers of texts set to music by her chapel royal composers suggests that her first choice was to use the Prayer Book of 1549, 'but political pragmatism and ecclesiastical realities coerced her into agreeing instead to the restoration of the Book of 1552'. This was the more Protestant Prayer Book revised by Cranmer on the advice of Martin Bucer. Elizabeth did not get her own way this time but she did exact certain concessions 'to her own conservatism'. These are to be found in the rubrics of the 1559 Prayer Book and certain of the 1559 Injunctions.[24] From its beginning the Elizabethan settlement of religion was a series of compromises and debates, especially with those radicals who had been abroad, at the fountains of the Reformation. There was speculation among the exiles as to the religion they would return to. There are many letters surviving but those between Thomas Lever and Thomas Bentham and Lever and Henry Bullinger, chief pastor of Zurich, are most relevant to our subject. On 8 August 1559 Lever wrote from London to Bullinger: 'On returning from you towards England, in the course of my journey I saw at Strasburgh a proclamation, that is, an edict published by the authority of queen Elizabeth, strictly prohibiting all preaching and exposition of holy scripture, or any change of religion throughout all England, until the great council which we call Parliament ... shall have come to a decision respecting religion.' In England Lever found 'masses and all the follies and abominations of popery' still sanctioned. The London congregation which he attended continued to conduct their reformed worship in private but were not allowed to use a public church. Nevertheless Lever and other reformists obtained licences to preach and Lever travelled to many places even in 'remoter districts' to which he intended to return. In the event, it was not a question of returning. He found that at Coventry there were many Protestants who begged him to remain; this he did, marrying and acquiring three young stepchildren before his own were born. Lever reported from Coventry to Bullinger on 10 July 1560: the 'true and sincere doctrine' was now freely preached but there was no 'discipline of congregations', some ornaments of the 'mass-priests' being retained. The Protestants of Coventry were maintaining Lever and his family 'liberally'.[25] One of the legacies of the Catholic church was the order of bishops, maintained by Elizabeth; Cecil played a major role in setting up the new bench. Ralph Baynes of Coventry and Lichfield was dismissed in June 1559, to be replaced by Thomas Bentham, consecrated on 24 March 1560. There were no preachers in the north Shropshire part of the diocese so in August 1560 Bentham asked Lever, whom he had made archdeacon of Coventry, to ride to Shrewsbury if he could, to preach. We do not know if he did but Bentham and Lever did visit the town on the weekend of 21-22 September. They found most churches in the area with altars still standing and images retained, contrary to royal injunctions: 'hopyng and lookyng for a newe day as may thereby be conjectured', something not to be countenanced by true Christians.[26]

The meeting that September weekend between the local Protestant elite and the officers of the Church was deeply significant. We might expect Shrewsbury, as usual, to go along with the state religion but in this case there were issues for which we have some evidence. For one thing, the town was still concerned with godly education: since the founding of the town's school in 1552 the master, 'Sir Morys', had been replaced by one John Eyton, in October 1556 the bailiffs were looking for 'an honest able and discreate person' to replace Eyton. It was presumably the same man, 'J. Heyton, ludimagister', who had signed to the oath at the ecclesiastical visitation of 1559. The council was still looking for another 'honest man' for the school in November 1559; an unnamed master and his deputy had taught the boys during that year and were paid £12 5s. This is bound to have been one of the issues at the September meeting.[27] The other chief need was for godly preaching, such as the visitors provided that weekend. Their concerns matched those of the borough officers who entertained them. Thomas Bentham, from Yorkshire, and Thomas Lever, from Lancashire, had long been evangelicals, from their respective days at Oxford and Cambridge, and they had both been exiles among continental

Reformed Protestants. In October 1554 Lever had written from Zurich to his fellow Lancastrian John Bradford with whom he had been ordained by Bishop Ridley (like Ridley, Bradford was a prisoner soon to be put to death): 'I have seen the places, noted the doctrine and discipline, and talked with the learned men of Argentine [Strasbourg], Basil, Zurich, Bern, Lausan and Geneva; and I have had experience in all these places of sincere doctrine, godly order and great learning.' Lever singled out Bullinger and Calvin for praise. During the next few years Bentham had the same experiences; after his return to London he wrote to Lever for advice. Lever in turn sought advice from Henry Bullinger, particularly when there was dissension among his Aarau congregation: 'Being supported by your authority, [I] shall persevere with much greater firmness and alacrity in taking care to avoid offences and useless controversies; so that every thing may be more easily and effectually accommodated to the peace, and concord, and edification of the church.'[28] It was in this spirit that both Bentham and Lever had to accommodate to the Elizabethan church, although Lever never wore the hated vestments ordered by the queen. Through her injunctions, writes Andrew Pettegree, 'Elizabeth was in effect reasserting the independence of the English church in matters of organization and ceremony' but, as she was aware, many of her leading churchmen had enjoyed first-hand experience of the Swiss Reformed churches: 'The ecclesiology of the "best Reformed churches" was to be a powerful and potentially irresistible model for England's reformers.'[29] Some at least of Shrewsbury's Protestants were in sympathy with this ideal of a church although others would be conservative in religion, like the queen herself.

One issue was settled: a new schoolmaster was engaged. It is likely that Thomas Lever gave advice: he had pleaded in Edward's reign for Sedbergh School, which was saved; in Switzerland he had worked with the headmasters of Berne and Aarau; his brothers John and Ralph were teachers (John was master of Tonbridge School); and the man who came to Shrewsbury was a former colleague at St John's College, Cambridge, Thomas Ashton. On 11 April 1561 Bishop Bentham wrote to Archbishop Parker asking that Ashton be allowed to stay in Shrewsbury: he was the only godly preacher in that part of the diocese of Coventry and Lichfield, and he had begun 'a good work to the furtheraunce of a schole in Shrewsberye'. On 21 June 1561 an entry in the exchequer book of the borough confirms Ashton's appointment with one other learned schoolmaster, their stipends to be £40 and £8 respectively. Ashton's salary indicates the value set on his work. Another master and another usher were to be appointed, suggesting the ambitions of the town (and of Ashton) for Shrewsbury School.[30] As well as being a godly preacher Ashton was an experienced administrator, having served five times from the 1530s as bursar of St

John's College. This was experience which the local elite would have appreciated and the School did indeed flourish: by December 1562 there were 260 boys registered, half 'oppidani' from the town, half 'alieni' from outside.[31]

This could not have been accomplished without local support. George and Thomas Bromley, kinsmen of Sir Thomas, and also lawyers of the Inner Temple, became friends of both Ashton and Bishop Bentham. They also had the friendship and support of the Corbet family: Sir Andrew's son Robert had completed two years at Clare Hall, Cambridge, when he and his brothers were entertained with Thomas Ashton by the bailiffs of Shrewsbury in May 1561. On 8 June Ashton stood sponsor at a family christening at Shawbury with Dame Elizabeth Corbet, matriarch of the family. Two of Sir Andrew's sons were among the earliest entrants to the School and two others entered in 1564, with their cousin Philip Sidney. Another early entrant was Andrew Downes, son of a yeoman of Moreton Corbet; later regius professor of Greek at Cambridge, Downes praised Ashton as 'a preceptor of whom all his scholars may be proud'. Boys from all ranks of society entered the school, entry fees ranging from ten shillings to four pence according to rank and place of origin of their families. The same humanist programme of education was followed as was prescribed at St John's, with works in Greek and Latin, and the St John's tradition of performing plays was incorporated into the curriculum: one afternoon each week senior boys would declaim and act a scene from a classical work. The education was Christian as well as humanist; prayers began and ended the day. Householders were also to take scholars to their parish churches for divine service and for sermons.[32]

Shrewsbury Castle with Shrewsbury School, now the library, in the background

Another contribution by Ashton was noteworthy: the production of vernacular plays in the Quarry at Whitsuntide. In 1561 his 'firste playe upon the passion' was put on, and he and another gentleman of Cambridge were entertained by the bailiffs. The borough assembly minute books for 1563-64 include a decision to confer with Ashton about the cost of the play in 1564; gilds and individuals contributed and the council met other charges so that Ashton should not be the loser. In 1564-65 the bailiffs' accounts include a payment of £25 to Ashton, a large sum which may have been for the setting up of a wooden frame in the Quarry; in 1565 *Julian the Apostate* was performed. Another 'great play' was put on in 1568, and *The Play of the Passion* was performed again in 1569. We are on familiar ground here with Whitsun plays but we are no longer in the medieval or Catholic tradition: Ashton's plays were part of his programme for instructing the whole of the town, and the many visitors (who were good for trade) in 'true' religion. The local chronicler wrote of 'a notable stage playe played in Shrosberie in a place callyd the quarrell [Quarry] which lasted all the hollydayes unto the which cam greate number of people of noblemen and others the whiche was praysed greatlye and the chyff aucter therof was one master Astoon being the head scoolmaster of the free scoole there a godly and lernyd man who took marvelous greate paynes therin'. The Shrewsbury-born poet Thomas Churchyard wrote of the crowds and of the amphitheatre where they saw the plays, adding in a marginal note: 'Maister Aston was a good and godly preacher.'[33]

It may be relevant that the Strasbourg reformer Martin Bucer, who had spent the last year of his life at Cambridge, wrote of plays in his *De Regno Christi:*

> The young will be able to take part in acting comedies and tragedies and thus provide their public with wholesome entertainment which is not without value in increasing piety: but religious men will be needed to compose these comedies and tragedies, men schooled in the knowledge of Christ's Kingdom and also endowed with discrimination.

This treatise, written by Bucer for Edward VI and his reformers, was published in Basel in 1567 but it had been available in manuscript before that. Ashton may have known of Bucer's teachings at Cambridge, where the reformer had many friends and gave many lectures; his funeral in 1520 was attended by some three thousand people. In *De Regno Christi* Bucer also left a pattern of the Reformation which might be effected in England: 'A sound relationship between Church and State can be achieved only if Christianity is not left to the Churches only, but if it penetrates and infiltrates all secular affairs.'

Parishes should be administered by well-educated and responsible ministers and abuses in rites and ceremonies must be rejected.[34] Ashton was later to write that it was the good providence of God that made the bailiffs 'committ the credit of such a mater to a weake person at the first whose purposed power should geave streingth to the same'.[35] He was committed to this mission.

Bucer may have inspired Ashton, Shrewsbury's reformist pastor: as schoolmaster he was educating the next generation in humanist and Christian principles and as preacher he was instructing and admonishing their elders. He was in fact more than a preacher, as certain references in Bishop Bentham's letters indicate. On 15 April 1561, in a letter to Richard Walker, archdeacon of Stafford and Derby, the bishop referred to a visitation when Walker was to instruct all curates to know certain texts of the New Testament – 'to be lerned withowt the booke' – and to explain some of the queen's injunctions. They must sing or say the two psalms in English with the litany and suffrages and with some sermon or homily of thanksgiving to God; they must be moved to temperance in their drinking; and they must avoid superstition and vain gazing, as they used the previous year: 'and in no case that they use crosse, taper, nor beades' as in previous Catholic practices. 'And yf my freynd Mr Aston do in any matter of myne conferr with you, I pray you helpe hym with your counsell as you knowe best in such cases.' The indication that Ashton was to act for the bishop in Shropshire is borne out in another letter, dated 29 May 1561, to James Weston, registrar, concerning a clerk, Richard Sherer, who was to appear before the bishop or his deputy at Shrewsbury 'to be examined of a matter towching my Lord of Hereford & me, before Mr Thomas Ashton preacher'. (The reference may be to Walter Devereux, viscount Hereford, of Chartley in Staffordshire.) In a letter to Ashton himself, of the same date, the bishop wrote about this examination: 'By reason the parson is aged & impotent thes are not onely to wyll you but also therewith to autoryse you in my name to take the examination accordyng to such articles as the bearer hereof shall minister or exhibyte unto you. Wherein I praye you most hartelye to use your diligence and so I doubt not but the wicked shalbe put to confusion.'[36] If more of the bishop's letter-books had survived we would doubtless know more about Ashton's activities and the state of the churches in Shrewsbury.

There was another sphere in which Ashton, as the public preacher and headmaster, was active: the secular affairs of the town. Again we are dependent on partial survival of documents. The headmaster's name occurs in the records of the Mercers, Ironmongers and Goldsmiths Company as surety for some members and supervisor of the examination of witnesses. The editor comments that Ashton 'seems to have been of great esteem in the Company as variances are frequently referred to his decision and judgment'.[37] When the Privy Council required the bishops to provide a survey of religious loyalties in 1564 Bentham took the advice of Sir Andrew Corbet, Sir Richard Newport and George Leigh, one of the bailiffs of Shrewsbury, in naming those favouring the new religion and meet to be made justices of the peace. For Shrewsbury the bishop recommended as aldermen and councillors fit to bear office Humphrey Onslow, Edward Hosier, George Leigh, Robert Ireland the elder and Robert Ireland the younger. He also named Thomas Ashton, 'Scholemaster, and a worthy man emongst them'. Lever, the archdeacon of Coventry, also named Ashton in his list.[38] In contrast, the archdeaconries of Derby and Stafford, and the diocese of Herefordshire, had many Catholics.

It was, of course, William Cecil who ran the business of the Council of State and who was concerned with the establishment of the English Protestant Church, and the threat of Catholicism. (In his absence from court, on account of his gout, in December 1571 the Commons failed to get the queen's assent to the bill establishing the Thirty-Nine Articles of Religion, already approved by convocation.) Thomas Ashton was probably known to Cecil who had been a student at St John's, Cambridge. Cecil had in his household one of Ashton's Shrewsbury pupils, Philip Sidney. By the end of the decade the headmaster was in contact with Cecil and the Council over matters relating to the School. It was another affair that occasioned a letter from Ashton to Lord Burghley (Cecil was ennobled in February 1571); the headmaster wrote to him in October. This time Ashton was of use to Burghley: the duke of Norfolk was involved in a plot to support the imprisoned Mary queen of Scotland and to help the Catholic cause. Norfolk was not himself a Catholic but he did hope to marry the Scottish queen. He had had interests in the north-west of England since his marriage to the widow of Thomas Lord Dacre in 1567; she died the same year. Her son, the sixth Lord Dacre, died in 1569, leaving three sisters who were Norfolk's wards and were married off to his sons. There had been Catholic risings in the north: the rebellion of the earls of Northumberland and Westmorland in 1569 and the Dacre rising of 1570. In that year Pope Pius V had excommunicated Elizabeth, 'the pretended queen', absolving her subjects from allegiance. The agent for Norfolk's Dacre estates was a Shropshire man, Lawrence Banister of Wem, another Catholic. Sir Andrew Corbet helped frustrate the plan to send funds for Mary Stuart, arresting Banister who was sent to London for questioning in September 1571. Sir Andrew sent his son Robert to Burghley and the earl of Leicester (Corbet's kinsman) with news of the interception of the money, while Ashton went to the north-west, possibly as far as Cumberland. He informed Burghley in his turn:

> I have travelled since Banister his apprehending in sundry counties especially where he had doing under the Duke. The people in general in these parts ... show in their countenance a misliking of the state and let not sometimes to utter the cankerdness of their hearts with the tongue, yet so that although the simple do it plainly, the other do it so cunningly, as no advantage can be taken of them ... The papists in this realm find too much favour in the Court ... The double faced gentlemen who will be protestants in the Court and in the country secret papists *frigidam suffundunt* [pour cold water on the government].

Ashton expressed the wish that Banister should be replaced by Sir Andrew Corbet, 'the only staid man, most secret, true and faithfullest to his prince, I know in all these parts of the realm'. Expressing the hope that Cecil would burn this letter (make a sacrifice of it to Vulcan), Ashton ends: 'God work with you as he hath done and give you long honourable life and health unto your noble heart's desire.'[39]

Although Ashton began a new career in the household of Walter Devereux, created earl of Essex in 1572, he won important grants and privileges for the School and made visits to the town. He had already helped to establish preaching in Shrewsbury, whose importance as a bulwark in a frontier zone was all the more important in the new politico-religious circumstances. The chief church for preaching and visitations was St Chad's, where Christopher Hawkshurst of St John's College, Cambridge was minister: in May 1573 the borough awarded him £5 extra a year 'in consideration of his travail and service in preaching and administration of God's word'; many years later the town

St John's College, Cambridge

would give his son money towards his maintenance at Oxford 'in respect of his father's pains ... late preacher of God's word in Salop'. A Welsh bilingual preacher, Thomas Price, was ordained by Bishop Bentham in 1570 and appointed to St Julian's in Shrewsbury. It was hoped to set up preaching 'exercises' in the town but Ashton's departure delayed this. He would have been the moderator as Lever was at Coventry.[40] These exercises or 'prophesyings' were a Zurich institution, begun by Huldrych Zwingli in 1525 and continued by Bullinger: the prophecy was the study of the Bible in Hebrew, Greek, Latin and the vernacular, and its exposition in a gathering of ministers and lay people – it was of central importance to education in the Reformed faith.[41] The Shrewsbury Chronicler records that in October 1573, following a special commission to see order according to the queen's injunctions, the exercise began at St Chad's. There was a condition: the wearing of 'seemly habits' and square caps as required by Injunction XXX: 'the clergy to be properly apparelled'.

> This yeare the mynysters in the churches of Shrewsberye against Christmas dyd all wear theire crosse capps and whyte syrplesyes which longe tyme befor dyd leave them off.[42]

Thomas Ashton and his supporters in the town also had plans for St Mary's, a royal peculiar not subject to episcopal jurisdiction, but they had to wait until new statutes for Shrewsbury School gave them control. In February 1578 the master and fellows of St John's, Cambridge were party with the headmaster and bailiffs of Shrewsbury, and the bishop of Lichfield, to the indenture tripartite confirming the statutes and formally linking Shrewsbury School with St John's. In August Thomas Ashton paid his last visit to Shrewsbury where he 'prechyd famously'; on 29 August he died near Cambridge. Bishop Bentham had preached at Moreton Corbet earlier that month, at the funeral of Sir Andrew Corbet. The bishop died in February 1579, in which year his son Benjamin entered Shrewsbury School. In March 1580 boys from the School performed in Thomas Legge's *Richardus Tertius* at St John's. The college hall saw the staging, in Latin, of a new development in chronicle plays, telling of the fall of the House of York, the sad demise of the princes, and the defeat of Richard by Henry Tudor, son of Lady Margaret, founder of St John's. His marriage to Elizabeth of York meant the happy uniting of both houses, 'of whome the Queenes majestie came and is undoubted heyre'.[43]

The exercises at St Chad's had been discontinued as they had elsewhere, forbidden by the queen in 1577 after she received adverse reports from some bishops. John Scory of Hereford complained that his chaplain had heard a preacher at Shrewsbury denounce 'the negligence, lordliness, tyranny, covetousness, and pluralities' of bishops; the bishop feared 'some colour of Cartwright's platform'. Thomas Cartwright had caused a sensation at Cambridge in 1570 by advocating a presbyterian programme of church government. The exercises were defended by Bishop Bentham but he had to transmit the order that they should cease, adding in his letter to Thomas Lever that 'the heavenly and most comfortable gift of preaching might still be used'.[44]

Godly preaching at Shrewsbury was enhanced by the establishment of a public preacher at St Mary's, the curate appointed by the headmaster and bailiffs. Christopher Hawkshurst had died in 1576, of 'plague', as had Roger Barnes, curate of St Alkmund's, but Thomas Price of St Julian's was promoted to the living of St Chad's. The two bailiffs

St Mary's (SA-IMG24340)

elected at Michaelmas 1579 were Robert Ireland the younger and John Perche, a wealthy Draper and parishioner of St Mary's. They acquired the services of Dr Edward Bulkeley for St Mary's: he was Shropshire-born, and a fellow of St John's, Cambridge, where he had refused to wear the surplice in the 1560s. The headmaster at this time was Thomas Laurence, former second master to Ashton; his letter of farewell to the bailiffs in 1583 reveals his attitude to his 'publicke charge', the School, 'which was in as flourishing an estate as any in all England.' This claim was endorsed by the judgement of William Camden, headmaster of Westminster School, when he visited Shrewsbury at about the same time: the school was the best filled in all England. Thomas Laurence was particularly glad that for twelve years, with the blessing of God, he had sent some hundred boys to Oxford and Cambridge, 'of whiche a greate number ... are as likelye men to prove good members in the churche of god, and worthie instruments in a Christian Commonwealthe, as any whosoever or whearsoever'. Bulkeley contributed to the godly regime of the town by setting up in 1581 a programme of weekday services on Mondays, Wednesdays and Fridays: at St Chad's at eight o'clock, at St Julian's at nine, and at St Mary's at ten. The Shrewsbury Chronicler calls this 'a good and godly begyninge the Lord be praysed for'. Bulkeley also had a chapel in St Mary's repaired so that schoolmasters and scholars could attend divine service and hear sermons. The borough council awarded him an extra £10, in addition to his generous stipend of £52 a year. He was also leased the splendid new Drapers' Hall, alongside St Mary's. The problem of papist images was in part solved by a great tempest which destroyed most of the stained glass. Bulkeley's successor in 1582, John Tomkys, continued this work by having an 'idolatrous' window of the Assumption removed, selling the two organs, and putting in pews for the convenience of those attending the sermons.[45]

Following the Catholic plots and the pope's bull of excommunication, a series of statutes was enacted to combat the Catholic and foreign danger. There were attempts to persuade the recusants to conform with fines and threats of prison. From 1581 there was legislation imposing a much heavier fine of £20 a month on convicted recusants. Informers and churchwardens were allowed to bring charges of recusancy and cases could be heard in secular courts. In the 1580s various statutes declared that priests could be declared traitors without need of overt act or statement; they could be executed or banished merely for being priests. One recusant family near Chirk was the object of attention of a select commission of the Council in the Marches in 1578/9. The Privy Council had been informed by Thomas Laurence and another master of Shrewsbury School, via George Bromley, chief justice of north Wales, of disorders in the house of John Edwards. Plas Newydd was a regular meeting place for recusants; masses were said there by priests returned from abroad; burials were conducted by night and children re-christened; and Mrs Edwards was in the habit of leading pilgrimages to Holywell. Her husband was imprisoned but his house continued as a recusant centre.[46]

If there were Catholics in Shrewsbury they were discreet, although those in country places might be undetected. Of the category described as 'Church Papists', conformists who were still Catholic at heart, it is difficult to say anything as their numbers and attitudes remained hidden. It might be difficult also to discriminate between such people and those content with Prayer Book Protestantism, not wishing for further reform. This group may account for the hostility to John Tomkys, who proved to be extremely harsh in dealing with his flock. He revered Bullinger, 'the learned and grave Father', some of whose works he translated; he wrote his own exposition of the Lord's Prayer for the Christian parents and godly householders of Shrewsbury; he drew up his own articles of inquiry; and he held a consistory court in St Mary's to punish offenders (such as the woman who spoke idle words about him and was imprisoned in chains). There was also a dispute over the election of a new parish clerk, recorded in full in the vestry book: parishioners assembled in church on Sunday 10 September 1587 were promised free election of one of three candidates, but when Tomkys found they had chosen a man not to his liking he simply overruled them. As a consequence, 'great unquietness was given to the said minister' and to his nephew and deputy. Godly parishioners begged for a friendly end to the dispute, accepting the ruling of a legal officer a month later. This incident contrasts with Thomas Price's emollient handling of complaints from his parishioners when he moved the ancient font and substituted a wooden one in the centre of St Chad's; he replaced the old font in its usual place at the entrance to the church, 'for that the moste parte of the parishioners did grudge against the remoovinge of the same'.[47]

Shrewsbury may be taken as a representative town. Its growth, in population and wealth, was reflected in its new buildings. William Camden praised it as a 'faire and goodly Citie ... well frequented and traded, full of good merchandise ... rich and wealthy'. Thomas Churchyard, revisiting his birthplace in 1587, found it 'as worlde were made anew'. The Council House was now a seat of the Council in the Marches but it was also leased to members of the town's elite. Our anonymous chronicler was by this time an eye-witness, sympathetic to the religious reforms and evidently proud of ceremonial. Elizabeth did not visit the town but the lord president of the Council in the Marches,

Sir Henry Sidney, represented authority in the two weeks he spent in Shrewsbury in 1581, from the eve of St George's feast. The long procession from the Council House, near St Mary's, to St Chad's included the bailiffs and the aldermen in their scarlet gowns. Sidney's stall was next to that prepared for the queen, with banners of other Garter knights in place. Divine service was sung 'by note to the glorifieinge of God and to the greate honour of the said Sir Henry'. Sidney kept open house while he was in the town, and the School played its part with 'a brave and costly bancket' on the first of May. The four masters presented ten courses each with accompanying Latin orations. On the next day the School put on a martial display with drums, trumpets and ensigns processing through the town to Gaye meadow where the scholars professed their willingness to fight

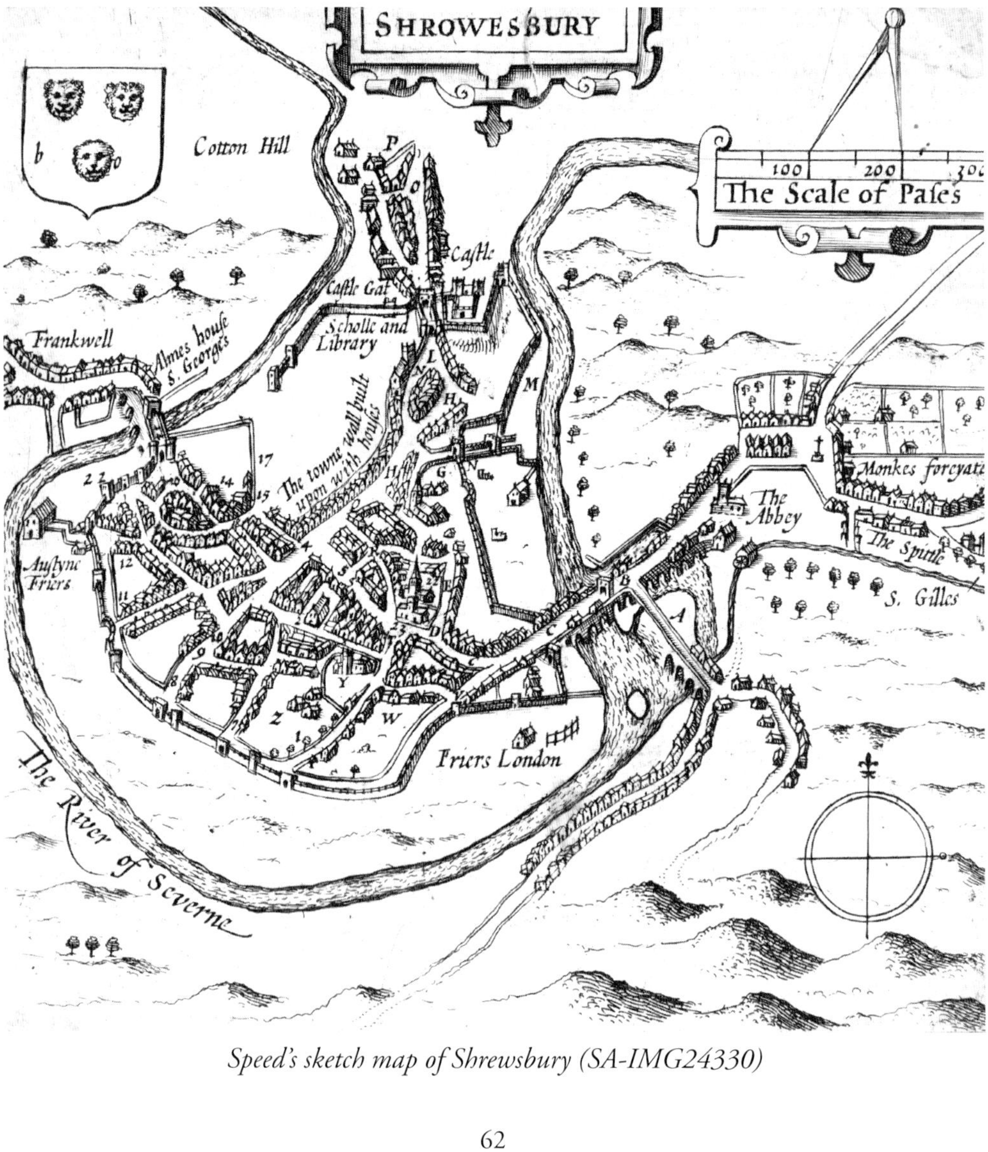

Speed's sketch map of Shrewsbury (SA-IMG24330)

and defend their country. A more lyrical display marked Sidney's departure by river: scholars dressed in green with willow branches lamented the departure, but 'because the oracions of the sayd nymphes are soomwhat tedious' the chronicler includes only the final verses.[48]

Three years later Sidney's brother-in-law the earl of Leicester visited the town, with his stepson the earl of Essex. Among other duties they attended a sermon given by John Tomkys at St Mary's. The fact that an episcopal visitation had taken place three weeks earlier, concerned to enforce the injunctions concerning the wearing of surplices and the christening of children, may be relevant, Leicester being a patron of puritan preachers. Tomkys preached on 16 May 1584, exhorting his hearers to 'walke in love, even as Christ hath loved us', and quoting the prophets, the apostle Paul and the gospels. The preacher discoursed on Adam's fall and God's covenant with his people, and the covenant of the New Testament. Through Christ God 'extended his mercy, in forgiving his elect their sinnes, and that through Christs Holines maintained his Justice, in punishing the nature of man'. He includes an anti-Catholic message: 'Judge ye then, whether the Papistes be nor of the number of those false teachers, whome Peter prophecied should come, whiche should denie the Lord that bought them, which undoubtedly they doe, when by bringing in the traditions of men, they deny the fulnesse of Christs prophecie'; he condemns the mass as a denial of Christ's sacrifice.[49]

Two months after the visit of the earls to Shrewsbury the chronicler records the performance of a 'notable' stage play in the Apple Market in the High Street put on 'openly and freely' by the earl of Essex's men. We are now in the age of the English Elizabethan theatre. The Poor Law Act of 1572 was particularly severe against vagabonds, 'a term widely defined to include unlicensed and wandering players, fortune tellers, fencers, bearwards, jugglers, and university scholars', as Penry Williams explains. After the northern rising and other alarms it was prohibited for any lord to give livery except to his household servants while the Act ordered the punishment of entertainers not belonging to any baron or lord of higher degree, the possible punishments including whipping, ear-boring, sentence to the galleys, or death for a third offence. Most reputable players had found patrons, strengthening their position. Essex's Men had first been maintained by Walter Devereux, the first earl, then by his widow from 1576 to 1578, in which year she secretly married the earl of Leicester and the players became her son's men.[50] In 1586, on 14 June, Shrewsbury's new charter was read out in the Guildhall. Principal articles requested by the town were granted: that the parish of Holy Cross with St Giles was to be under the government of the bailiffs of Shrewsbury and that the town had liberty to

St Giles (SA-IMG24342)

buy land worth not more than £100 per annum to maintain the public preacher (money from interest on capital not being considered a suitable source of his income). On 8 September the School put on another martial display 'against the popes army and other rebells whom they triumphantly vanquished to the greate reioysinge of the beholders'. The date was significant: in the Catholic calendar it was the nativity of the Virgin Mary but the Protestant replacement was the queen's birthday on 7 September. The timing was particularly appropriate as there had been more popish plots in favour of Mary Stuart, whose complicity was now proved.

On 8 September Burghley wrote to Francis Walsingham: the queen had refused to send Mary to the Tower, suggesting Fotheringhay in Northamptonshire instead, but she had agreed to put her on trial, naming a panel of peers. Elizabeth informed Mary and proceedings began on the 14 October. There were delays and bouts of indecision, especially on the part of Elizabeth: 'It seems it was not Mary's death that troubled the queen, but her own unavoidable responsibility for it.' The sentiment, writes David Loades, does her little credit. Mary was executed on 9 February, having shown sufficient dignity to elevate her cause 'into one of Catholic martyrdom'. Burghley 'could console himself for his temporary rustication with the thought that he had masterminded the demise of the woman he had regarded for nearly 20 years as the single greatest menace to Elizabeth and her crown'. On 19 September in 1588 a solemn day was kept in Shrewsbury to thank God for the defeat of the Spanish Armada, 'to the greate rejoisinge of all England. God be praysid. Amen.'[51]

Such victories over Catholics did not guarantee harmony in religion in England since there were still many who wanted a thoroughly reformed church, often referred to as 'Puritans'. In Shrewsbury in 1589 there was what the chronicler described as 'soom contraversie' in the town about the setting up of maypoles, the making of bonfires, and the putting up of trees before the Shearmen's Hall and other places. The shearmen with their tree were the main protagonists on the side of festivity, with John Tomkys preaching against them. At about the same time the bishop's ordinary came to St Chad's to reform sundry faults contrary to the queen's injunctions – once again it was the requirement to wear surplices at divine service which was being ignored, and continued to be ignored in the chronicler's account. What we have here is a demonstration on two fronts that the town was divided on religious matters. The shearmen were a large and rowdy component of the population, employed by drapers whose Company dominated the town's government, but there was another factor: the Shearmen's feast was kept at about the time of Corpus Christi, indeed their accounts still referred to Corpus Christi although Trinity Sunday was now the official reference point. Nor was the trouble of the kind experienced at election time in October, when apprentices and schoolboys were meant to be confined at home.[52] The dispute went on for two years, matters coming to a head in 1591 when the shearmen kept their feast on 6 June, the first Sunday after Trinity. Tomkys was followed mockingly through the streets to his home at Drapers' Hall. The leading apprentice, Richard Fearnes, was put in prison, accused of 'not having God before his eyes but seduced by the instigations of the devil'; he claimed to be defending 'lawfull customes of our

Shearers' Hall (SA-IMG24334)

company'. The bailiffs that year, Thomas Shearer and Thomas Burnell, stressed to the lord lieutenant that they were concerned for public order, but their deposition reads:

> for sondry yeares in former times the Sonday next after Trynyty Sonday yearely was so prophaned from morning to evening by the freemen jorneymen and apprentizes of divers occupacions by unlawfull and riotous assemblyes by excesses of eating and drinking ... the most parte of them especially of the youthfull sort absenting them selves from their parish churches.'[53]

Burnell, a leading Draper, had been the town's emissary to invite Edward Bulkeley to Shrewsbury in 1580. On the other side was Thomas Owen of Lincoln's Inn, recorder of Shrewsbury, who declared in favour of the tree which could be used 'as heretofore' as long as it was done 'civilly and in lovinge order without contention'. Tomkys died on 23 June 1592, leaving a divided town behind him: his death caused 'great lamentacion' among the 'perfect protestants'.[54] The question posed by Patrick Collinson, at the end of his study of the affair, is: 'did Tomkys represent that mysterious substance, or factor, '"charisma"; or was he no more than the paid agent of something called "social control"?'[55] It is an intriguing question.

Social control was part of the intention and effect of godly government, but during the Elizabethan phase of Shrewsbury's Protestant history religion was the main motive in the pursuit of suitable preachers. The first was Thomas Ashton, who was not always supported by the borough council. In 1576 he wrote letters to the then bailiffs complaining of delays in agreeing to the School statutes: 'I will take a new course, both to defeat the purpose of those ill-meaners, and establish the thing more surely for learning, though less beneficial for the Town hereafter.' Bulkeley had sufficient status, academically and socially, to impose his will on the town. Tomkys probably lacked the same advantages: he had, for example, to undergo a probationary period of preaching in the town before his appointment was confirmed, although after his death he was described by the then bailiffs, Richard Powell and Edward Ireland (son of Robert the elder), as 'the golden candlestick of Doctryne which hath shined amoungst us now divers years by his ministry'. This they wrote in a letter to Edward Bulkeley, asking him to return 'for the continuance of the word of truth being the food of our souls'. Bulkeley had moved of his own choice to Odell in Bedfordshire, a more prestigious living. He did not intend to return to Shrewsbury, but he went to Cambridge on the town's behalf and found 'a bachelor of divinity of 4 years' standing ... a man greatly recommended by the best in Cambridge for his learning, good and godly behaviour, wisdom and disposition'. How much trouble this took we do not know, but the group in Shrewsbury were anxious to have a continuing godly ministry. Thomas Laughton at St Mary's joined Thomas Price at St Chad's in the spiritual care of the town during the difficult 1590s when floods and ruined crops caused great hardship. Their care for the poor was a familiar feature of godly religion but was now statutory, according to poor law.

On Sunday 11 August 1594 the two preachers, with the consent of the bailiffs, appointed a general fast in Shrewsbury, held at St Mary's where most of the inhabitants, in the chronicler's account, prayed for seasonable weather to bring in their crops, 'lamentinge their synns and callinge to God with sooche godly sermons made there of the preachars', from 8 in the morning until 4 in the afternoon. Laughton resigned in 1596, possibly joining Bulkeley whose son-in-law he became. The bailiffs wrote to both men who replied in 1597 that they had tried to find a suitably qualified minister but those asked declined 'on account of the stipend being too slender for these hard times'. When Thomas Burnell was again serving as bailiff, in 1597-8, William Bright BD of Emmanuel College, Cambridge, was appointed (January 1598) as curate of St Mary's and public preacher, having spent sixteen days in the town when he preached 'divers times'.[56] All this suggests the initiative and persistence of certain Protestants in Shrewsbury. The appointment of Humfrey Leech to St Alkmund's in 1598 was outside their control, being a Crown living.[57]

The reigns of the two daughters of Henry VIII spanned well-nigh fifty years. Mary, queen for little more than five years, was clear in her aim of restoring England to the Roman Catholic Church, persecuting Protestants mercilessly in the process. Elizabeth is a more enigmatic figure, ready to accept the presence of non-seditious Catholics in her realm, until the actions of Pope and missionaries, and the plotting of followers of Mary Stuart, forced a more severe policy. Her relations with her bishops and her opposition to preachers shows us another side of the queen. Patrick Collinson writes that it was 'an odd sort of Protestant who nursed a negative prejudice against the preaching ministry' and wished it to be reduced. He quotes the famous rebuke by her second archbishop of Canterbury, Edmund Grindal, when she exerted her own will by suppressing the prophesyings: 'Alas, Madam! is the scripture more plain in any one thing, than that the Gospel of Christ should be plentifully preached; and that plenty of labourers should be sent into the Lord's harvest?'[58] After the Injunctions of 1559, which largely followed those of her brother Edward VI, Elizabeth did not endorse further articles of Archbishop Parker in 1566 (they were issued as 'Advertisements'), or the canons and articles of convocation in 1571. She approved the Acts against Jesuits and Seminarists (1585) and those against Recusants and Puritans (1593), but in 1595 she ordered Archbishop Whitgift to withdraw the nine Lambeth articles calling for an end to religious controversy at Cambridge. 'Even at the height of his power, the archbishop could not rely upon crown support.'[59] Many of the preachers who praised Elizabeth as a Deborah were, in the way of prophets, also admonishing her that her entitlement to the crown was 'contingent upon the commitment she demonstrated in extirpating idolatry and erecting a true Church in her realm.' If she failed, 'England might once again find herself in penal servitude to Rome'. As early as 1583 Archbishop Edwin Sandys, in an Accession Day sermon at York, praised Elizabeth as the restorer of religion and liberty but pointed out her further responsibilities. There was also oblique criticism of the queen in parliament. Nevertheless, as Alexandra Walsham argues, if Elizabeth was 'a disappointment as a proactive reformer' her survival despite numerous plots confirmed her as 'the Lord's anointed'. So the myth of Elizabeth survived her reign: on her death in March 1603 an anonymous poet extolled her virtues:

> How God's religion which herself professed
> She did establish; banished Popery,
> With superstition and idolatry.
> Her hearty zeal sought both by deed and word,
> To build the ruined Temple of the Lord ... [60]

Chapter 4
Puritans and Laudians

As Elizabeth I lay dying she had at her side John Whitgift, archbishop of Canterbury, as her father had had Thomas Cranmer with him. Whitgift, 'like the queen ... had become something of a survivor of a bygone stage in the English Reformation'.[1] At Cambridge in the 1570s he had opposed Thomas Cartwright, the leader of the English presbyterian movement; as bishop of Worcester and vice-president of the Council in the Marches of Wales he had encountered Roman Catholicism; as archbishop he wanted to maintain the integrity of the Church of England, against puritan and papist alike. In 1596 he had drawn up but not publicised the so-called Lambeth Articles, intended to reinforce Reformist theology, which was faced with a challenge from certain Cambridge divines who believed not in predestination but in free will as a means to salvation. Whitgift may also have been anticipating the accession of James VI of Scotland 'whose own confessional commitment was then still ambivalent'.[2] In Shrewsbury there was a legacy of those Cambridge disputes in the person of Humfrey Leech, vicar of St Alkmund's, a living in the hands of the Crown and administered by the Lord Keeper Thomas Egerton, who liked to appoint godly preachers, especially if they were from his native Shropshire. Leech fulfilled the criteria: he was from Market Drayton and was educated at Shrewsbury School, having John Tomkys of St Mary's as a catechist. A graduate of Queens' College, Cambridge, he moved to Emmanuel, a college founded specifically to train godly preachers, where he took his MA. But Leech changed his religious position, possibly on account of the theological disputes while he was at Emmanuel in the mid-1590s. He wrote later of his 'perfit hatred, that from my innermost soule, I ever conceived against Puritanisme (the very bane of ancient Christianity)'. While he was at St Alkmund's, from 1598 until 1607, there were two Reformist preachers in Shrewsbury: Thomas Price of St Chad's had been in the town since the early 1570s while William Bright, BD, of Emmanuel College, was appointed to St Mary's in 1598.[3] The religious disputes in

St Alkmund's church (SA-IMG24350)

sixteenth-century Shrewsbury were set to continue in the reign of James I, which began on 24 March 1603.

The term 'puritan' as used by Leech was one of the derogatory labels applied in factional disputes, just as 'popish' or 'papist' were used of Roman Catholics. The term Catholic, however, was used by theologians of the Church of England to encompass their Church as deriving from the early Church for the term 'Anglicanism' had not yet been coined – the *ecclesia anglicana* was the English Church. Article XIX of the thirty-nine, in translation, reads:

> Of the Church. The visible Church of Christ is a congregation of faithful men, in the which the pure word of God is preached, and the Sacraments be duly administered according to Christ's ordinance in all those things that of necessity are requisite to the same. As the Church [*sic*] of Jerusalem, Alexandria, and Antioch have erred, so also the Church of Rome hath erred, not only in their living and manner of ceremonies, but also in matters of faith.

Article XXII is specific: 'The Romish Doctrine concerning Purgatory, Pardons, Worshipping, and Adoration, as well of Images, as of Reliques, and also Invocation of

Saints, is a fond thing vainly invented, and grounded upon no warranty of Scripture, but rather repugnant to the Word of God.' (These issues within the Church of England were to become paramount in the seventeenth century.) Calvin defined the visible church as 'the multitude of men diffused throughout the world, who profess to worship one God in Christ; are initiated into this faith by baptism; testify their unity in one true doctrine and charity, by participating in the Supper; have consent in the Word of God, and for the preaching of that Word maintain the ministry ordained of Christ.'[4] The term 'Calvinist' thus became a label, used in the 1550s when Calvin was engaged in various debates:

> While a few of those attacked as Calvinists accepted the label for the purposes of public debate, most rejected it as the appropriate name for the party or church of which they were a part. They preferred to call themselves variously the evangelical, reformed, evangelical reformed, or reformed Catholic churches, the term *reformed* emerging as the most common label ... *Reformed* is thus for several reasons a more historically accurate and less potentially misleading label than *Calvinist* to apply to those churches and to the larger tradition to which they attach themselves.[5]

We find instances of such usage in the context of early seventeenth-century Shropshire, one being the inscription devised by Andrew Newport for his tomb at Wroxeter: he described himself as a 'true professor of the doctrine according to the best reformed churches'.[6]

Reformists among the English clergy hoped that the new king would grant some of their petitions, the more extreme demands being for a presbyterial form of church government, but James himself remarked that if he wanted presbytery he could return to Scotland. Crowned king of Scotland when he was only a year old, in 1567, his troubled reign had seen disputes with the Kirk, the Reformed Scottish Church of which John Knox was a leader in the 1560s. James did call a conference of divines in January 1604 at Hampton Court, where an unfortunate use of the word 'presbytery' by one of the Reformists provoked the king's famous outburst 'No bishop, no king'. An anonymous account of the conference quotes James as saying: 'I will have the Bishops to governe the churche, and they only shall have to do with the censure of excommunication being assisted with the deanes and the gravest preachers.' (This was in direct contrast to presbyterial church discipline.) There was an implied threat to make the reformists conform but James agreed with them about the need for preachers. One commentator, the diplomat Dudley Carleton, observed of the two sides in the debate that 'as they differ in opinions so doe they in fashions, for one side marches in gownes and rochets [surplices worn by bishops], and th'other in clokes and nite-caps'.[7] The old dispute over clerical garb persisted.

Archbishop Whitgift had already written to the bishops for lists of clergy and preachers, their academic qualifications and place of residence: such a list survives for the diocese of Lichfield. Of 89 ministers in the archdeaconry of Salop, 22 were preachers. At least one name is missing, that of William Bright of St Mary's in Shrewsbury, perhaps because of that church's status as a royal peculiar. Thomas Price is named for St Chad's and Humfrey Leech (not officially a preacher) for St Alkmund's; assistant clergy are not named. Shrewsbury's ratio of ministers to population (then about 5,500) was in fact reasonably high in comparison with other provincial places.[8] Richard Bancroft, bishop of London, was a leading figure at the Hampton Court Conference, representing the church hierarchy; on the death of Whitgift soon afterwards (February 1604) Bancroft was appointed archbishop of Canterbury. He took up the task of ensuring ceremonial conformity and rectifying abuses such as non-residency and the shortage of qualified preachers, opposing puritans and papists alike. This was a time when there were fears that James might grant toleration to Catholic recusants, the queen, Anne of Denmark, being allegedly a convert to that religion, but the Gunpowder Plot of November 1605 altered the case. During the summer Shrewsbury had been a stopping-place on the pilgrimage to Holywell of a group of thirty or so pilgrims, led by the Jesuit Henry Garnet. They set out on 30 August on a journey 'which took them across the whole recusant arc from Enfield in the east ... [to] Norbrook near Stratford, Huddington Court near Worcester, a tavern at Shrewsbury and finally into Wales itself'.[9] Unfortunately we do not have an account from anyone in Shrewsbury, where recusants had to remain well hidden.

Humfrey Leech moved to Oxford in 1607, having already been appointed a chaplain there in 1603/4. The religious milieu was hostile: 'The character of Oxford divinity, until the reign of Charles I, was militantly Protestant, generally Calvinist, in the sense of adhering to the Reformed theology of grace, and strongly evangelical.'[10] The friends left behind in Shrewsbury were suspected of popery when Leech became a Roman Catholic in 1608. In January 1609 Archbishop Bancroft deplored the storm created at Oxford by Leech's preaching, his apostasy, and the 'shipwrack of a good conscience'.[11] In 1609 Leech published *A triumph of truth* which was answered in 1610 by *The defence of truth* by Daniel Price, an Oxford scholar and a son of Thomas Price of St Chad's in Shrewsbury; like Leech he was an alumnus of Shrewsbury School. In the light of the question of labelling it is worth quoting Price:

> The scornful aspersion you cast upon us by the byname of Calvinists we neither reject nor receive. Reverend, Learned, holy Calvin was the greatest glory of the French Church that ever was ... and though our Religion seek neither antiquity or confirmation by him ... yet we reverence him.

The same thing might have been said by another group, labelled 'Arminian' after Jacob Arminius of Leyden (died 1609): in the English context this group is represented by churchmen such as Lancelot Andrewes and Richard Neile. These clerics rejected the harsher aspects of the doctrine of predestination, laying 'greater stress on the sacraments and upon the history of the "visible" Church in the form which it took in England. There was now almost definitive stress upon the apostolic succession of bishops.'[12] These clerics did not rely on Arminius for their identity or origin but are best seen as part of the Catholic tradition in the Church of England, as opposed to the Reformed. This was exemplified particularly by the tradition of ceremonial and beauty of the church and the liturgy at Westminster Abbey under the dean, Lancelot Andrewes. Neile was made dean of Westminster in 1605 when Andrewes became bishop of Chichester.[13]

In 1610 Neile was appointed to his second bishopric, Coventry and Lichfield, but it was as a Visitor on behalf of St John's College, Cambridge that he was drawn into a dispute over an appointment at Shrewsbury School. In 1607 the second master, John Baker, died; in the normal course of events the third master would have been promoted, as headmaster John Meighen wished, but the bailiffs refused to promote Ralph Gittins who had been associated with Leech during his tenure at St Alkmund's. In 1608, 60 townswomen made a protest against the bailiffs' refusal by occupying the School for four days and three nights. The bailiffs took Gittins before the Court of High Commission, where Archbishop Bancroft pronounced him 'unworthy of the second place in respect of his wavering and unsteadiness in religion'. At this point the king ordered Bishop Neile to visit Shrewsbury where, as the bishop informed the master of St John's, there had been 'much adoe' about the second mastership.[14] Neile's visit was made during Lent 1611. He examined Gittins for 'four long hours', concluding that all the accusations against the schoolmaster were either 'surmises or malicious aspersions without good ground' (the School ordinances forbade dismissal on such grounds). He found Gittins entirely conformist in religion, despite accusations of 'popery'; the master was promoted in 1612. We are in 'Arminian' territory now and a further point of interest is the possible presence of another young cleric of this persuasion, the bishop's chaplain William Laud. Much later, when he was archbishop of Canterbury, Laud stated that, to his own knowledge, the School had been troublesome 'these thirty years'. If he was not actually at Shrewsbury he certainly knew of the affair. The bailiffs persisted in their view, however, bringing the case before Lord Chancellor Ellesmere (Thomas Egerton) and getting Gittins dismissed in 1613 as 'a dangerous suspected papist' who associated with others 'ill affected to religion'. By this time Leech had been ordained, again, at Rome, but Gittins remained within the Church of England.

Daniel Price dedicated *The defence of truth* to Prince Henry Frederick, the eldest son of James I:

> The infection of Popery spreads too far: some come not to our Church, others fly our Land and Church. The eyes, and hearts, and hopes of all the Protestant world, be fixed upon your Highness, all expecting your Gracious faithfulness, and readiness in the extirpation of that man of sin.

The reference is to the Pope, Paul V. Fear of the Catholic influence at court caused zealous Protestants to turn their hopes to the heir to the throne. In June 1610, the year of his sixteenth birthday, Henry was made prince of Wales; Daniel Price was one of his household chaplains. In that year three bishops were sent from Scotland to be consecrated: since Archbishop Bancroft had no jurisdiction over Scotland the ceremony was performed on 21 October by the bishop of London, George Abbot, with Andrewes of Ely, Neile, then of Rochester, and Thornborough of Worcester. The Scottish bishops were to return home to consecrate their fellow bishops. 'Abbot was also assiduous in policing the Roman Catholic community in and around London.'[15] It is noteworthy that a visiting Irish bishop (not named in the account by Samuel Clarke) should have been in London that same year when he ordained certain evangelical young men who could not in conscience subscribe to the required oath of supremacy and obedience (number 36 of the 1604 canons). This reads (in the Lichfield subscription book):

> The king is the only supreme governor under God over all things spiritual as well as temporal; the Book of Common Prayer, with the ordering of bishops, priests and deacons, contains nothing contrary to the word of God; the Articles of Religion (1562) are agreeable to the word of God.

One of the young men, Julines Hering, would become a preacher in Shrewsbury seven years later, brought there by the lay group who were concerned to maintain preaching in the town.[16] After Leech's departure Lord Chancellor Ellesmere, having had enough trouble in Shrewsbury, allowed the town to choose a successor for St Alkmund's; Leech's assistant, Thomas Lloyd, was promoted. Prince Henry, the Protestant hero, died in November 1612. By chance it was Daniel Price's turn to attend the prince, so he used the occasion to preach to the household, extravagant sermons which he published early in 1613. His younger brother Sampson, almoner of the chapel royal at the time, also preached; in October 1613 he published *London's Warning to Laodicea's Lukewarmedness,* warning of the dangers of toleration and attacking atheists, papists and puritans. He claimed that the death of Prince Henry, 'the expectation of all the Christian world', was God's punishment. In *Ephesus Warning before her Woe* (1616) he preached against the moral decay of London. Abbot conferred London livings on Sampson.[17]

In September 1617 Dr. Sampson Price returned to Shrewsbury, where he preached before the new bishop of Lichfield, John Overall (another 'Arminian') at the opening of the school chapel: his theme was *The Beauty of Holinesse.* He appealed to the bishop:

> Reverend and Honourable Father of this Diocesse, Be as hetherto you have been to this religious towne, a faithfull Patron to Church and School ... This towne yet flourisheth in many blessings; and so it will, if faction and schisme prevayle not against the peace of it.[18]

During this year Julines Hering, ordained in London in 1610, had been persuaded to come to Shrewsbury by William Rowley, 'a wise religious man' (in the words of Samuel Clarke). Rowley was a wealthy brewer and merchant, a member of the powerful Drapers' Company, who worked with fellow members to maintain godly preaching in Shrewsbury. Among these were John Nicholls, bailiff in 1608 and 1616, and his brother-in-law Richard Hunt, bailiff in 1613, 1622 and 1631. Their wives, Ann and Eleanor, were sisters of Rowland Heylyn, Shrewsbury born and educated but now a wealthy London merchant: master of the Ironmongers' Company of London in 1614 and 1625, and sheriff of London in 1624. The particular significance of this connection is that Heylyn was a patron of puritan preachers and that he funded a lectureship at his former Shrewsbury parish of St Alkmund's – this would not require swearing the oath in the Lichfield subscription book before the bishop that institution to a living would entail. Hering had been a preacher in Derbyshire, at Calke, where he enjoyed similar freedom through the influence of Arthur Hildersham, a famous preacher, survivor of the Elizabethan presbyterian movement, as was Humphrey Fen, who trained Hering in divinity at Coventry after his graduation from Sidney Sussex College, Cambridge. Another of that puritan group was John Oxenbridge whose granddaughter, Christian, married Julines Hering; their daughter, also called Christian, was baptised at St Chad's (the parish of William Rowley) in February 1617/18.[19] Could the activities of this group have motivated Sampson Price's appeal to Bishop Overall? It is quite likely since another petition dates to this time: Sampson's father Thomas Price, now old and with failing eyesight, made a plea to the borough council that his son should be promised the next admission to the living of St Chad's. Such assurance would 'be the cause of his more frequent repayre from the university to tender his services in that charge by preaching: and the cause in *my* old age and weakness, of rejoicing'.[20] Sampson Price preached another sermon in Shropshire in 1617: 'The Clearing of the Saints Sight' was preached at the home of Sir William Owen of Condover and dedicated to his sister-in-law, 'The right worshipfull and truly religious my very good the lady Owen, wife to the Worthy Sir Roger Owen', the erudite legal historian and former MP for Shrewsbury.[21] Later events suggest that the Owens, as patrons, chose opponents of puritanism for vacant livings.

It is as well at this point to consider the Jacobean regime in the religious context. The king made a clear distinction between radicals and moderates, requiring subscription (to the canons of 1604) but prepared to compromise. 'Under James I, therefore, subscription but not strict ceremonial conformity was reinforced by the episcopate.' The bishops could, however, indicate their satisfaction or dissatisfaction in their articles of visitation. Archbishop Abbot merely asked if the surplice was 'commonly' used while Bishops Neile and Overall enquired if the minister wore the surplice 'always and at every time both morning and evening ... and doth he never omit to wear the same?'[22] Overall was allied with Lancelot Andrewes in what Hugh Trevor-Roper called 'the neo-Erastian movement' of the late sixteenth century, already noted at Cambridge University: 'a movement which led to an enhanced ceremonialism in worship and high claims for episcopacy as the indispensable sign of a true Church'. (The term 'Arminian' emerged as a label in the early 1620s.) A significant episode was the meeting in 1614 of Overall with a Roman Catholic defecting archbishop, Marcantonio de Dominis. Archbishop Abbot would not see him but the king referred him to Overall, 'who easily persuaded him that the Church of England was the ideal leader of a new ecumenical Church'. This reflects the new concept of the English Church as a *via media* between Reform and Catholic. Making notes of the meeting was Overall's secretary, John Cosin who was to be a leading figure in the Church of England. As Trevor-Roper writes, in the voice of an Arminian:

> Who would not wish to ... listen to the golden voice of Andrewes or Overall, appealing to the cultivated Greek Fathers – Basil and Gregory of Nazianzus and John Chrysostom (newly edited and splendidly printed by Sir Henry Savile) – rather than reiterate the horrible doctrine of "double predestination" and rummage in unintelligible prophetic books in order to prove the Pope to be Antichrist?[23]

The rise of this party in the Church met a setback at the Synod of Dort in 1618 when King James openly supported the Calvinist cause. The variety of theological views produced faction and conflict at court: 'At stake between Calvinists and anti-Calvinists was much more than conflicting views on the theology of grace. Each was offering the king a different vision of the English Church.' The Reformists or evangelicals wanted an increased preaching mission and persecution of papists, while the opposite party complained that Reformists had corrupted English Protestantism, neglecting the liturgy in favour of excessive preaching. The king 'throughout his reign chose not to adopt either and thereby forfeit the unity he had so laboriously constructed'. His aim was conciliation of moderates.[24] Events in Shrewsbury must be seen against this wider background, and with reference to the particular bishop occupying the see of Lichfield at any time: John Overall from 1617 to 1618 and Thomas Morton from 1619 to 1632.[25]

From the documentary evidence we can draw a vignette of religious affairs in the town in 1617. (Speculation will be confined within parentheses.) The incumbent of St Mary's, William Bright, had been appointed in January 1598 at the instance of Laurence Chaderton, master of Emmanuel College, Cambridge, who made the college 'a puritan seminary in all but name' and established for himself a great reputation. As public preacher Bright was paid the usual stipend of £46 13s 4d.[26] Thomas Price had been at St Chad's for 41 years and was now in ill health. He had always opposed the wearing of the surplice but this was probably unavoidable when a bishop visited the church, as John Overall did on Saturday 9 September, the eve of his visit to Shrewsbury School. The bishop preached on stewardship, as Sampson Price reminded his hearers next day. (With such a learned bishop to entertain and impress, Sampson larded his sermon with Latin quotations as well as scriptural references. No doubt he took advantage of his situation and the support of his aged father to play host to Overall at St Chad's.) We do not know the response of the leading parishioner of St Chad's, William Rowley, who had by now brought Julines Hering to the town (and may have put the family up at his Mansion). St Alkmund's had Thomas Lloyd as vicar, but he was paid £5 simply to read the morning prayers. The annuity of £20 provided by Rowland Heylyn was for Hering who was to preach 'every Tuesday morning and upon the Sabbath also ... which Sermon was at one o'clock, that neither the Ministers of the town might be offended, nor other Congregations emptyed, by the peoples flocking unto his Ministry', as Hering's friend Samuel Clarke was to write. In charge of the money, which may have been supplemented by local followers, was Richard Hunt. Before Hering's arrival visiting preachers were paid, including a Scot.[27]

The prospective curate of St Chad's was, as we have seen, Sampson Price, holder of two London livings and a preacher in the city and at court. (There would have been misgivings on the part of some parishioners, and perhaps a sense of superiority on the part of Sampson, among his native provincials. The bishop's feelings are not known.) John Nicholls, as one of the bailiffs, attended the ceremony in the school chapel, where Sampson Price reminded the magistrates of their duties: 'Let Learning be countenanced by you ... I shall hereafter give you a more ample charge out of another Text of Scripture.' Price was to preach later than month, before the election of new bailiffs. Nicholls and his

Rowley's Mansion (SA-IMG24349)

Shrewsbury School Chapel (SA-IMG24331)

fellows were looking to the future, sending their sons to Cambridge, unsurprisingly, but choosing Queens': Thomas Nicholls entered in September 1616, Thomas Hunt at Easter 1617, Rowland Hunt at Easter 1622. The attraction was the presence of John Preston whose pupils came from all parts, 'but the Politicians assured, it was some inclination unto Puritanisme, a name now odious at Court'. In October 1622 Preston moved to Emmanuel and Rowland Hunt moved too.[28]

In October 1618 William Bright died. Immediately Richard Hunt was sent by the town council to ask Dr Chaderton at Cambridge 'to make choise and commend unto the corporation such a Learned Divine as he should think fitt to this Town to be Publicke Preacher'. The Drapers' Company, of which Hunt was warden, leased their vacant Hall to Julines Hering, while Bright's successor, Samuel Browne, was paid an extra £6 13s 4d a year for another house (it was a generous sum). Browne was appointed in March 1619 and had among his parishioners Hering, who was described in St Mary's register as preacher or minister of the word of God, which suggests concord between the two men. Hering attended the services at St Mary's and was in this way a conformist. By this time a new bishop had been installed at Lichfield: Thomas Morton, a preaching pastor who had shown leniency to a group of nonconforming ministers in Lancashire and Cheshire and thereby forfeited the see of Lincoln. To win back royal favour he published *A defence of the innocencie of the three ceremonies of the church of England ... the surplice, the crosse in baptism and kneeling at the receiving of the blessed sacrament* (1618). This is a very gentle and eirenic work, demonstrating the same spirit which Morton showed when there were complaints made against Hering for similar 'nonconformity' in Shrewsbury:

> Hereupon Doctor Morton ... referred [Hering] unto two neighbour-ministers for satisfaction, and in pursuance of this order, Master Herring gave in his scruples in writing, and also replyed upon their answer. The consequence of this paper-dispute was a Certificate to the Bishop from the Ministers, that they believed Master Herring from conscientious grounds, in his own apprehensions remained unsatisfied, and the Bishop himself told Masters Herrings friends that he was satisfied in his integrity.[29]

We are not told the names of the neighbour-ministers who supported Hering but the preacher clearly had support from people in Shrewsbury who were accepted by Bishop Morton as reliable advocates for Hering; others in the town were opponents, as we shall see. The bishop was willing to accept conscientious objections to non-puritan ceremonialism, as he had already done in his previous diocese, Chester. The spokesman for the ministers in Cheshire had been Thomas Paget, minister of Blackley in Manchester: he would in time become co-pastor with Hering at Amsterdam, and come to Shrewsbury as minister of St Chad's – but much was to happen before then. Change came with the death of Thomas Price in 1620, and the appointment of his son Sampson in the same year. Wishing to pursue his London career, Sampson Price obtained from Bishop Morton a letter to the bailiffs asking them to reconsider their strict residence requirement, 'except one month only', and to allow a longer absence. The borough council refused, Price was forced to resign his curateship, and by May 1622 the council were looking for another curate.[30] Because the living was treated as a 'corporation donative' subscription was not required, so neither Price's name nor that of his successor can be found in the Lichfield subscription book. It is the borough records which supply the information about Price. The next incumbent of St Chad's was Peter Studley, of Shrewsbury School and Oxford (MA 1617), formerly apprenticed to a mercer.[31]

Again, we need to look beyond Shrewsbury, considering the background to events and developments at Cambridge and in London. At Cambridge anti-Calvinism was growing and Calvinists were being dubbed 'Puritans'. There and in London the influence of John

Preston must be set against that of the Church hierarchy: in addition to his mastership of Queens' and then Emmanuel, in 1622 he was made preacher at Lincoln's Inn, 'where he was assured many Parliament men and others of his best acquaintance would be his hearers'. Preston also formed a strong party in the City where, we may recall, Rowland Heylyn was prominent. Christopher Hill has written of the 'deep political game' of Preston and his friends. He was influential not only as a politician but as a populariser of covenant theology, the essence of which was 'that God had bound himself to the elect by an explicit bond, to stand by them if they would stand by him'. The terminology of a legal or business bond is important, this covenant theology freeing men 'from the blind and incomprehensible decrees of an unknowable God' and establishing moral obligation 'on a clearer, more rational basis'. It was the duty of members of parliament, lawyers, magistrates and electors to oppose sin. At Lincoln's Inn in 1625 Preston preached:

> The Church of God hath times and seasons, and the Common-wealth hath some seasons and times when men should be set aworke to doe more than at other times; and you all know this is such a season ... You must be men of contention ... for the common Faith ... and the good of the Church.

Another influential cleric, a friend of Preston, was Richard Sibbes, preacher at Gray's Inn from February 1617; so popular were his sermons that by 1624 the chapel had to be enlarged. Among students at Gray's Inn were Thomas and Rowland Hunt and Humfrey Mackworth, who had already inherited an estate at Betton Strange near Shrewsbury and who was also an alumnus of Shrewsbury School and Queens' College, Cambridge, which he entered at Easter 1619, during Preston's mastership. Sibbes 'understood the church to be a covenant community far more extensive than the elect, intended to be filled by people in various spiritual states'. Richard Sibbes was one of a group of London ministers, lawyers and businessmen set up in 1625 to purchase church livings in various parts of the country where they could establish godly preachers, preaching being paramount in the work of religion. The Feoffees for the Purchase of Impropriations, or the Collectors of St Antholins, had among their number Rowland Heylyn (uncle of the Hunts), who in 1629 made a personal acquisition of the advowson of St Alkmund's in Shrewsbury, where he had anticipated the feoffees by a decade when he provided an annuity for a preacher at St Alkmund's.[32] The Salopians, who would become leading figures in their native town, were being educated, guided in religion, and politicised, ready to play their part in the time of contention forecast by John Preston.

On 27 March 1625 King James died and Charles I became king. The new reign was to see increasing conflict between the Puritan and Arminian parties in the Church of England, with the king unequivocally supporting the latter. 'Anti-Calvinists who had prospered in the last years of his father's reign now received a more exclusively royal patronage.'[33] Peter Studley seems to have been in tune with the times, to judge from his report at the bishop's visitation of 1626. Thomas Morton had attended in person the first two visitations of his tenure, in 1620 and 1623, and may well have attended at Shrewsbury in 1626 when that archdeaconry was being examined. St Mary's was of course exempt from this procedure as a royal peculiar, there is little about St Alkmund's, and St Julian's seems to have been in the care of Studley, along with St Chad's (they were just across the road from each other), and it is Studley who is prominent in the proceedings, at the time Laud was still bishop of Bath and Wells, not yet archbishop of Canterbury). The parishioners of St Julian's voiced their objection to this minister reading the service when there were sermons in other parishes (which they could not, therefore, attend) but he did not himself preach or even read homilies. Most of the dissatisfied parishioners were said to go to the 'other places'. Clearly, St Julian's was a divided and discontented parish. Among the charges for St Chad's was one that the wife of Humfrey Sandford was a recusant, but clearly most of Studley's attention was on 'puritans': 'Mr George Wright and Mr William Rowley do admit the people of divers families into their houses to hear the sermons repeated to sing psalms and [say] prayer[s], most Sunday nights in the year.' But, adds Studley, strongly hinting his opinion, 'whether Action of gathering together may be termed a conventicle we refer to your honorable Court to judge and determine.' (The wording suggests Morton's presence.) Studley also named Rowley along with Daniel Chidlowe (Chidley) and his wife for not frequenting church. George Wright and Rowley both served as bailiffs.[34] Looking from the Puritan perspective we can see that Hering was active in preaching the Word:

> He continued in Salop for the space of seventeen years, sometimes enjoying, and sometimes wanting liberty for the exercise of his Ministry in publick: But when the Pulpit-door was shut against him, he was the more frequent in keeping private Fasts, and in expounding the Scripture three times a day in his own family, by which exercise some of the neighbours were edified also.

These exercises would have taken place at Drapers' Hall, but Hering also attended divine service at St Mary's; the parish register records also the baptisms and burials of Chidley's children. St Chad's register has entries for the christenings of eight little Chidleys between 1618 and 1629, and the burial of one, Daniel, in June 1621 before his first birthday. Another Daniel, born in February 1626, was the occasion of his mother's defiance of Studley.[35]

Katherine Chidley, Judith Wright (wife of George) and five other women refused to be 'churched'. This ceremony might be no more than a thanksgiving and a pleasant social gathering, but as conducted by some clerics it was offensive to women. The original Hebrew tradition of 'purification' survived, along with Catholic practice, in the veiling of the woman and her separation from the rest of the congregation until the ceremony was over. Moreover, Studley demanded a fee. 'Puritan suspicions were not allayed by the recitation at the ceremony itself of Psalm 121, with its strange incantation: "The sun shall not smite thee by day, nor the moon by night"...'. The ceremony was derided by John Milton. Katherine Chidley and her son Daniel were to become notable separatists but the family had to leave Shrewsbury for London before they found support; Hering refused overtures to separate, regarding this as 'a Gangrene' in the Church. The last Chidley child christened at St Chad's was John, on 26 October 1629. Later Katherine wrote *The Justification of the Independent Churches of Christ* in which she states:

> For my owne part, considering that the Church of England is governed by Canon Lawes (the Discipline of Antichrist) and altogether wanteth the Discipline *of* Christ ... I hold it not only lawfull, but also the duty of all those who are informed of such evills, to separate themselves from them ...[36]

This suggests the hostility that Studley could arouse in some of his parishioners. Mrs Chidley was an extreme case but other leading members of St Chad's parish avoided that church. The borough council of Shrewsbury was divided too. The opposition to Rowley and his fellows came from, among others, Sir William Owen of Condover whose support on the council is indicated by the fact that he was elected bailiff in the autumn of 1621. It may have been his influence which brought Studley to St Chad's (he was his patron later, as we shall see), and caused the council to appoint another lecturer to St Alkmund's. Samuel Greaves, an Oxford MA and rector of Berrington (not far from Condover), was to be paid £10 a year for a weekly lecture on Wednesday mornings. Thomas Owen (no relation of Sir William) was another of this group: an Old Salopian and a lawyer of Lincoln's Inn, he was appointed town clerk in 1624. At Michaelmas 1628 two opponents were elected bailiffs: William Rowley and a wealthy lawyer named

Richard Gibbons, brother of Dr Francis Gibbons, since 1611 the vicar of Holy Cross, the former abbey. At street or tavern level there were also differences, revealed in records of the sessions of the peace at Shrewsbury. In 1627 an apprentice was alleged to have said that Thomas Lloyd of St Alkmund's was not worthy to preach before a dog and that Peter Studley was not as good a preacher as Mr Brown and Mr Hering, 'neither was he soe well liked of in the towne as they were'. In early July 1629 we find William Rowley in action, putting a stop to an evening's entertainment in a private house – it was on the Sabbath. A 20-year-old apprentice baker named Ozias Lloyd admitted missing morning prayers at six, the morning service at nine and the morning and afternoon sermons. Instead of making the customary humble submission he declared his wish to remain in gaol until Master Bailiff Gibbons came home.[37]

The presence of Hering in Shrewsbury drew other preachers to the town, from Cheshire, Herefordshire, perhaps Staffordshire where his lifelong friend John Ball had a patron in Edward Mainwaring of Whitmore, and even further afield. Samuel Clarke was first in Cheshire and then in Warwickshire and may also have visited Shrewsbury. These ministers 'were put upon preaching once or oftner, before they departed thence, whereby knowledge was much increased, and the power of godlinesse much cherished and promoted there'. It was when 'envious ill-affected persons, (amongst whom Master *Peter Studley* was the chief) were stirred up, to lay in complaints against him as a Non-conformist' that Bishop Morton asked for the opinion of two other (unnamed) ministers and was satisfied about Hering's integrity.[38]

At the opening of parliament on 17 March 1628 William Laud preached on Ephesians 4:3 on 'endeavouring to keep the unity of the Spirit in the bond of peace'. In June the Commons presented a Remonstrance to the king expressing their fears of popery (the queen for one was a Catholic), relaxation of laws against recusancy, and the suppression of pious preaching. As leaders of 'the faction of the Arminians', bringers in of 'innovations' in religion, Bishop Neile of Winchester and Bishop Laud of Bath and Wells were named. In June, however, Laud was promoted to the see of London; he was also a privy councillor. With Archbishop Abbot under a cloud since his shooting of a gamekeeper instead of a deer in 1621, Laud was in effect Charles's leading cleric. It was apparently on Laud's advice that the king published a Declaration asserting his rights as supreme governor of the Church and his intention to ensure 'the settled continuance of the doctrine and discipline of the Church of England'. In January 1629 the Commons entered into a 'vow': 'We ... do claim, protest and avow for truth, the sense of the Articles of Religion which were established by Parliament in the thirteenth year of our late Queen Elizabeth ... And we reject the sense of the Jesuits and Arminians, and all others wherein they differ from us.' On 10 March parliament was finally dissolved and the eleven years 'personal rule' of Charles began.[39]

Laud had followers among the younger clerics, of whom Peter Heylyn merits mention. During a divinity disputation at Oxford he maintained that the visible succession of the English Church derived from that of Rome. In July 1630, on Act Sunday when he was sure of a large congregation, he exposed the activities of the Feoffees for Impropriations, condemning these patrons of puritan preachers as patrons of faction, a term which reflects the growing animosity which was to develop into 'party' hatred. In 1633 the attorney-general, briefed by Heylyn, ordered the Feoffees to cease their activities. Heylyn was a great-nephew of Rowland Heylyn, who died in February 1632: he left property to his Shrewsbury nephews but did not mention his great-nephew Peter.[40] Another family split between factions was that of Peter Studley. On his mother Lucy's side of the family he was the grandson of Peter Wright, a Shrewsbury shoe-maker, whose son Robert was a pupil of Thomas Ashton and, like his mentor, a tutor in the Devereux family, becoming steward to the second earl of Essex. Wright and his brother George were Calvinists while their nephew Peter Studley was an outspoken anti-puritan. He found support in Shrewsbury after the departure of Bishop Morton to Durham and his replacement by another Robert Wright, an Oxford graduate who was promoted by Laud: Wright supported the religious initiatives of Charles I and Archbishop Laud.[41]

Bishop Wright's visitation of Shrewsbury in the autumn of 1633 coincided with Laud's elevation to the see of Canterbury. On Sunday 8 September the bishop preached at St Chad's on the text 'Fear God and honour the king' (1 Peter 2:17). This, wrote Studley, was a suitable theme for a place of 'factious schism'; he hoped that the bishop would move against the 'factious Brotherhood' of Puritans. The visitation records include Studley's denunciations of the heads of twenty families in the parish of St Chad's. William Rowley, Bailiff George Wright and Humfrey Mackworth, now a leading lawyer in the town, were cited for not bowing at the name of Jesus and not kneeling at communion: they were 'wilful refusers to communicate for the gestures sake'. Numerous parishioners of St Julian's were said not to frequent their own church, one of them being further accused of 'deriding and mocking our minister in the perambulation'. This practice, like churching, was contentious, with pagan and Catholic elements; ministers were not supposed to wear a surplice but Studley may have done so. The annual perambulation of the parish ('beating the bounds') was 'the sole survivor of the many medieval ceremonies which had been conducted in the open to secure fertility and good weather', as Keith Thomas explains. Although the ceremony was intended to maintain parish boundaries, many saw the intercessions as too 'medieval' (i.e. Catholic). Puritans were particularly hostile to the custom. On Sunday 15 September Studley read out injunctions concerning the adornment of churches. All these details reflect what may now be described as Laudianism: the greater emphasis on ceremony and reverence in church had its positive side but it also had theological overtones unacceptable to those of a Reformed or evangelical persuasion. Laud was anxious too to suppress subversive preaching. He had an ally in Peter Studley. During the visitation Bishop Wright was entertained to dinner by Sir William Owen; Studley was also a guest. This may have been the occasion for hatching the idea of a book to be written by Studley. *The Looking-Glasse of Schisme* was completed in Shrewsbury on 4 November and published in London in 1634.[42]

The ostensible reason for writing the book was a double murder at Clun in Shropshire which Studley attributed to the puritanism of the deranged young yeoman who killed his mother and brother. This interpretation of the crime was abhorrent to the godly and was fully answered by one of the laymen in that parish, Richard More. More's book, however, was not licensed for publication: *A true relation of the Murders committed in the Parish of Clunne* did not see the light of day until 1641 whilst *The Looking-Glasse* was reissued in 1635. Studley had a personal motive: to attack the godly of Shrewsbury, whom he referred to as Puritans:

> They are a generation of men strongly addicted, to heare no other Ministers, but those of their owne character and print, and such men, though of lightest talents and meanest parts, they extoll and advance up to the clouds in raptures of admiration; runne after them from place to place to be partakers of their sanctified gifts and holy exhortations.

Studley's rancour had been brewing for thirteen years (his estimation) as rival preachers, in particular Hering, drew the crowds and the private finance ('underhand maintenance'). At Wright's visitation there had been another 'factious' minister present, Samuel Fisher, ordained by Bishop Morton in December 1630. On the Friday after the visitation Fisher preached in Shrewsbury, presumably at St Mary's where Dr James Betton, a Queens' man appointed by the borough in 1632, was now public preacher. Fisher deplored the suppression of nonconformity and of the 'free passage of our blessed Gospel' fearing this might lead to a revival of popery.[43]

The links between politics and religion in Shrewsbury become clearer at this time. Laud himself had his suspicions about the town, perhaps from earlier years, and perhaps from informers in the town. In November 1634 he wrote to attorney-general Sir John Bankes of Grays Inn: 'I heare the Towne of Shrewsbury are about to renew thyr Charter, and I am informed from a very credible hand, that they doe it of purpose to hedge in some Priviledges of the Church.' Laud had been well briefed. The bailiffs elected at Michaelmas 1634, Charles Benyon and Thomas Hayes (one of the protesting parishioners of St Julian's), were taking advice as to 'how to retain the jurisdiction of St Mary's to the bailiffs and burgesses'. The chief counsel for their party was Humfrey Mackworth. The following April, at the Shrewsbury quarter sessions when the sheriff, justices, lawyers and men of substance were present, there was a heated debate on the levying of charges to pay the muster-master for training the militia: this was described by the grand jury as a 'great greevance and oppression', as other forced levies had been. The Shropshire lawyer Timothy Tourneur, a barrister at Gray's Inn and a Master in Chancery, rebuked the grand jury. Sir John Corbet of Adderley and Robert Charlton of Apley defended them, Corbet demanding that the clerk of the peace read out the Petition of Right – the document asserting the supremacy of parliament over the royal prerogative. News soon reached London. Corbet was put in the Fleet prison for several months, Charlton for two days. Both men were supporters of parliament and of Reformed religion.[44]

In 1635 Laud instituted a visitation of all the dioceses within his province. His Articles express his vision of the Church of England: united, orderly, seemly, comely. He dealt with the physical maintenance of churches, and their economic maintenance, with the conduct of clergy, churchwardens and parishioners, and with the liturgy. The stone font should be in its ancient place and the altar covered with 'decent stuff' and placed conveniently for the minister to be heard and the people to communicate, which they should do kneeling. The minister should use the sign of the cross in baptism, observe all the orders, rites and ceremonies of the Prayer Book, and wear a surplice, according to the existing canons. Parishioners should attend on Sundays and holy days at morning and evening prayers, and behave themselves reverently, using 'all due and lowly reverence, when the blessed Name of the Lord Jesus Christ is mentioned'. Information was to be given about parishioners who usually go to other parish churches than their own, and about 'any conventicles or private congregations'. No one should speak or write against the Book of Common Prayer, Articles of Religion, the king's supremacy, or any rites of the Church of England now established. These are just some of the points but they indicate the criteria for conformity which was to be more strictly enforced than before. Only a few requirements are actually 'innovations' but they were anathema to evangelicals. Nathaniel Brent's report on the diocese of Lichfield shows that he suspended Richard Lee of Wolverhampton for nonconformity and that there were many papists in Staffordshire. The dean of Wolverhampton, Matthew Wren, had complained to Laud of Lee's 'factious' behaviour. On 20 May 1635 Brent reached Shrewsbury: 'The magistrates here were extraordinarily observant of me, being always ready to go with me when I went abroad. The people here about are somewhat addicted to preciseness, but not very much.' Dr Betton of St Mary's protested against the visitation but Brent insisted: he was not impressed by the church itself. 'In all the churches in Shrewsbury many things were out of order, especially about the communion table.' He wished to suspend Mr Bedford, curate of St Mary's, for nonconformity, but Bedford protested and was merely admonished because Brent could find no witnesses against him.[45]

Early in 1635 Julines Hering and his family were forced by the new severity of conformity to leave Shrewsbury; they went first to Wrenbury in Cheshire, the home of their sister-in-law, the widow of the preacher Robert Nichols. One of the preachers suspended by Brent, William Peartree of Bury St Edmunds, shared the pastoral work at Wrenbury with Hering. Richard Lee was elected by the parishioners of St Julian's to be a 'lector'. Churchwardens' accounts show that some work was done after the visitation: repairs were made at St Mary's and at Holy Cross a rail was set up around the communion table. The most extravagant response was at St Chad's, as noted by the Cheshire puritan Sir William Brereton in August 1635: it was 'gaudily painted, wherein you may find many idle, ridiculous, vain and absurd pictures, representations and stories, the like whereunto I never saw in England'.[46] It might be thought that Peter Studley had triumphed but perhaps his was a pyrrhic victory: in 1636 he was given the second portion of the living of Pontesbury, in the gift of Sir William Owen; he was also to act as parish priest; he resigned from his Shrewsbury living. Dr Francis Gibbons of Holy Cross held the first portion of Pontesbury and Samuel Greaves the second. The question of Studley's replacement caused a great conflict in the town with accusations of an irregular election, celebrated rowdily by pro-Studley supporters; there was also the involvement of the king and Laud. It was found that the town did not in fact have the right of appointment to St Chad's, and the living was taken back into royal hands. Negotiations for the new charter also involved conflict between the opposing groups, described by the privy council as the 'parties' of Thomas Nicholls and Thomas Owen, the town clerk. The latter called their opponents puritans; the 'puritans' described themselves as 'the religious party'.[47]

It needed the mediation of Sir Richard Newport to settle the matter of the 1638 town charter. Newport, the leading landowner in north Shropshire, was a graduate of Brasenose College, Oxford, and had served as MP for the borough or the shire in five parliaments, between 1614 and 1629. His family had a long association with Shrewsbury. There was to be a single mayor instead of two bailiffs: a request that the 'auncientest alderman' be made mayor may have been an attempt to install Rowley or Richard Hunt but another choice was made. Thomas Jones, with an estate worth £30,000 or £40,000 (a huge sum) wished to be mayor and for this honour he promised to 'give liberally to St Paul's [Cathedral in London] and will draw his friends to do the like'. 'Rich Jones' as he was nicknamed was accordingly elected on this cash for honour basis. (The restoration of St Paul's was important to both Laud and the king, who described the cathedral as 'the imperial seat of this his realm'. Inigo Jones was the architect.) The number of aldermen and assistants was doubled to 24 and 48. Both parties were represented: Richard Hunt, Thomas Nicholls, Humfrey Mackworth, Thomas Knight, William Rowley, John Prowde of the 'religious' party and of the other group Robert Betton, Richard Gibbons, John Studley, Simon Weston and others. Timothy Tourneur was made recorder and Thomas Owen was confirmed as town clerk, despite a petition from Christopher Whichcott, of the court of king's bench and a Shrewsbury resident, which pointed out that Owen was 'an aged man' and guilty of electoral miscarriages of justice. Two clauses inserted into the charter by Laud caused offence to the godly: that the bishop and his commissary or chancellor should be appointed justices of the peace for the town and that the borough sword should not be borne upright in any church.[48]

A new witness to the consequences of the policies of the king and the archbishop was Richard Baxter, whose early schooling had been helped by Sir Richard Newport. Baxter was born on 12 November 1615. 'At last at about 20 years of Age, I became acquainted with ... very zealous godly Nonconformists in *Shrewsbury*, and the adjoining parts, whose fervent Prayers and savoury Conferences and holy Lives did profit me much.' Chief among these was William Rowley; Baxter also met ministers ejected from their livings by bishops. He became an assistant to the preacher William Madstard (a kinsman of Rowley) at Bridgnorth, where he witnessed the protests of Shropshire clergy to the 1640 canons, especially the 'Etcetera Oath', approving the government of the Church 'by archbishops, bishops, deans, and archdeacons &'. The May canons were contested in parliament in November 1640 by the 'Root and Branch Petition' which objected to ceremonies and

'Romish' elements in the Prayer Book. In July 1641 Acts were passed abolishing the courts of Star Chamber and High Commission. William Laud had already been in the Tower since 1 March, charged with treason.[49]

James Betton of St Mary's had also been arrested but was saved from punishment by the abolition of the Court of High Commission. Richard Lee was promoted to be curate at St Julian's, where the altar rails were pulled down, as was the altar at St Mary's; and in May 1642, at last, Thomas Lloyd died. A letter of invitation was sent immediately by Rowley, Mackworth and others to Julines Hering, now pastor at Amsterdam. In the event he could not return but he was 'one of Gods special Remembrancers, in behalf of England, begging fervently that the Lords and Commons in Parliament, might be preserved from the two destructive rocks of pride and self-interest'. The corporation of Shrewsbury were alarmed at developments: on 30 August 1642 they agreed 'that considering the great distractions that are now in this Kingdom and the great Feare that the Inhabitants of this Corporation are in' they must join together against 'all unlawful force that might be attempted against the town'. No one was to wear partisan colours and all suspicious strangers were to be sent from the town. But, 'if the Kings Majesty come to this Town ... he shall have free access into the Town and ... the Town [shall] make the best entertainment as these Troublesome times afford'. The king had moved from Nottingham, where he had raised his standard (a sign of war). In Staffordshire he received information that the town of Shrewsbury was 'at his devotion' and that rumour of his approach had driven away those most inclined to sedition:

> His majesty therefore resolved to go to Shrewsbury, which, as well as being in a strong and pleasant situation (one side being defended by the Severn and the other having a secure passage into Wales), was conveniently placed for correspondence with Worcester, of which city he hoped well. He also expected that by being at Shrewsbury he would be as well able to secure Chester as he would by going there himself – an action that might also have given some apprehension of his going into Ireland, which had been formerly mentioned. [50]

Chapter Five
Civil War and Regicide

The King had indeed been invited to Shrewsbury, as recounted by Edward Hyde, who was with him, drafting most of the royal proclamations. Charles had left London in the hands of Parliament in January 1642 and journeyed north, where he was disappointed in failing to gain support. In March, Parliament passed a Militia Ordinance for the mustering of trained bands but the King had to rely on the medieval system of commissions of array, issued to individuals to raise and train men. In Shrewsbury both sides were mustering but the Royalist sheriff, John Weld, tried to prevent the opposition's activities. On 16 July a petition was sent to the Commons by several aldermen and others: 'Many volunteers ... have entered themselves to be exercised in military discipline under the command of Thomas Hunt', but the sheriff was discouraging the men. The lawyer Hunt was now an alderman, his father having died in 1640. In response, the Commons issued a warrant of indemnity, authorising the training 'for the defence of the town', and sent three Shropshire MPs to declare the King's commissions of array illegal. These were Sir John Corbet, William Pierrepont and Richard More: Corbet and More have already figured in this narrative as resisting the King and Laud in the 1630s. The Drapers' Company in Shrewsbury organised the sending of their contribution of horses, plate, money and arms to Parliament. The Royalist muster was planned for 2 August, the Parliament muster being held the day before. The Royalists were drilled as planned at Atcham by Sir Vincent Corbet of Morton Corbet, who had served with the King in the recent Scottish campaign; he commanded a troop of horse. Other younger members of the gentry were also active, above all Francis Ottley, who with his followers disrupted the Parliament muster. Letters between him and his friend Tom Eyton of Eyton reveal how their overtures suggesting the King came to Shrewsbury were made. Eyton reported to 'Cosen Franke' on 4 September: he had been to the King at Nottingham and Ottley was to go to the King next day. By the time Ottley arrived, the King was at Uttoxeter in Staffordshire. A royal

Prince Rupert (SA-IMG24335)

address was drafted for King Charles to deliver at Wellington, in Shropshire. At the same time Sir Richard Newport wrote to his brother-in-law Sir Richard Leveson of Trentham in Staffordshire urging him to use his influence with Lord Strange (heir of the dying earl of Derby) so that Newport might mediate between supporters of the King and the supporters of Parliament as he had done before. There was a strong neutralist party in Cheshire but at Shrewsbury support for the King increased. This was especially so when Newport, possibly influenced by his heir Francis, appeared wearing Ottley's colours. This influenced the many tenants and associates of the Newports. Ottley assured the King that the town was 'at his devotion'.[1]

The King with his sons and followers arrived in Shrewsbury on 20 September. Four days later the King's nephew Prince Rupert attacked a small force of the Parliamentary army near Worcester – this was unplanned and did not prevent the earl of Essex and the main body of his Parliamentary army from occupying Worcester. Rupert withdrew, going via Ludlow to Shrewsbury,[2] where his younger brother Maurice also attended the temporary court. The King, based at the Council House in Shrewsbury, visited Chester and Wrexham, taking his twelve-year-old heir, Charles, with him. On their return the King addressed gentry, clergy, freeholders and 'substantial inhabitants of the county ... in a meadow called the Gay' on Wednesday 28 September. The three weeks spent in Shrewsbury were in effect a recruiting campaign, for both men and money, as a result of which many soldiers came to the town, requiring billets. Local supporters were honoured, Ottley being knighted while Sir Richard Newport was made a baron, in return for a contribution of £6,000. By the time the King left Shrewsbury he had a field army, and Shrewsbury a garrison. Taxes were levied and provisions of all kinds bought or seized. A Royalist officer in Shrewsbury, Basil Waring, wrote on 18 October:

> The King did go from hence on Wednesday last to Bridgnorth ... The King is about 16,000 strong of foot, besides horse, and every day more and more come to him, by reason (as we are informed about us) the Parliament forces do so plunder as they go ... The last Sunday the King took a protestation, and the Sacrament upon it, in St Mary's Church, in our town, to defend the true Protestant religion, established by Queen Elizabeth and his Royal father.

At Bridgnorth on 14 October the King declared three men traitors: Thomas Hunt, Humfrey Mackworth and Thomas Nicholls. He ordered other disaffected men to be removed from the council in Shrewsbury, amongst them William Rowley, John Prowde, Thomas Wingfield, John Betton and Owen George.[3] In the circumstances it is understandable that the three 'traitors' vanish from Shrewsbury at this time. We will try to pick up their trail later.

These puritans had naturally opted for Parliament, religion being 'far more decisive than any socio-economic correlations'. When it came, the Civil War not only split communities but divided families: 'in many cases, if not all, [this] derived from genuine differences of opinion over the political and religious issues at stake in the war'. Poor men were mere cannon-fodder, like the villagers of Myddle, Marton and Newton, near Shrewsbury: 'Out of these three towns ... there went noe lesse than twenty men, of which number thirteen were killed in the warrs.'[4] The 'traitors' and others of their party in and near Shrewsbury had not been inactive. Newport's neighbour Robert Charlton of Apley had 'much solicited' him to support Parliament, without success. Charlton himself raised two hundred men for the militia and joined with his cousin Walter Barker of Haughmond in an attempt to send 'thousands of pounds' by way of the Severn to Parliamentary supporters in

Coins of Charles I minted at Shrewsbury (SA-IMG24327)

Bristol, but the money was intercepted at Bridgnorth by the sheriff. On 17 September John Prowde of Shrewsbury had written in reply to a letter of Humfrey Mackworth from London: Mr Charlton was thought to be at Bristol but Barker had been detained. Mackworth's letter had been delivered by a Mr Walsh as the mayor was intercepting the regular post and opening anything suspicious. After the King's stay in the town Rowley was put into the custody of the provost martial.[5] Thomas Nicholls, then sheriff of Montgomery, was absent from Shrewsbury, where his house was ransacked. He is found in 1643 in Hertfordshire where he became tenant of Balls Park and served as colonel of the Hertfordshire Militia Regiment.[6]

With the growing partisanship Lord Newport, as he now was, feared for the future, as he wrote to his brother-in-law Leveson on 29 November: if the war continued it would bring ruin and desolation. Leveson's neutralist policy failed, as the King sent an order to the sheriff of Staffordshire to suppress all local forces raised without royal warrant. Meanwhile a 'Resolution of the Clergy of Salop' promised to defend the King's royal person, the established Protestant religion in the Church of England, the due rights of Parliament, the laws of the land and the liberties of the subject. This indicates the problems of allegiance.[7] Mackworth remained for the present in London, where he could work on behalf of Shropshire, now wholly under Royalist control. Thomas Hunt disappears from view for the moment but his younger brother Rowland, a London lawyer, went to Lancashire where he became a member of the Parliamentary Committee.[8] Late in 1642 over thirty 'of the Principal Gentlemen of the County of Salop' swore a resolution to raise a troop of dragoons at their own expense 'for the defence of his Majesty, their country, and more particularly the Fortunes, Persons, and Estates of the Subscribers undernamed'. These included men recently honoured by the King: Sir Vincent Corbet, knight and now baronet, Sir Francis Ottley, Sir Thomas Eyton, and other knights and esquires, Sir William Owen among them. Sir Vincent Corbet was to be the chief commander of the dragoons. All contributions of horses and money were to be in by 20 December, 'all in the battlefield'. There was a stress on their 'particular safeties', their families and fortunes, not just their loyalty to the King.[9]

In October 1642 the King had declared in a letter that Cheshire, Shropshire, Denbigh and Flintshire should be associated 'for the mutuall security of one another'.[10] Sir Francis Ottley in the meantime maintained a strong garrison in Shrewsbury to keep in check 'the element of discontent which existed in the town', discontent evidenced by the fact that all ten prisoners on the calendar for the spring 1643 assizes were charged with speaking 'ill and malicious speeches against the Kings majestie' or were suspected of disaffection in not holding the earl of Essex and his party to be rebels. A document dated 17 March 1643 ordered the arrest of a further 43 disloyal persons for actively displaying contempt for his majesty's person and power.[11] Shrewsbury had clearly not gone over entirely to the King despite its occupation.

Sir William Brereton, 1647 engraving (Grosvenor Museum, Chester)

A swathe of Royalist territory now stretched south-east from Shropshire through Worcestershire and the Cotswolds to Buckinghamshire, Oxfordshire and Berkshire. The King was himself based at Oxford where peace negotiations began in February 1643 but collapsed in April. The main Parliamentary towns between Shropshire and London were Coventry and Northampton. Coventry, the base of the Warwickshire Parliamentary Committee, was to be important for the Shropshire men. In April Parliament appointed a committee 'for the Association of the Counties of Warwick, Stafford and Salop': this included Sir John Corbet, Richard More and Thomas Hunt (MPs for Shropshire, Bishops Castle and Shrewsbury), Thomas Mytton of Halston, Robert Corbet and Humfrey Mackworth. By the summer of 1643 troops were being assembled in London under Mytton and Mackworth. In May Sir William Brereton captured Stafford for Parliament, which became the base for the Staffordshire Committee, and Wolverhampton. The new Parliamentary commander in the north-west midlands was Basil Feilding earl of Denbigh. He led his forces from London at the end of August, following the Shropshire men, but was recalled amid accusations of disloyalty. On 6 September Mytton and Mackworth wrote to him: they hoped that when this stain was wiped away his honour would shine the brighter. They urged him to resist 'subtle and clandestine practices' against him and to pursue the course of 'devotion to his oppressed country'.[12] Denbigh was however to prove slow to react to pleas for help, partly because of the many demands on him, partly because of hostile rivals; on occasion he showed a reluctance to leave his home in London.[13]

These were hard times for civilians as well as military men. A Shrewsbury man trapped in Birmingham, Jonathan Langley, wrote to Sir Francis Ottley, governor of Shrewsbury, and Henry Bromley, sheriff of Shropshire, to ask for their help – he was concerned about his father, his wife and his children. He protested:

> I never had any intention, nor yet have, of taking up Arms of neither side, my Reasons this my protestation already taken, binds me both to King and to Parliament. I am not senseless ... that there are two Armies each seeking to destroy the other, and by oath bound to preserve both, each Chalenging the Protestant religion for their Standard yet the one takes the Papists the other the sismatikes for their Adherents, and (for my part) my conscience tells me they both intend the Protestant Religion, what reason have I therefore to fall out with either.[14]

This letter was dated 22 February 1643. Birmingham was to suffer in early April from 'Rupert's Butcheries', committed by his soldiers in the defiantly Parliamentary town. Less bloody problems concerned Samuel Woodds, steward of Sir John Trevor of Trevallyn in Denbighshire: the disruption of the markets in Shrewsbury was affecting his work; he had not set the pear and lime trees in that year.[15]

In February 1643 Parliament appointed a committee of its Shropshire supporters, mostly magistrates; its leaders included Thomas Hunt, Humfrey Mackworth, Thomas Mytton of Halston and Andrew Lloyd of Aston. By the end of September 1643, with the help of Sir William Brereton of Cheshire and Sir Thomas Myddleton of Chirk in Denbighshire, the Shropshire Committee had established a base in its own county, at the small market town of Wem, between Whitchurch and Shrewsbury. Thomas Malbon, a gentleman of Nantwich in Cheshire, gave an account of this move: the Cheshire troops, except for the Nantwich trained band, marched to Wem and fortified the town, quartering the men in adjoining townships and villages. On 28 September a Royalist attack was repulsed. Next day the Nantwich-trained band marched to Wem to assist. Other attempts on the town were made by the Royalists but, as Brereton reported to Parliament on 21 October, Colonel Mytton, Mr Mackworth, Captain Thomas Hunt and other of their friends in Wem had achieved significant success. 'Thus you may evidently perceave how God hath helped us, and in what case wee now stand for the reducinge of the whole countye of Saloppe.'[16] Brereton's help was essential for the regaining of Shrewsbury.

The earl of Denbigh's Civil War correspondence deals with events in the north Midlands. Among particular fears were the threat of Prince Rupert's moves and the arrival of a large force from the army in Ireland, following the King's truce with that country, English soldiers that were described as 'Irish' or even 'papist' by Parliament men. Their arrival on the Welsh side of the Dee estuary threatened Wales and it was hoped that Sir Thomas Myddleton would take action against them. At Coventry in October Denbigh's soldiers had to swear to the Covenant, lately published by Parliament, in St Michael's church. They had also to attend morning service on the Lord's Day, fasts and other holy days; they were to refrain from swearing and drunkenness and were to behave civilly in their quarters. The swearing to the Solemn League and Covenant was of immediate and future importance. It was a condition of the help promised by the Scottish Estates and involved an oath to preserve the reformed religion in the Church of Scotland and to advance the reformation in religion in England, along with the extirpation of popery and prelacy – 'government by archbishops, bishops, their chancellors and commissaries, deans and chapters, archdeacons, and all other ecclesiastical officers depending on that hierarchy'. The Covenant also included a promise to preserve the rights and privileges of Parliament 'and to defend the King's majesty's person and authority ... we have no thoughts or intentions to diminish his majesty's just power and greatness.' There was a promise to discover those 'evil instruments' who were dividing the King from his people or making factions. 'We shall also, according to our places and callings, in this common cause of religion, liberty, and peace of the Kingdom, assist and defend all those that enter into this league and covenant, in the maintaining and pursuing thereof.' The final long clause relates to the covenant between God and his people. 'And this covenant we make in the presence of Almighty God, the Searcher of all hearts, with a true intention to perform the same.' It was imposed by Parliament on all Englishmen over eighteen years of age, in part because a Scottish army was to be sent into England in its support, although fighting was continuing in Scotland.[17]

One of numerous preachers in Coventry when Denbigh's soldiers were swearing the Covenant was Richard Baxter, who was persuaded by Hunt and Mackworth to go to Wem. He did so for a short period and was, he wrote, followed by about thirty neighbours who went to join 'Colonel Mackworth's Troop'. Before the end of the year a preacher was sent by Parliament from London to Wem: he was Andrew Parsons, a Somerset man and an Oxford MA. The Shropshire Committee had ejected Nicholas Metcalfe from his living at Wem and James Fleetwood from nearby Prees, whilst Dr John Arnway, rector of Hodnet, took refuge in Shrewsbury. On 21 December two of the Wem Committee (Andrew Lloyd and Robert Corbet) wrote to Humfrey Mackworth, who seems always to have been on the move and had gone to London to make depositions against Laud in January 1644 – the archbishop was to be put on trial. Lloyd and Corbet informed their colleague that the enemy were potent in Cheshire, that Nantwich was surrounded,

Wem, the base for Salop parliamentarians (SA-IMG24347)

and the countryside round about plundered. More Irish soldiers had come over. They entreated him to 'represent our forlorne condition to the Parliament, for whom we have desperately engaged our estates and lives'. They hoped they would not be suffered to perish 'in the midst of merciless men'.[18]

The garrison at Wem was under constant threat and Nantwich was under siege during January 1644. Sir William Brereton and Sir Thomas Fairfax went to the relief of the town, helped by the besieged force under Colonel George Booth of Cheshire. Most of the so-called 'Irish' officers were taken prisoner. Meanwhile, Thomas Mytton had defeated a Royalist force at Ellesmere on 12 January. In response Prince Rupert was put in charge of the Royalist forces in the area. He wrote to Sir Francis Ottley, governor of Shrewsbury, on 25 January, a letter that suggests doubt about Ottley's performance: the loyalty of the town was not without some suspicion at that time, with a considerable party which did not support the King. There was a rumour of a plan to take the town, causing numerous people to be imprisoned. No doubt aware of these concerns, Rupert left Oxford on 6 February, arriving in Shrewsbury on the 18th. The King appointed his nephew President of Wales and adjacent counties, echoing the remit of the traditional Council in the Marches. Rupert now replaced Ottley as governor, appointing in his place Sir Fulke Hunckes, one of the officers who had brought troops back from Ireland. The town had to raise £1,000. On 4 March Rupert took about 300 horse and 600 foot with him to visit Royalist garrisons, entering Chester on the 11th. Next day he returned to Shrewsbury to collect extra forces before going into Cheshire and Lancashire.[19] The earl of Denbigh meanwhile was being kept informed of Royalist troop movements; 'persons from Shrewsbury and from Wales frequently came to him at Coventry', urging their

Sir Francis Ottley and family (SA-IMG24321)

need for help. When Mackworth returned to Coventry he wrote to warn Denbigh that that town was in imminent danger. The earl promised to return soon. On 27 March Mackworth was writing again about the 'bleeding condition' of Shropshire. Denbigh was at Coventry by 6 April when he wrote to the Committee of Both Kingdoms with complaints against some of the soldiers. On 17 April the Committee at Nantwich wrote warning that the enemy, under Rupert, were making great preparations at Shrewsbury and Chester against Nantwich or Wem or both.[20]

Richard Gough of Myddle has one anecdote of the wars in the early summer of 1644. Parliament had passed an ordinance that all native Irish found in arms in England should be hanged. Thirteen prisoners were treated this way although they were English:

> which thing, when Prince Rupert heard, hee vowed, that the next thirteen that he tooke should be soe served, which hapned not long after ... The next day the Prince caused these prisoners to be brought before him, and ordered thirteen of them to be hanged. They cast the dice on a drum head to see who should dye, and amongst them there was one Philip Littleton, who had been servant and keeper of the parke to my old master, Robert Corbet of Stanwardine, Esqr. This Phillip saw Sir Vincent Corbett, of Morton Corbett, ride by, and said to some that stood by, 'if Sir Vincent Corbett did know that I were here, hee would save my life.' Upon this a charitable soldier roade after Sir Vincent and told him ... Hee came back

immediately, and seeing Phillip, hee alighted from his horse and fell on his knees before the Prince, (who sate there on horsebacke to see the execution,) and begged for the life of Phillip, which was readily granted on condition hee would never beare arms against the King. Phillip promised and escaped, and afterwards noe more Irish were hanged.

Not only is the savagery of war tempered by humanity in this episode but the latter instinct cut across partisan divisions: Sir Vincent was a devoted Royalist but his kinsman Robert Corbet was on the side of Parliament. Even the formidable Rupert is shown as capable of a degree of mercy.[21] We are reminded also that many, perhaps most, people got caught up in a war they did not want. John Morrill has written of the beginning of the Civil War: 'The realisation that the country was drifting into a civil war sank in gradually and reluctantly. The reaction of the majority was to keep the war at arm's length.'[22] That was no longer possible by 1644. There were also divisions within the Shropshire Committee, mainly between Mytton and other members. While Wem was being attacked by Rupert, its governor, Mytton, withdrew to London. He returned on 24 May, just after Rupert had marched most of his forces east, to the relief of York. The next week, as Thomas Malbon of Nantwich records, Mytton and his brother-in-law Myddleton took Oswestry. Myddleton then returned to Nantwich, where Brereton and Denbigh had also arrived with their forces, ready to march into Lancashire only to receive letters from Mytton that he was once more besieged. Denbigh marched to his relief on 1 July, some of the besieging Royalists fleeing to Shrewsbury.[23]

On 2 July 1644 the Royalists were defeated at Marston Moor, Rupert and his force being allowed to march away, 700 soldiers with colours flying, heading west to Wales. In Shropshire there was still fear of Rupert. Mytton meanwhile was made governor of Oswestry, answerable only to Denbigh, even though he was still at odds with other

Morton Corbet (SA-IMG24348)

members of the Shropshire Committee and Thomas Hunt appears to have taken charge at Wem. Richard Baxter wrote that Colonel Hunt was 'a plain hearted, honest, godly Man, entirely beloved, and trusted by his Soldiers for his Honesty'.[24] There were to be repercussions from the quarrel with Thomas Mytton, as there were from the capture of Francis Newport, taken at Oswestry. On 5 July the Committee at Wem asked that Newport and two other 'considerable' prisoners should be removed, 'in regard of an especiall respect this place bears unto my Lord Newport and his friends'. On the same day Francis Newport was writing to Denbigh from Eccleshall Castle: 'Our accommodation is soe untoward at present that we have scarce philosophy enough to undergoe it.' Newport asked to be returned to Stafford or sent to London, but if to London not to the Tower or Peter-house, another London prison; he said he would prefer to be in a private house on parole. He was a prisoner at Stafford in October 1645, but gained his release and went to France where his father Richard lived. High Ercall was one of the last Royalist garrisons to fall in Shropshire, in March 1646, but it had been slighted and its moat drained. Lord Newport described it in his will: 'By the malignity of recent times, my family is dissolved, my chief house at High Ercall is ruined, my household stuff and stock sold from me for having assisted the King.' He and his son were heavily fined.[25] Francis Newport would not forget what he and his family had suffered.

In the late summer of 1644 there was still much activity in Shropshire and the Welsh Marches as Rupert and his brother Maurice tried to raise another army at Bristol and Chester. There was little welcome for their soldiers, the townsmen of Bridgnorth shutting the gates against them and the people of Much Wenlock denying them food, whilst countrymen at Shifnal overpowered the Royalist troops from Tong Castle who were

High Ercall (SA-IMG24346)

trying to exact a tax. In Shrewsbury Hunckes was deeply unpopular for 'being too much a soldier' and in August Rupert replaced him with fellow officer Sir Michael Erneley. He too found the population hostile, writing to Rupert on 21 October: 'The edge of the gentry is much blunted, the county's loyalty is strangely abated; they begin to warp to the enemy's party.' Elsewhere, in south Shropshire in December 1644: risings of 'clubmen' first occurred against plundering soldiers.[26]

Shrewsbury had been occupied by Royalists for just over two years and there had been a Parliamentary garrison at Wem for over a year, yet communications between these towns had continued in clandestine ways. A typically colourful note is provided by Richard Gough:

> This Richard Clarke was the son of Richard Clarke of Myddle Wood. He was naturally ingeniouse. Hee had a smooth way of flattering discourse, and was a perfect master in the art of dissembling. Hee was listed for a soldier on the Parliament side in Wem, whilst hee was yett but a mere boy ... hee was serviceable to the officers of the Garrison by carrying of letters to their friends ... Hee had an old ragged coate on purpose which he would putt on, and goe as a beggar boy.

Carrying a short stick such as was thrown to a dog he would mingle with other beggars and get by unnoticed: the stick was hollow and was the means of carrying letters. A more official source is the letter book of Sir William Brereton which contains correspondence with the Shropshire Committee at Wem.[27]

On the last day of January 1645 members of this Committee wrote to Brereton; the letter was signed by Robert Clive, Andrew Lloyd, Thomas Hunt and Robert Charlton. They were somewhat guarded in what they said but a reference to Colonel Mytton 'who carries himself crossly towards us on all matters' indicates the reason: they did not intend to inform the governor of Oswestry of their plan to retake Shrewsbury, referring instead to Atcham, a nearby village. The situation had become urgent and they were 'in a sad condition', as they explained to Brereton:

> For eight weeks we have detained 130 more foot than we can pay, in the expectation of carrying out a design that might enable us to enlarge our quarters and so our contribution, and now we will have to part with them. We are sure our horse, lacking necessary accommodation, will leave us and we will be compelled to sleight our two petty garrisons [Stoke upon Tern and Moreton Corbet] that we cannot provision for three days ahead. These gone, it will be no easy thing to continue in

> a defensive posture and, if we fail, it will be very prejudicial to you and the public service.

But if they were to achieve their long-held aim they would need help. Brereton's own aim was to take Chester but, as he informed the Committee of Both Kingdoms on 22 February, there was danger from Prince Maurice's army, now numbering about 5,000 and quartered at Wrexham. Earlier in the month the prince had been in Shrewsbury whose force he had depleted and Brereton saw the opportunity. Thus it was that on 21 February the Shropshire Committee wrote again to Brereton:

> Thanks be to God for enabling us to gain possession of Shrewsbury. This morning about break of day we entered – horse, foot and all – and are now staying the soldiers from plundering. We have not yet time to give you a list of the prisoners but there are many of quality, including the governor and Sir John Weld ... We doubt not of your assistance as occasion shall present and thank you for the great favour you have afforded us.

Brereton had lent some Cheshire and Staffordshire troops, whilst the tactics had been planned by the Dutch professional soldier they had at Wem, William Reinking. Under cover of darkness one group went around by the encircling river, entering the town below the Council House and going through its gardens to open the main gate for the rest of

Shrewsbury Castle from the river behind the town

The lower gateway of Shrewsbury Castle

the force. It does not emerge until later in the records that the tenant of the Council House, Sir William Owen, had been aiding them secretly; he was taken as a prisoner so his cover was not blown. Surprisingly, Mytton's is the first signature on the letter, for he had joined the enterprise, uninvited; his own account of the affair exaggerates his role. The official account was written by Reinking.[28]

The re-taking of the county town was of enormous importance to the Shropshire Parliamentarians, and a great blow to the King. Brereton wrote from Tarvin, his base near Chester, to the Committee of Both Kingdoms. The surprising and taking of Shrewsbury 'this Saturday morning about 5 o'clock' was attributed to 'that God which heareth prayers and giveth success to those that seek him and make their whole dependence upon him'. The Shropshire Committee wrote to Brereton on 23 February 'concerning God's wonderful goodness and mercy', but they still needed practical help. 'Did you know the condition of this place, the disaffection of most and how poor and faint the spirits and resolution of such are as seem to wish well to the cause, you might well conceive what our just fears and dangers are.' They asked for forces to secure them against Prince Maurice and to strengthen Wem: 'at least 2-300 more foot and one good company for Wem'. In addition to Mytton, Hunt, Charlton, Clive and Lloyd, one member of the Committee who signed the letters was Samuel More, son of Richard More, MP for Bishops Castle, who had died a few years earlier. Samuel had been a prisoner at Ludlow but had been exchanged. There was a public thanksgiving but no jubilation as the situation was still dangerous: within the town the Cheshire and Staffordshire troops were causing trouble, while beyond it Prince Maurice was reported as sending troops as far as Chirk, 'and it is probable he will advance this way'. The danger continued and in May the King himself with Rupert and their army passed through Shropshire, stopping at Market Drayton and Newport. On hearing that the siege of Chester had been raised and Maurice was no longer in need of their assistance, the King turned eastwards. The Royalists stormed Leicester on 1 June but on the 13th came defeat by the New Model Army at Naseby. On 5 August, from Brecon, Charles wrote to his eldest son: 'It is very fit for me now to prepare for the worst.' He then turned north towards Chester.[29]

The men of the Shropshire Committee were entrusted with the government of Shrewsbury, the garrison as well as the town. Thomas Mytton may have hoped to be made governor, his family having long been associated with the town, but he played little part in the town's affairs. On 26 March 1645 the rest of the Committee wrote to the Speaker of the Commons: 'Wee have upon serious consideration made choyce of Collonell Humfrey Mackworth ... one of known fidelity ... who hath engaged himself and his estate as farr as any in this Countrey to further the Publique services.' Mytton was not a signatory; on 12 May he succeeded Myddleton as commander in chief in north Wales.[30] Thomas Nicholls' 'party' of the 1630s was now in control. The borough assembly minutes resume: on 2 May 1645 it was agreed that the aldermen and assistants sequestered by the King should be restored; in December four of the Parliamentary commissioners (Lloyd, More, Clive and Charlton) were made burgesses without fine or fee 'in regard of their great affection for the town' – they were not Shrewsbury residents. It was also decided early in the year that the public preacher should be restored and James Betton returned to St Mary's. William Rowley survived to see this restoration and it was probably he who wrote to Julines Hering asking him, once again, to return, but the minister was now seriously ill in Amsterdam. The register of the Begynhof shows that Hering had died by 18 May 1645. Rowley died that summer, his burial at St Chad's being recorded on 2 July.[31] During this year Mackworth was made recorder of the town as well as its governor. Thomas Nicholls was chosen to be mayor, for an extended term. Thomas Hunt was chosen as MP in place of Francis Newport, and his brother Rowland became town clerk, returning with his family to his native town to join in the work of the godly restoration. There is a reference to Rowland in Baxter's memoirs: Mr Rowland Hunt of Harrow on the Hill, then living in Manchester, was 'a man of most exemplary Holiness ... without self-seeking, Hypocrasie or Guile'.[32] The events since 1640, and the invitation to Hering, indicate the turning to a presbyterial system of church government, the 'religious party' picking up where it had left off before the war, even when this was not official policy for the whole country.

In May 1645 Joshua Richardson, a young Oxford graduate from Broughton near Myddle, was made minister of Holy Cross. In 1646 Peter Studley was ejected from Pontesbury, where he died in 1648; Samuel Greaves was deprived of the third portion there but was allowed to keep Berrington. On the ejection of Dr Seddon from the valuable living of Worthen, Dr Betton was presented there ('was by a troop of horse put in possession'). St Mary's was now vacant. The borough assembly appointed Samuel Fisher who since preaching his 'factious sermon' there in 1633 had been first at Upton Magna and then in London. He was to be paid the usual salary of the public preacher, £46 13s 4d, plus £20 a year from lands purchased with an existing bequest. Thomas Blake of Tamworth was placed at St Alkmund's. Richard Pigot, formerly master of Northwich School in Cheshire, was appointed headmaster of Shrewsbury School, now described as being 'under the Government of the Saints'.[33]

There remained the appointment to St Chad's, the largest church and parish. In 1646 the parishioners elected as their minister Thomas Paget, co-pastor with Hering at Amsterdam. Decades earlier, Paget had been one of those ministers who opposed 'ceremonies' and explained their reasons to Bishop Morton at Stockport in 1617. Paget had been a minister in Cheshire and then in Manchester; ejected from that living, he joined Hering when his brother John Paget, whom Hering himself had joined in Amsterdam, died there in 1641. It was also in 1641 that Thomas Paget presented a book to Parliament: *A Defence of Church-Government exercised in Presbyteriall, Classical, & Synodall Assemblies*, written by his brother John Paget, 'late able and faithfull Pastour of the Reformed English Church in Amsterdam'. He had a book of his own published in 1643: *A Demonstration of Family Duties*, a guide for godly households. Paget was to be a magisterial figure in Shrewsbury so what we can glean of him is valuable. He married Margery Goldsmith in 1613, but she died in 1628 and was buried at Bowdon in Cheshire, where Thomas Paget was vicar. By this marriage he had three daughters and a son, Nathan, physician and friend of John Milton. By a second wife he had a son named Thomas, born in 1635, and a son named John and daughter named Hanna, who were buried at St Chad's in November 1646 and May 1648. He must have been elderly when he made Shrewsbury his home.[34]

In August 1645, after Naseby, the King told his army: 'I resolve by the grace of God, never to yield up the church to this government of Papists, Presbyterians or Independents, nor to injure my successors by lessening the crown of that ecclesiastical or military power which my predecessors left me.' Yet the Laudian church was now being dismantled, Laud himself having been executed on 10 January 1645. In January 1647 the King was a prisoner of the English army.[35] In the same month the Book of Common Prayer was replaced by the Directory of Public Worship, drawn up by the Assembly of Divines at Westminster. John Morrill argues that this ordinance was 'almost wholly a dead letter' with probably fewer than 10% of parishes acquiring the Directory in the ensuing months. He also claims that the new church organisation, a parochially-based version of the presbyterial and synodical pattern of church government, 'never really got off the ground'. It was intended to have 'classes' or groups of parishes in each county, with provincial assemblies above this and a national synod at the top of the pyramid. The national synod never met and only some areas chose to have presbyterial classes. London and Manchester were among them; eight counties attempted to put the scheme into practice and six more presented other schemes which were approved. Shropshire was in the former group of counties, with six designated classes. Shrewsbury was meant to head the first *classis*, containing 36 parishes with eight named ministers: Dr Betton of Worthen, Thomas Paget of Chad's (the appellation 'Saint' was dropped, except for Biblical saints), Thomas Blake of Alkmund's, Samuel Fisher of St Mary's, Francis Garbet of Wroxeter, James Smith of Upton, Francis Wright of Wellington and Samuel Smith of Cound. Elders included Thomas Knight, mayor of Shrewsbury, Humfrey Mackworth, Thomas Nicholls, Rowland Hunt, John Langley, John Prowde, Richard Pigot, Thomas Hunt, John Corbet and Robert Charlton. There is no evidence, such as minutes, to show that the *classis* operated but in 1648, 26 *classis* ministers were among the 57 from the county who signed a paper against the Independents and their wish for toleration: 'A Testimony of the Ministers in the province of Salop to the Truth of Jesus Christ, and to the Solemn League and Covenant: As also against the Errors, Heresies, and Blasphemies of these times and the Toleration of them'. This was sent to the London province as were testimonies from other presbyterians, in Cheshire and Lancashire for example, some worded more strongly than others. Thomas Paget's name is unaccountably absent. The only one of the six classes in Shropshire to be fully functioning was the fourth, based on Whitchurch and Wem; Thomas Porter, pastor of Whitchurch, and Andrew Parsons, pastor of Wem, were among those who signed.[36]

Independency or congregationalism was an alternative model of Reformed church government. Philip Benedict points out that as early as 1635 'New England ministers like John Cotton had begun to draft justifications for the distinctive practices that took shape in that part of the world in response to letters containing queries and criticisms from colleagues back in England.' One such letter was signed by Simeon Ashe and William Rathband; Ashe's friend Julines Hering was also a signatory. An unsatisfactory reply meant that only one of the 19 ministers who drafted the questions chose to go to New England; Hering went to Holland. Another figure from the Shrewsbury scene wrote one of the tracts defending the Independent position: Katherine Chidley's *Justification of the Independent Churches of Christ* was published in 1641. Then, in 1647, the lawyer John Cooke published *What the Independents Would Have,* 'a tract which sought to define more carefully, and less threateningly, a movement which was already being condemned as "fanatical" – The answer was obvious: they wanted what the Puritans sought vainly from James I, namely liberty of worship'. Cooke's biographer, Geoffrey Robertson, refers also to the importance of Richard Sibbes, preacher at Gray's Inn where Cooke studied:

> The message from the Gray's Inn pulpit was that Kings might be held to account for leading their people astray and it was superstition, not true religion, that immunised them from punishments for breaching the law. Over such challenges to sovereign immunity, hostility between [Charles I] and his Parliament would quickly develop.[37]

Cooke's contemporaries at Gray's Inn in the 1620s were the Hunts and Humfrey Mackworth. The two lawyers and the Member of Parliament would be concerned in developments in 1647-9. In December 1647 the King secretly signed an 'Engagement' with the Scots; this duplicity led Parliament to vote for 'No Addresses' to the King, putting an end to negotiations. Risings in Wales, the south-east of England and the north soon followed and constituted the 'Second Civil War' of 1648, Parliament blaming the King for the renewed bloodshed. There were also attempted risings in Shropshire, in which Sir Francis Ottley and Lord Byron were active. On 25 June the Committee of Safety (the renamed Shropshire Committee) ordered that Shrewsbury be put in a posture of defence, this task to be referred to the 'well-affected' of the town who should recommend six commanders, they in turn to enlist 'well-affected' persons. The mayor at this time was Rowland Hunt. The walls needed rebuilding so a note in the register of Shrawardine church is of interest: the stonework of the castle was to be pulled down and sent to Shrewsbury to repair the castle there and the walls. On 5 August Humfrey Mackworth reported to Parliament on a Royalist plot to gain entry to the town during the Lammas fair: 'Many were listed within the Walls and more in the Suburbs; the number not yet discovered.' Constant watch had to be kept and Mackworth wanted to raise two companies of one hundred men each, 'and to add fifty of my own'. He noted that the Lammas plot had been foiled by God's help: 'by special Providence' the Royalist messenger had been captured and information 'extorted from him'. Details of the encounter between the two sides followed. This seems to have been the end of Royalist endeavours in Shropshire for the time being.[38]

There still remained the question of dealing with the King, the army becoming impatient with him and with those Members of Parliament who still wanted to negotiate. On the morning of 6 December, as Cromwell, Lieutenant-General of Horse, was marching back from the north after besieging Pontefract, Colonel Pride and his troop excluded from the Commons those of the 471 active members who were in favour of a treaty with the King, others simply abstained from attending. Of the Shropshire MPs Robert Charlton, Sir John Corbet and Thomas More were 'secluded'; Thomas Hunt was absent; Humphrey Edwards (another Gray's Inn man) has subsequently been classed as a 'revolutionary' in David Underdown's categories. Cromwell's part in the Purge is equivocal. Austin Woolrych describes Henry Ireton as the 'mastermind' behind the army's moves: 'It is scarcely conceivable that Ireton kept his father-in-law [Cromwell] and immediate superiors in the dark about his intentions, but Cromwell probably took care not to know too much and timed his arrival so as not to be personally involved in the day's business.' In the following weeks, as Lucy Hutchinson recalled, many petitions were sent in to Parliament from the 'well-affected' in cities, counties and the army. Colonel Mackworth and other Shropshire officers wrote to General Fairfax, their letter being read out in the Commons on 26 December. They concurred with the Remonstrance of the army, against a treaty, asking 'that justice may be done upon the Authors of our troubles and bloodshed in the three Kingdoms'. They would depend upon the ordinary remedy by Parliament 'till God declare by evident demonstrations of His will in the passages of His providence, that the extraordinary is to be resorted to'. Geoffrey Robertson finds several ideological supports in the revolutionaries' arguments for a trial:

> The soldiers' cry for justice on the "man of blood" had a respectable pedigree not only in biblical blood-guilt, but in the common law of incitement to murder ... English criminal law was based on the notion of individual responsibility and Charles Stuart was the individual who was most responsible.

A trial was decided upon and counsel was needed; most lawyers left for the country but John Cooke remained, awaiting the will of God. On 10 January 1649 a messenger from Parliament found him at his Gray's Inn chambers and presented him with 'history's most fateful brief', to prepare the case against Charles Stuart. The trial began on 20 January, the King refusing to acknowledge the authority of the court. Another Gray's Inn lawyer presided, John Bradshaw of Cheshire. On the 27th Charles Stuart was condemned as a tyrant, murderer and public enemy. On 30 January he was executed after a public trial, not murdered or assassinated.[39]

Cooke's case against the King was published as *King Charles: His Case*. John Milton's *The Tenure of Kings and Magistrates* uses language that echoes the indictment of the King: it is 'an illuminating register' of the poet's political thought at the time.

> But this I dare owne as part of my faith, that if such a one there be, by whose Commission, whole massachers have been committed on his faithfull Subjects, his Provinces offered to pawn and alienation, as the hire of those whom he had sollicited to come in and destroy whole Citties and Countries; be he King, or Tyrant, or Emperour, the Sword of Justice is above him ... to avenge the effusion and so great a deluge of innocent blood.

Thomas Paget, of St Chad's in Shrewsbury, also published a pamphlet, 'by Authority', in defence of the purge and the regicide, presumably echoing his sermons:

> The Law and Minde of God, touching the capital punishment of the polluting and crying sin of wilful murder, whosoever is the committer of it, yea, though he be a blood-guilty King, may not be by a Magistrate looked upon as one to be dispensed withal.

He concluded with the analogy of the Babylonish captivity of Israel. 'Their course shall not be in vain. The valley of Achor is given for a door of hope.' This reference (Joshua, 7) is to Achan, who had stolen some of the treasure of Jericho and was stoned to death in the valley of Achor; God approved of this punishment, meted out by Joshua. A very different work was put out by the Royalists, and attributed to the King. *Eikon Basilike* was edited by John Gauden, possibly to seek an accommodation with Parliament, then published after the King's death. It appeared as a martyr's testimony and contributed greatly to the sentimentalisation, beatification even, of Charles Stuart. Its principles of royal and episcopal authority would also be passed on to his heir.[40]

Chapter 6
Commonwealth Controversies, 1649-1660

Kings had been deposed before, and violently murdered, but the trial and execution of Charles I was something new and shocking. A protest, written in French, came from certain lords, presumably some exiled Royalists who were at the court of Henrietta Maria (Charles I's queen) at St Germain, 'against the late perfidious, traitorous, and tyrannical usurpations of some members of the House of Commons, who are trying to overturn the fundamental laws and Kingly government of this country, and to make its subjects the slaves of this insolent tyranny'. The news of his father's execution came to the prince of Wales at the Hague where he was the guest of his brother-in-law Stadtholder Wilhelm II, husband of Mary Stuart. One account had one of the prince's chaplains breaking the news by addressing him as 'Your Majesty'. The English government was now in the hands of a truncated Commons (the Rump) which appointed a Council of State, including lords and army officers, notably the commander-in-chief Thomas Lord Fairfax and his deputy, the cavalry commander Oliver Cromwell. Any nine of them could form a quorum 'to oppose the pretensions of Charles Stuart, eldest son to the late King' and to direct the militia and deal with affairs of state. The Act instituting this Council was dated 13 February 1649. On the same day there was a public declaration by excluded members of the Commons protesting against the usurpation of power, the murder of the King, and the disinheritance of Charles Stuart. They disclaimed all acts done under the army's power and stood by the Solemn League and Covenant. The new institution went ahead, however, ordering that Whitehall be prepared and two seals made, having the arms of England and Ireland and 'The Council of State' as inscription.

Two days later, on 19 February, the proceedings of the Council of State included a report that not every member had subscribed the new oath of Engagement, the objectors including the earl of Denbigh and Lord Fairfax: 'They had served Parliament faithfully, and were willing to do so still ... but they cannot subscribe engagement, as it looks backward, and is contrary to what they acted as peers in the House of Lords.' That House, and the monarchy, were abolished, but the Engagement oath proved a major point of controversy: 'I do declare and promise that I will be true and faithful to the commonwealth of England, as it is now established, without a King or House of Lords.' Fairfax had not agreed to the regicide and would later lament it in verse: 'Oh lett that Day from time be blotted quite', though he accepted it as God's will, to which they must acquiesce.[1]

There were other disputed issues, such as the role of the army. Some believed that the militia should again be under the control of county gentry. Robert Clive was of this opinion, which may explain his reaction to the billeting of troops destined for Ireland in north Shropshire. Their captain was a young man from Denbighshire who had entered Shrewsbury School in 1640. The Council of State received the report of events in August 1649: Captain Lumley Thelwall's troop of horse 'were seized on by a tumultuous multitude led on by Colonel Clive, and reviled as traitors and rebels for being in the service of Parliament, and their horses openly sold in the markets'. Clive was summoned to London to answer for his action. Others on the war-time Shropshire Parliamentary Committee were among the justices of the peace named as commissioners for providing money to maintain forces raised by authority of Parliament: Sir John Corbet, Robert Corbet, Thomas Hunt, Rowland Hunt, Thomas Nicholls, Thomas Mytton and Humfrey Mackworth are all familiar names. In July the Council of State had written to the governors of certain towns about the necessity of defence against any attempts by 'the malignant party'. Shrewsbury was one of the towns where it was decided that the castle must be repaired, 'by advice of a skilled engineer', and maintained – a small garrison should suffice (Plate 3). The governor, Mackworth, had the responsibility. In December there were complaints by Staffordshire officers about the behaviour of the earl of Denbigh during the war. He was said to have been at odds with Mackworth, threatening to run him through with his sword and swearing not to go to Shropshire until Mackworth was removed from the Committee. Denbigh remained under suspicion but Mackworth was cleared of any condemnation, continuing to serve as a reliable local commander for the Council of State. Among other orders we find, in February 1650, that Colonel Mackworth, governor of Shrewsbury, should 'use his judgement about opening packets that he shall judge to contain matter prejudicial to the commonwealth'. He and Mr Nicholls were also to 'examine the business concerning Mr Porter [of Whitchurch], and whether the engagement ought be entered into, and send up the examinations'. Thomas Cooke of Market Drayton was also to be examined.[2] This controversy exercised many people. Richard Baxter, who preached in Worcestershire against the oath, wrote:

> the Rump presently drew up a Form of Engagement, to be put upon all Men ... So we must take the Rump for an established Commonwealth, and promise Fidelity to them. This the Sectarian party swallowed easily ... But the Presbyterians, and the moderate Episcopal Men refused it ...

Presbyterians had scruples that subscribing the Engagement would mean forswearing the Solemn League and Covenant, which entailed loyalty to the King.[3]

The controversy was particularly evident in Shrewsbury, where Thomas Paget preached in favour of the Engagement. However, Samuel Fisher and Thomas Blake preached openly against it. These ministers 'preach much against the present Government, and to encourage the people to sedition', wrote the London lawyer Bulstrode Whitelocke: 'at the day of the publicke Fast kept in one of their churches [Chad's], there was another mock fast kept in the other two [Mary's and Alkmund's]'. Paget also defended the Engagement in a new edition of *A Religious Scrutiny*. Using arguments from Scripture he exhorted 'religiously affected Common-wealths-men' to pray and seek for a settled peace and prosperity: the 'main and chief scope and end of the oaths of Supremacy and Allegiance formerly; and of the Protestation and Covenant lately, and likewise of the Engagement at the present was, and is the just safety and preservation of the Common-wealth of England'. In religion he still advocated the presbyterian way.[4] Debates were also going on in neighbouring Cheshire. In March 1650 Richard Bradshaw, mayor of Chester, reported to the president of the Council of State, his kinsman John Bradshaw, that the delay in sending in returns for the taking of the oath was due to preachers' arguments from pulpits. John Bradshaw was Chief Justice of Chester and Humfrey Mackworth was his deputy. Adam Martindale of Rostherne, near Knutsford, wrote that all the ministers of any account that he knew, save only one, were for subscribing; there were debates in which he took part, and he signed, though he was troubled about it. Another minister, later to be associated with Shrewsbury, was Henry Newcome of Gawsworth, near Macclesfield: 'I went to Chester and on Christmas-day, 1650, I did subscribe ... and it was long on my heart as one of my great transgressions.'[5]

Sir Robert Harley (SA-IMG24345)

Another episode hinged on the oath of Engagement, which Sir Robert Harley had refused to take. A sad letter from him to his kinsman Humfrey Mackworth is dated 29 April 1650. After recounting his service to Parliament and his sufferings – with the loss of his Herefordshire estate and his house at Brampton Bryan – he refers to his request to settle in Shrewsbury, conveyed by his servant Samuel Shilton. The 'faire acceptance' of Mackworth's reply 'did much incourage me to accellerate my repair to a place soe advantageous to me'. But he had had another letter from Shilton to the effect that Mackworth would gladly serve Harley in any way he could 'but as for your coming to live at Salop, he must let you know that it is a divided place and that you being persons of eminence [Harley and his sons] and not compliers with the present proceedings, the eyes of [dissenters] might be upon you'. This might strengthen dissent. On 8 May Mackworth wrote to Harley, explaining: 'I am now entrusted by the Parliament for the security of this garrison, and in pursuance of some private instructions I have received I shall desire that if you be not fully "satisfied to the subscribeing of the engagement", that you will at present rather forbear than retain your intention of coming to reside here.' The private instructions can have come only from the Council of State, which at this point approved Mackworth's proceedings. The divided loyalties of Shrewsbury, and the fears of the Council of State, forced its governor to refuse his kinsman's request, which he had it seems been ready to grant. Sir Robert Harley settled instead at Ludlow (where he died in 1656). His sons Edward, Robert and Thomas were imprisoned, at Hereford and Bristol, for not taking the oath, and Edward wrote later that he had been prevented for ten years from living in Herefordshire.[6] In 1653 there was a recommendation in the Commons to abolish the oath but the House voted merely to abolish the legal disabilities of those who refused to take the Engagement: it still stood as a political test.[7]

We learn a little more about Shrewsbury in the summer of 1650 from Samuel Fisher and Thomas Blake. Fisher wrote a few years later about meditations on death 'when he with Reverend Mr Blake, stayed in Shrewsbury (in the time of Gods last visitation of that place by Pestilence) to execute their Pastoral Office amongst their people that did abide there in that doleful time when they were under the continual expectation of arrest'. In August Mackworth was ordered 'to turn out of the garrison all such persons as either in pulpit or elsewhere by seditious words endeavoured to stir up sedition and uproar among the people'. Blake and Fisher were counted among these. Fisher still remembered the harsh treatment he had suffered from Peter Studley twenty years earlier. Now the party he had long supported was driving him out. But he and Blake found temporary refuge at Myddle where the minister Joshua Richardson, formerly of Holy Cross, allowed them to preach – he too had refused the oath. They were welcomed also by another Presbyterian minister in Shropshire, Samuel Hildersam, and his wife Mary: to them Blake dedicated *A Treatise of the Covenant of God Entered into with Mankind,* written at Tamworth in 1652. Blake recalled that for many months they had 'free and liberal entertainment' at West Felton, with leisure to study in Hildersam's library. Samuel, we may recall, was the son of the puritan preacher Arthur Hildersam, mentor of Julines Hering.[8]

At the time of the ministers' expulsion from Shrewsbury the Council of State ordered the Governor to prepare for possible invasion by foreign or domestic enemies. The main reason for the government's anxiety was the return of Charles Stuart to Scotland in June 1650. He was to receive the Scottish crown in return for swearing to the Solemn League and Covenant. In the same month Cromwell came back from subduing Ireland. At the prospect of having to invade Scotland, Thomas Lord Fairfax resigned his commission and Cromwell was promoted to commander-in-chief.[9]

Charles Stuart was crowned at Scone on 1 January 1651:

> The Scottish Army under their King crossed the Border ... on August 6th and on the 7th Major-General Thomas Harrison forwarded letters from Newcastle-on-Tyne ... to the Commissioners of the Parliament in Chester, Salop, Stafford, and other English counties in the North and West, and in the six counties of North Wales, to give them timely notice thereof.

Shrewsbury was thus warned. Mackworth's elder son, Thomas, was one of the officers entrusted with command of troops in the town On 16 August it was reported from the castle that the town was 'in good posture'. On his journey southwards, Charles Stuart and his army camped at Tong Heath in Shropshire. Perhaps the prince remembered his earlier stay in Shrewsbury, in 1642, for he sent an optimistic summons requesting

Mackworth to yield the town up. 'I cannot but persuade my self you will do it, when I consider you a gentleman of an ancient house, and of very different principles from those with whom your employment ranks you at present.' In the event the prince was answered in forthright terms by Mackworth who addressed his letter 'For the Commander-in-Chief of the Scottish Army':

> What principles I am judged to be of I know not, but I hope they are such as shall ever declare me honest, and no way differing (as I know) from those engaged in the same employment with me ... I resolve to be found as I am, unremovable, the faithful servant of the Commonwealth of England. H. Mackworth

The Scottish army had to pass on, to Worcester and defeat by Cromwell on 3 September. One traitor discovered in Shrewsbury was John Benbow. He was shot in a cabbage garden outside the walls, at the point where he was said to have taken part in the regaining of the town in February 1645. After Cromwell's 'crowning mercy' at Worcester in September Shropshire was full of fugitives, including Charles Stuart who famously escaped from Boscobel House with the help of the Catholic network in the area.[10] His ally the earl of Derby was less fortunate. He was tried at Chester before Mackworth on 1 October and executed on the 15th at Bolton, being held responsible for the massacre there in 1644.[11]

The religious situation in Shrewsbury now needed attention after the problems over the Engagement. The borough council wasted little time. The register of the Commissioners of the Great Seal records the grant of the vicarage of Alkmund's on 23 June 1651 to Richard Heath, recommended by Colonel Mackworth and Mr John Milton. Heath was a scholarly cleric, ensconced in south Shropshire since leaving Cambridge where he had been at Milton's college. Austin Woolrych writes: 'This is Milton's sole appearance in this register, whose eighty-seven folios record some hundreds of presentations.' The poet had helped the younger man with his studies and Heath would play a part in the production of the great Polyglot Bible, financed by the Commonwealth. Milton was now a man of importance: the Council of State's Secretary of Foreign Languages, or Latin Secretary. This link between the great man and the minister called by Richard Baxter 'holy humble Heath' may surprise us. There was the Cambridge connection, but perhaps the Paget connection had a part to play too. Thomas Paget's son Nathan, a distinguished London physician, was married to a first cousin of Cromwell and was the friend and doctor of Milton.[12] The borough council in Shrewsbury had already recorded the departure of Samuel Fisher and had instructed the mayor, John Prowde, to write to Dr Whichcote and to Mr John Corbet 'to find out a Minister for St Maries and to procure an Augmentation for the same'. (The renowned (Cambridge scholar Benjamin Whichcote was a native of Shrewsbury.) They hoped first to entice Dr John Bryan from Coventry, paying for his hiring of horses and charges of travel to Shrewsbury. But Coventry would not release him and the borough officials had to turn for help elsewhere to find a public preacher.[13]

Portrait of Richard Baxter (SA-IMG24724)

The friend they turned to was Richard Baxter. He was in a slightly awkward position because the people of Coventry had asked his help in persuading Dr Bryan to stay there. Perhaps to compensate, Bryan's eldest son, John, became minister at Holy Cross in Shrewsbury; at the age of 24 he was presumably considered too young to be public preacher. In 1650 Baxter had dedicated the fourth part of *The Saints' Everlasting Rest* to his 'dearly beloved friends in the Lord, the Inhabitants of the town of Shrewsbury, both Magistrates, Ministers and People'. So he did what he could to persuade Francis Tallents to come to Shrewsbury. Tallents was a Fellow of Magdalene College, Cambridge, where 'it pleas'd God to call him by his grace'. (He may have been recommended to the council in Shrewsbury by Whichcote.) He had been ordained by the third London Presbyterian *classis* in 1648. The parishioners of St Mary's, without a pastor for two years, wrote an address to Tallents with an invitation from the elders. Baxter added his voice: 'My desire of the prosperity of Christ's Church in Shrewsbury causes me to be solicitous for their present breach in regard of a minister ... I do assure you, impartially, that were I loose, I know not one congregation in England that I would sooner choose.' (He was not free because he had accepted the call to Kidderminster.) The Governor, he assured Tallents, was 'very Godly, Judicious, Orthodox'. The Governor's son, Thomas, would help get a further £50 a year from the London committee, in addition to the salary of £150. The Shrewsbury headmaster, Richard Pigot, conveyed an assurance from Samuel Fisher that he had renounced the place and was desirous for Tallents to come there. The borough council agreed on 18 August 1652 'that Mr Francis Tallents BD be publick preacher of this Town and curate of St Mary's': he was to preach the Thursday lecture weekly and conduct the Lord's Day services. Among the advantages described by Baxter was the presence of many godly ministers in the area. One of these was Samuel Hildersam, whose niece Anne Lomax married Tallents at West Felton in June 1653, only six months after his formal appointment to St Mary's on 4 January. Tallents, like John Bryan the younger, was to enjoy a long ministry in Shrewsbury.[14]

The presence of these ministers in Shrewsbury in addition to the doyen Thomas Paget was important at the time when independent sects and individuals were flourishing. In October 1652 William Taylor of Bridgnorth wrote to Baxter for help in finding a minister to assist him: neither of the two men who had preached 'on tryall' was satisfactory, one, named Fidge, from Shrewsbury, preaching sermons that savoured of antinomianism. This belief that the moral law was not binding upon Christians under 'the law of grace' had a long history. Stephen Geree, in 1644, condemned it as a plausible but dangerous doctrine, lacking discipline. Baxter argued strongly against it but Tallents judged it merely as 'a company of bad conclusions drawn from good principles'.[15] Mr Fidge was not the only preacher to worry more orthodox ministers. In Cheshire Henry Newcome was troubled by 'an erroneous fellow, one Harrison' who was in the area in the summer of 1651, infusing dangerous tenets among the people: 'he asserted desperate blasphemous things – as that the soul within a man was God, and that there was neither heaven nor hell but in a man's own self'. In contemporary terms Harrison would no doubt have been considered a 'Ranter'. Newcome had him charged under the Blasphemy Act of 9 August 1650, aimed against the denial of civil and moral necessity and tending to 'the dissolution of all human society'.[16] Harrison was committed to prison at Chester until the assizes of April 1652; the judges were Humfrey Mackworth and Thomas Fell. The case was remitted to sessions, where Harrison had his supporters while Newcome felt deserted (except by God). Colonel Henry Bradshaw, brother of John, arrived to support the minister. The justices abhorred these heterodox beliefs but would 'hear no more of the business'. When Thomas Fell returned to his home at Swarthmoor in Furness after being absent on circuit in 1652 he found that his wife Margaret had opened their home to a group of 'Seekers'. Such groups (sometimes associated with Ranters) were strong in Westmorland. Mrs Fell claimed to have been one of them for twenty years.

At Swarthmoor Hall in 1652 the Seekers, especially Mrs Fell, found their messiah in a newcomer: George Fox claimed to have had a vision on Pendle Hill of a multitude waiting to be gathered in. With Mrs Fell as their manager the wandering preachers became a movement, going in pairs to spread the word and reporting back to her. Her husband did not become a Friend but he gave the group his protection, as when Fox and James Nayler were summoned to Lancaster in October 1652 to answer charges of blasphemy. In 1653 they published their defence: *Saul's Errand to Damascus, with his Packet of Letters from the High Priests against the Disciples of the Lord.* A copy of this soon reached the village of Cound near Shrewsbury. The sect of Quakers had come on the local scene.[17]

Even where there was agreement on doctrine and the need for church discipline controversy might arise, as between Presbyterians and Independents, the latter rejecting any prescribed liturgy. The main body of parishioners included those formerly devoted to the Prayer Book, those opposed to its 'popish' elements, and a number of the indifferent. The first group would have felt deprived by the withdrawal of the Prayer Book, and they and the indifferent would certainly have regretted the loss of saints' feast days and communal enjoyment. Only the committed godly would have welcomed the discipline of ministers and lay elders who controlled entry to the sacrament, now something to be attained by worthiness rather than a parish celebration. Then there was the observance of the Lord's day, sabbatarian measures having been passed in the 1640s. The Act of April 1644 was steered through Parliament by Sir Robert Harley who stipulated that the sabbath should be sanctified by the exercise of 'piety and true religion, publickly and privately'. Everyone, including vagabonds, should attend church, commercial work and travel were banned, as were sports, bell-ringing, wakes, church ales, dancing and maypoles, and even leisurely walks. In January 1645 the *Directory for Public Worship* declared that the whole day was to be spent in public worship, reading of scripture, meditation, repetition of sermons, catechisings, conference for prayer, singing psalms, visiting the sick and helping the poor. Known profaners of the sabbath were to be excluded from receiving communion. Responsibility for enforcing the Act was placed upon JPs, constables and churchwardens, who were liable to heavy fines if they defaulted. The degree of enforcement depended on the size of the godly faction and the outlook of officials. Some of these were exceedingly zealous. A French visitor to London reported that 'the religion of England is preaching and sitting still on Sundays'.[18] We may be reminded of Shrewsbury in the 1620s under magistrates such as William Rowley who arrested the leader of the merry-making apprentices, and of the private devotions conducted at Rowley's Mansion and Drapers' Hall under Julines Hering which had so impressed the 20-year-old Richard Baxter.

By the 1650s Richard Baxter was steering his own course, setting up an Association of ministers in Worcestershire. Jarvis Bryan, uncle of John the younger of Chad's, was one of them. Baxter did not approve of lay elders: the ministers were to perform all pastoral duties. His own practice was to teach his flock 'personally, interlocutorily, & in smaller subassemblyes', as he interpreted Paul in Acts 20:20: 'I kept back nothing that was profitable unto you, but have shewed you, and have taught you publickly, and from house to house.' The propositions and profession of the Association were published in 1653 as *Christian Concord or the Agreement of the Associated Pastors and Churches in Worcestershire.*[19] The same principle was adopted in Cheshire in the autumn of 1653 but this Association may have been the revived presbyterian *classis* since ruling elders were admitted; it was accepted by the Manchester *classis*.[20] It is no surprise that, especially in country areas, ministers often found their flock absent when they made a house-visit. Even though Baxter did not approve of the presbyterian system he had high regard for its ministers (especially those who sought or listened to his plentiful advice). We have seen his empathy with the ministers and godly people of Shrewsbury. There was a demonstration of the borough's political stance in the celebration in February 1653 of the anniversary of recapturing the town:

> Yesterday our Governor, with the wel-affected of this place, solemnly kept the whole day in commemoration of the great mercy in taking this garrison. Many petitions were put in the behalfe of our councels and armes, and to strengthen the resolutions of those whom God hath made instrumentall for his glory and the propagation of the Gospel, that they may be carried on for the welfare of them that are faithful in and to the Commonwealth.[21]

The Rump Parliament had considerable powers but was ineffective in promoting religious and social reform. It was summarily dismissed by Cromwell on 20 April 1653. David Smith's summary may be quoted: 'Believing that the Rump had betrayed the godly, the Army now devised a Parliament *consisting of* the godly. This institution, based on the ancient Jewish Sanhedrin or assembly of 'saints', was unique in English constitutional history.' Devised by Thomas Harrison, it was adopted by Cromwell: the army officers would take in nominations from separatist congregations, selecting 139 'persons fearing God, and of approved fidelity and honesty'. A further five members, including Cromwell and Harrison, were added. Cromwell's address at the opening of the Nominated Assembly on 4 July has been read by Robert Paul as suggesting that he was thinking of the Assembly 'in these terms: England was to be governed by a "Church Meeting" set within the parish of the whole nation'. There were two members for Shropshire: William Botterell of Ludlow and Thomas Baker of Sweeney Hall near Oswestry.[22]

Richard Gough of Myddle wrote scathingly about Baker although he evidently went often to Sweeney to hear preachers, such as Vavasor Powell 'who commonly preached every day in the weeke. I have heard him pray and preach four houres togeather in the dineing room att Sweeney, where many persons came to heare him'. After the lengthy religious meeting everyone would be given a twopenny bun or cake and a half a pint of beer. Powell represents another strain of religious activity, an unaligned preacher taking as his exemplar Paul and the early apostles. He was brought up in Shropshire, where his great-uncle Erasmus Powell was vicar of Clun. Erasmus Powell was one of the puritan circle which included Richard More (defender of the godly against Studley) and Richard Heath, in his first post after Cambridge, at a chapelry of Clun. It was probably Heath who brought with him a book by his Cambridge tutor, and Milton's, Joseph Mede. This was an influential millenarian work, *Clavis Apocalyptica,* translated by Richard More as *The Key to the Apocalypse,* which reached a wider audience. Vavasor Powell was presumably one of them. So we must weave into our account this concept of the coming of the end of the world (as promised by Christ to his followers) and Christ's own imminent monarchy (the fifth by calculating ancient empires). The belief influenced Cromwell and Milton, among many others. Vavasor Powell saw the saints' support of Parliament as a sign of God's approval. He asked the new Assembly to have regard for the poor and oppressed, to administer justice, and 'to be tender also to some tender consciences'. He declared:

> Christ begins to take his great power, and to reigne, and now the Judgement is set, and power put into the hands of the Saints, and one of the ten Hornes [of the beast in Revelation, 13: 1] is cut off, and never to be put on againe.

On 25 April 1653 the London preacher John Rogers wrote to Cromwell: 'This is the day to be much observed, the rather for that in the revolution of times the changes will run their round out, and then the Lord will come to reign.' Cromwell opened the Nominated Assembly in a similar fervent manner: 'Truly you are called by God, to rule with him, and for him ... this may be the door to usher in things that God hath promised and prophesied of ... we are at the threshold.' Unfortunately for all these hopes there were differences within the Assembly, and when the emotive issue of religion was under discussion the moderate majority withdrew, tendering their resignation to a surprised Cromwell, the Assembly eventually dismissing itself in December.[23] Cromwell remembered the experiment with sadness and a sense of his own failure, his 'weakness and folly'. Robert Paul reads in the failure a lack of understanding that 'to govern a nation on the basis of an ethic to which the majority of people cannot or will not aspire, is an imposition'. The attempt bred resentment.[24]

One of the statutes passed during the six months' life of the Nominated Assembly concerned the marriage ceremony, which was now to be performed before a JP. Francis Tallents was one of the ministers who objected to this Act, but he had a way around it, as he wrote to Edmund Calamy: 'I and others have married many before a Justice, he saying nothing but only declaring the marriage valid.' Official registers were also to be kept. In Shropshire there were various expedients: at Donnington the parishioners asked their minister to be the registrar; at Newport the parish clerk was chosen; at Ashford Carbonell the schoolmaster was elected for this duty.[25] The Assembly (or Short Parliament, as Ronald Hutton calls it) was divided between radicals and those less radical.

When Cromwell had dismissed the Rump on 20 April 1653 he had taken everyone by surprise but, writes Hutton, it was a feature of this later coup, 'so brilliantly and mysteriously contrived', that a new constitution had been prepared in advance. Its author was John Lambert, cavalry commander of a quality to rival Cromwell, and statesman. In Hutton's words: 'His instinct was to replace the old trinity of King, Lords and Commons with one of King, Council and Parliament, each limiting the others' powers.' A monarchy would not be acceptable to the army so Cromwell became Lord Protector, with a system of checks and balances generally acceptable. (Millenarians, however, accused Cromwell of usurping Christ's reign.) The Engagement was now repealed, and the taking of such oaths condemned (which would satisfy sectaries and Quakers). At Shrewsbury the Protector was proclaimed 'with great rejoicing' on the day of his inauguration, 16 December 1653.[26] Some of the 42 clauses in Lambert's Instrument of Government dealt with religion: the Christian religion as contained in the Scriptures was to be 'held forth and recommended as the public profession of these nations'. Provision would be made for appointing able preachers. No one should be compelled to the public profession of religious beliefs by penalties or other means; there would be liberty of worship except for popery or prelacy, or for those who practised licentiousness. The anti-Catholic and anti-Laudian prejudice was of long standing, whilst accusations of licentious behaviour were levelled at sectaries such as Ranters. Quakers were to present something of a problem, as we shall see. The national Church referred to in ordinances was the Presbyterian state church, but Independents and certain sectaries were allowed their own church government or worship. In March 1654 the system of Triers was instituted, to approve preachers and fill vacant benefices. In August Ejectors were appointed to remove unsatisfactory clergy.[27] The 21 Shropshire Commissioners appointed as Ejectors included Humfrey Mackworth, his son Thomas, Thomas and Rowland Hunt, Richard Pigot (the schoolmaster at Shrewsbury) and Thomas Baker of Sweeney. The Ministers Assistant, local clerics appointed to give advice, included the four Shrewsbury ministers, ministers of the fourth Shropshire *classis* and others – Samuel Hildersam, for example.[28]

On 7 February 1654 Humfrey Mackworth was appointed to the Council of State, the 'Protector's approval being signified': he was to be a regular attender at meetings and to serve on committees dealing with religion and the law. He was also elected as a member of the first Protectorate Parliament which opened on 3 September 1654. Mackworth represented the county along with Thomas Mytton, Robert Corbet of Stanwardine and Philip Yonge (Mackworth's son-in-law); Humfrey Mackworth the younger sat for Shrewsbury and his uncle Colonel William Crowne was returned for Bridgnorth. The Mackworth interest was clearly strong. Shrewsbury may not have been typical, in the light of Ronald Hutton's statement that this Parliament consisted mainly of 'Civil War Parliamentarians who would never have supported the regicide'. In November Parliament was considering the reduction of forces and garrisons but Shrewsbury was one of those listed by Cromwell as meriting further consideration, along with Chester, Bristol and Hereford. His comment on the town was doubtless influenced by Mackworth: 'It was a place of strength ... if any enemy should get into it, and possess it, all the forces of England and Scotland could not be able to force them out.' With his new responsibilities as member of the Council of State Mackworth and his wife had lodgings at Whitehall where he died suddenly (at least, he died intestate) at about Christmas time. He was buried in Westminster Abbey at night on 26 December 1654, his burial paid for by the state, at a cost of £300. Mackworth's servant Edmund King was paid £30.[29] Subsequent orders from the Council of State addressed to Colonel Humphrey Mackworth, Governor of Shrewsbury, are presumably addressed to the late governor's younger son and namesake, born in May 1631; he had the assistance of a more experienced soldier in his uncle Colonel William Crowne. Royalist risings were being planned for early March 1655 and the garrison of Shrewsbury was small, so there was danger to the town and a challenge for the new governor.

The plan devised by Major Nicholas Armorer, former Royalist governor of High Ercall, was to seize the most important towns and garrisons: Chester, Shrewsbury, Ludlow and Denbigh. Sir Vincent Corbet and his kinsman Colonel Scriven promised their support. Backing was also needed from Francis Lord Newport: he had failed to help Charles Stuart in 1651 (he claimed to repent this) and now he passed on assurances of loyalty but did nothing (Plate 7). His younger brother Andrew was, however, an active agent for the Royalist cause, collecting funds, but he seems not to have taken part in the present action. Corbet also failed to take part. The leader in Shropshire was now Sir Thomas Harris of Boreatton, an energetic 26 year old. A more senior Royalist was Sir Thomas Myddleton of Chirk. Another Montgomeryshire man, Ralph Kynaston, was to attack Shrewsbury. News of the plot reached Mackworth at the last minute but he took decisive action: a small force was sent to arrest Harris at Boreatton, where a rich haul of arms and a number of ready-saddled horses were captured; a warning was sent to Chirk; and local forces were alerted to prevent Kynaston coming into Shropshire. The Royalist design was abandoned. On 10 April an order came from the Protector to Governor Mackworth to disband the Shrewsbury garrison and receive another from Worcester: 'that the place may be in better security, for you have many townsmen who cannot be relied on for exact duty as strangers'. In July the Council of State advised Cromwell to bestow on Humfrey Mackworth the first company of foot that could be spared. In addition, members of the Owen family in Shrewsbury were arrested for disaffection to the present government and the Newport brothers were put in the Tower.[30]

For the people of Shrewsbury this must have been a worrying time, some fearing and others hoping for a successful Royalist rising. For the governor and his assistants there was the knowledge that many in the town could not be trusted. At the national level there was fear and perhaps overreaction: during the autumn of 1655 a new regime was established whereby eleven leading men in the army were commissioned as major-generals to each supervise a group of counties. They also conducted elections for the Parliament of 1656: Thomas Mackworth again represented the shire, along with Philip Yonge, Andrew Lloyd and Samuel More. Humfrey Mackworth the younger was again chosen to represent Shrewsbury, along with a merchant of the town, the rich Samuel Jones. There was a new MP for Bridgnorth: Major Edmund Waring, a captain under Major-General James Berry who had Shrewsbury as one of his headquarters in his allotted area: Herefordshire, Worcestershire, Shropshire and Wales. The duties of the new officials included security and moral reform, putting down drunkenness and other vices.[31]

On his arrival in Shrewsbury on 28 November 1655 James Berry was entertained by the mayor and aldermen at the Red Lion; on 3 December, as he set off on a tour of duty, he was given a feast costing £14 at the Pheasant. He was in the town again in early January and during May and June. Early on he persuaded a reluctant Thomas Hunt to become sheriff: 'he is an honest man and will doe good', Berry wrote to Secretary of State John Thurloe whose remit included control of a well-financed espionage system and censorship of the press. From now on Thomas Hunt became more prominent as a leader of the Presbyterian community in Shrewsbury, working with Berry who was an Independent in religion. On 12 January 1656 Berry wrote to Thurloe:

> I am now at last become civell and have taken my place among such magistrates, in the Quarter Sessions at Sallop; where hath been the greatest appearance that hath been seene there for many Cessions and that you may see who were there and what hearts they have for reformation I have sent you the Copy of an order or declaration that we made and subscribed and read publiquely ... we are not without hopes that magistrates shalbe a terrour to evill doers and a prayse to them that doe well.

One order, for the suppression of undesirable alehouses, was signed by Berry, Thomas Mytton, Humfrey Mackworth the younger, Philip Yonge, William Crowne, Richard Bagot, Robert Corbet, Robert Clive and Edmund Waring (who succeeded Hunt as sheriff). At the spring assizes, when Hunt was still sheriff, Richard Baxter preached before his good friend on the obligation of magistrates to assist the Church in promoting virtue and suppressing vice. This was part of Berry's programme but Baxter was now critical of his former friend. Berry had lived in the same house as Baxter in Dudley when Baxter began his preaching career and had accompanied him to Worcester when he was ordained by the bishop and received his licence to preach. But during the civil war Berry, Baxter complained, had not invited him into his army quarters nor visited him:

> He was a Man, I verily think, of great Sincerity before the Wars, and of very good Natural Parts ... and affectionate in Religion ... But when Cromwell made him his Favourite, and his extraordinary Valour was crowned with extraordinary Success, and when he had been a while most conversant with those that in Religion thought the old Puritan Ministers were dull, self-conceited, Men of a lower form, and that new Light had declared I know not what to be a higher attainment, his Mind, his Aim, his Talk and all was altered accordingly.

In Baxter's critical, seemingly resentful view, to follow such new light, instead of the light of the study of divinity, was to take error for truth and evil for good. Baxter was particularly angry at Berry's lenient treatment of Quakers.[32] This individual experience may serve to illustrate how sharp differences could be between 'orthodox' religion, whether presbyterian or episcopal, and the beliefs of radical sects.

Berry was harsh in his treatment of one group: dangerous papists – 'desperate persons and divers of them fitt to grind sugar or plant tobacco' – but to others who were not dangerous or did not create disturbance he showed tolerance. When Thurloe and Cromwell expressed concern at the preaching in Wales and the borders of Vavasor Powell they instructed Berry to examine him. The manner of his examination of Powell says much about the character of James Berry, who wrote to his friend the Protector: he had invited the preacher to dinner (at Worcester) and been assured that there was no plot against Cromwell, merely criticism which might 'worke upon your heart'. Powell's criticism was published and delivered to Cromwell in the form of a pamphlet, *A Word for God.* Berry gave Powell leave to preach and met him again, suggesting to his superiors that they might show 'a little more understanding' of 'our British zeal'. A letter from Shrewsbury on 5 January 1656 expressed Berry's conviction that people would not 'be wrought up to any comotion ... they [the Welsh] are an affectionate tender-spirited people that want judgment'. He and Powell 'parted friendly'. Berry had a sense of humour as well as common sense, and appears to have empathised if not identified with Powell and his fellow Welshmen – 'our British zeal'. Berry had also been able to persuade Hunt and other Presbyterians to work with him, but they too feared the influence of the Quakers, who were established in Shrewsbury by 1655. In the spring of 1656 a leading Quaker preacher visited the town perhaps three times: Alexander Parker, well educated and aged 27, was a formidable rival for the local ministers. Another Quaker preacher reported back that summer to Swarthmoor (the Quaker base and home to Mrs Fell) that he had visited Shrewsbury 'where we found some soldiers (that quarter there) newly convinced ... and we were informed that the townspeople begin to come in much to meetings'. The group from Cound were among these.[33]

Both the Quakers (or Friends) and the earlier sect of Baptists flourished during the Commonwealth and Protectorate, especially in the Welsh borders. There were similarities and differences. Scripture was the final authority for Baptists, the Holy Spirit for Quakers; both shared the Calvinist doctrine of total dependence upon divine providence, but the General Baptists (unlike the Particular Baptists) and Quakers dissented from the doctrines of election and predestination; both were democratic in their forms of church government; both were iconoclasts, rejecting pomp, coercion and formality. Both insisted on 'gathering' the Christian community from the world at large, symbolised in the case of Baptists by the baptism of believers – a profession of faith followed by submersion in water, such as a river, drowning the old Adam – while Quakers required outward tokens of inward change such as refusal to bear arms, take oaths, or doff hats in deference to authority. Baptists followed the Independents but rejected infant baptism; Quakers eliminated all sacraments. The groups were of course rivals in trying to convince others. There were many pamphlets published and debates between Baptists and orthodox groups, often on the subject of infant baptism. There was one such in April 1656 (we are still in the year regarded as apocalyptic by millenarians) at Ellesmere in north Shropshire, between Thomas Porter of Whitchurch, in the fourth *classis*, and the Baptist Henry Haggar of Stafford. The biographer and former pupil of Francis Tallents relates that 'Mr Tallents was pitch'd upon to be Moderator ... beginning and ending with Prayer, and directing the Progress of the Dispute (which continued five hours) with Prudence and Candour, that is, like himself'.[34]

The Presbyterians of Shrewsbury had some serious competition but they also had problems of their own. When Baxter was in the town in 1656 he had a meeting with John Bryan of Holy Cross, following this up with one of his neatly written and very long letters of advice. Holy Cross had always been conservative in religion and Bryan had not been able to administer the sacrament because his parishioners refused to elect elders; he was afraid of dissenting from his fellow ministers in Shrewsbury. Baxter acknowledged that Bryan would have a hard time, but insisted that elders were not necessary – the minister could judge who was fit to receive communion. Thomas Hunt also engaged Baxter in a scheme to strengthen the Presbyterian presence in Shrewsbury: he hoped to bring Henry Newcome to the town. This diffident young minister was evidently inspirational in the pulpit – something needed to combat the Quakers. Newcome had preached in Shrewsbury during some of his summer tours and in June 1656 Hunt invited him back. Newcome preached the Thursday lecture at St Mary's and stayed until Monday. He recorded:

> I preached twice on the Lord's day at Alkmonde, Mr Hildersham exchanging on the Lord's day with Mr Talents; and so being in the town, I had the society of both those worthy persons at this time.

Hildersam accompanied Newcome to Wem on the Monday and they met several ministers of the area 'to advise about personal instruction, the business that precious Mr Baxter had set on foot at that time.' Baxter had recently published his work on catechising and personal instruction of parishioners, *Gildas Silvianus: the Reformed Pastor,* a greatly influential work.[35] Newcome then returned to Gawsworth in Cheshire where his wife was expecting their fifth child.

Shrewsbury had only one vacant living, Julian's, then neglected, although they had visiting preachers – John Bryan came over from Holy Cross and it seems they would have liked him to transfer to them. With the hope of Newcome taking the living the parishioners spent money on the refurbishment of the pulpit, stairs and reading desk, the clerk's seat and the mayor's seat, and on 'beautifying the church': Mr Benjamin Prowde of London, draper, gave a green velvet cushion with a silk and gold fringe. Over £100 was spent in repairing the north and south aisles and the steeple. They even paid for a horse for Captain Hunt (one of the parishioners, not one of Thomas Hunt's family) to ride to see 'Mr Nucum'.[36]

In September an offer was made through Baxter that Newcome should have a salary of £80 or £100 a year as an interim measure. Baxter went beyond his brief, in undiplomatic fashion, by suggesting that Newcome might then succeed Mr Paget, 'who is old and sickly, if God shall so order it, in the greatest congregation, where there is a

St Julian's church (SA-IMG24341)

fuller maintenance'. Paget knew nothing of this and his reaction would be forthright since he was reputed to be 'froward'; Baxter for the moment avoided meeting him. He asked Newcome to destroy the letters; fortunately he did not, and we have a rare insight into the town's affairs.[37] The September letter begins: 'Though I am yet a stranger to you and unmeet to meddle in your affairs, yet at the request of some friends in Shrewsbury I shall presume to offer you their thoughts and mine own.' His own thoughts included comments on ministers:

> They have very godly, humble, peaceable, judicious ministers. But I may tell you (in secret) what the people say – that it is a thousand pities but such a place as Shrewsbury should not have one that hath a lively, convincing, awakening way of preaching, and is more eminently fitted to the conversion of souls – though they highly reverence those that are more fit for building up.

Newcome had reservations: he felt he lacked learning and even an adequate library, and he was fearful of Mr Paget. Although Baxter had not yet confronted Paget he assured Newcome that 'he is not altogether so morose as some report him'. When he did meet him, Baxter found him 'very fair and placable', or so he told Newcome. We have no comment from Paget, but other ministers wrote in a friendly and welcoming way, offering 'the right hand of fellowship in feeding the church of God and labouring to propagate his eternal gospel'. At this point an offer came from Manchester, which Newcome, after some heart-searching, accepted. Despite this Thomas Hunt and his wife Elizabeth remained his friends and welcomed him back as a visiting preacher. Francis Tallents ended his last letter in the sequence: 'Let us be helped by your prayers, that we may be faithful in our places. Farewell, dear Sir, Your hearty friend and unworthy fellow servant.'

The year 1656, according to calculations based on events in the Bible, might bring the millennium or herald the Second Coming. This belief was held by many, not just a lunatic fringe. A prerequisite of the millennium was the conversion of the Jews. As it happened, this was the year when Cromwell gave tacit assent to the already existing Jewish community in London to have a synagogue and their own burial ground.[38] In Shrewsbury that year two newcomers must have caused interest: converted Jews named Paul Isaiah and Peter bar Samuel, formerly Eliazar ben Israel and Abraham bar Samuel. Perhaps Richard Heath of Alkmund's, the scholar of ancient Biblical languages, got to know the men. Hebrew was held by many to be the language of the Garden of Eden, and

Heath worked on the Polyglot Bible. Eliazar, still a young man, died the following spring and was buried at Chad's; the parish register records the burial in March 1657 of 'Paul Isaiah, a converted Jew'. In 1663 Elias Ashmole noted a tombstone at St Chad's inscribed 'Mr Paul Isaiah, a learned Jew, converted to the Faith', with a Hebrew addition signifying 'may his memory be preserved in the life of the world to come'. In fact, Eliazar had a colourful history. Born in Muscovy in 1626, he was baptised by a Jesuit at Antwerp, then by Baptists in England in 1652 in order to marry a widow. Having received money from her congregation he moved on to the officially suppressed Church of England and more 'temporal refreshings'. With his friend, Peter bar Samuel, he also published and sold books, receiving contributions from Magdalen College, Oxford, and from people in Coventry. They moved into Gloucestershire, where Peter was accused of trying to rape a maidservant at an inn in Dursley, then to Shrewsbury.[39] Clearly they took everyone in, adding an exotic touch to the mixture of religious groups.

In the summer of 1657 George Fox, the leading Quaker, was in the Welsh borders with his companion and interpreter John ap John. Turning into England they came to Shrewsbury, 'where we had a great meeting'. The Shrewsbury Quakers began to keep their register that year. On 11 August the marriage was recorded of William Trattle and Katherine Broughton: 'our Brother and Sister ... both Members of the Meeting of the Lord's people at Shrewsbury and inhabitants of that place'. It was in 1657 that Richard Davies of Welshpool walked the 18 miles to Shrewsbury in search of the Quakers. He had found no satisfaction in his parish church, nor eventually in the preaching of Vavasor Powell, but he had met one of the Quakers and adopted their customs. In Shrewsbury he went first to the house of John Millington, on St John's Hill (this remained a main meeting place):

> When the first day of the week came [Sunday, a name not used by the Quakers], we went to a meeting at W. Pane's, at the Wild Cop, where we had a silent meeting, and though it was silent from words, yet the word of the Lord was among us.

Then John ap John came to the town and another meeting was held: 'I staid that meeting, where I heard the first friend that was called a Quaker, preach in a meeting, and when I heard him, I thought he spoke as one having authority.'[40] The town was still a place where non-Catholic sects could worship as they wished, although the regime of the Major Generals had come to an end earlier that year when Parliament failed to vote them finance.

There is also an indication of the continued if surreptitious activity of the Church of England from the case of the minister appointed to Julian's in March 1658: Zachary Mayne had scruples about serving as a minister without being ordained. Henry Hammond of Worcester, chief proponent in England of what would be Anglicanism, tried to persuade him to be ordained secretly by the former bishop of Bangor, William Roberts, then living as 'Dr Roberts of Llanelidan' in his native Denbighshire. Instead Mayne decided to resign and became a schoolmaster in his native West Country. It was said that 'he gave no disturbance to the town, but ... had a fair reception and acceptation' in Shrewsbury. Dr Roberts was not the only bishop to ordain in secret – Thomas Morton, former bishop of Lichfield, was another. This was not a survival of Laudianism but of Cranmer's Prayer Book and the principles of episcopacy. In Shropshire there was what Richard Baxter called the episcopal or diocesan party, with clerics such as Thomas Good and Thomas Warmestry. Some of the most loyal members of the Church of England were to be found in Wales: Jeremy Taylor was given a home by the earl of Carberry at Goldengrove, while in Brecon the poet Henry Vaughan condemned the usurpers and

The Abbey Church in 1658 (SA-IMG24336)

lamented the suppression of his beloved church, celebrating her feasts and composing his own prose devotions. A poet and physician, he was answering his people's spiritual as well as bodily needs.[41]

Cromwell died on 3 September 1658, to be succeeded by his son Richard. A sense of things falling apart is reflected in a petition from Humfrey Mackworth, governor, on behalf of the garrison and the well-affected of Shrewsbury, dated 26 October that year. It concerned John Tench, a Royalist, late marshal of the town and court:

> Such is the unhappy state of the town that John Betton, lately chosen mayor, though formerly set aside for refusing the engagement, has displaced the marshall put in by the well-affected magistracy, and restored Tench to the office, and tries to turn out of office all who took the engagement ... he has (contrary to the judgement of the Recorder) released Jasper Lloyd, ever a bitter cavalier, committed for speaking treasonable words. We beg that Tench be removed, and that the friends of the old interest may not be turned out of their places.

Tench had sworn not to cut his hair until Charles Stuart reigned again in England – we do not know if he kept this oath. Lloyd had been committed for 'speaking words against the now Lord Protector'; the associated document was signed by Thomas Hunt.[42] The revival of Royalist confidence was indicated as well by the return of Sir Thomas Harris to Boreatton; having been released from the Tower he was now distraining his tenants for money they had already paid to the local authorities. There was another conflict, between the old Commonwealthsmen (republicans) and supporters of the Protectorate. One of the former, John Bradshaw, was restored to influence on the death of Oliver Cromwell; he promoted Thomas Paget to the living of Stockport, the scene of the minister's long-ago dispute with Bishop Morton over ceremonies. Paget reminisced about this when Henry Newcome visited him on 29 April 1659. Paget's move allowed the transfer of John Bryan from Holy Cross to Chad's, on 27 March. The political in-fighting resulted in the recall of the Rump Parliament on 6 May, and the resignation next day of Richard Cromwell. This was the last phase of the Commonwealth.[43]

In August there was a Royalist rising in Cheshire, led by Sir George Booth, but this was put down by John Lambert. In October a group of army officers (including James Berry) set up a 'Committee of Safety'. Events at the centre again influenced the localities. For a short while Major Edmund Waring was governor of Shrewsbury. He wrote to the Speaker of the Commons, William Lenthall, to say that only three JPs had as yet taken the Engagement; he himself was busy 'securing persons that have been in the late rebellion, that are of this county, and are now lurking in holes'. With another turn of the wheel Parliament prevailed over the army: the Long Parliament reassembled in February and Thomas Hunt was made governor of Shrewsbury: he would oversee events leading to the Restoration. The Long Parliament dissolved itself in March and in April a Convention (not an elected body) was assembled. Restoration of the monarchy seemed the only way to bring both security and stability.[44]

General George Monck, in communication with the Stuart court in exile, had brought his English regiments back from Scotland at the New Year, 1660. Edward Hyde was guiding the actions of the exiled court, with a careful eye to reactions at home. The Declaration of Breda of April was drafted, most probably by Hyde, for the King to publish – it is a masterly composition:

> Charles, by the grace of God ... to all our loving subjects, of what degree or quality soever, greeting. If the general distraction and confusion which is spread over the whole Kingdom doth not awaken all men to a desire and longing that these wounds which have so many years together been kept bleeding, may be bound up, all we can say wil be to no purpose.

He refers to his rights in God and nature, his daily prayers to Divine Providence, his wish for his subjects to enjoy their rights – a free and general pardon was extended to all subjects who accepted it within forty days, publicly stating their return to loyalty and obedience – 'excepting only such persons as shall hereafter be excepted by Parliament':

> And because the passion and uncharitableness of the times have produced several opinions in religion, by which men are engaged in parties and animosities against each other (which, when they shall hereafter unite in a freedom of conversation, will be composed or better understood), we do declare a liberty to tender consciences, and that no man shall be disquieted or called in question for differences of opinion in matter of religion, which do not disturb the peace of the kingdom ...

He promised an Act of Parliament to be considered 'upon mature deliberation' for the granting of that indulgence. 'Given in the twelfth year of our reign.' This was read to the restored Parliament which, on 1 May, voted the King home. Among the municipal records of Shrewsbury is a bundle of parchment slips – the original declarations of those in the town and neighbourhood who accepted the King's pardon. Subscribed between 6 and 9 May, they were signed (probably with some formality) in the presence of Hunt, or the mayor or a former mayor. 87 acceptances survive, all but 14 signed with their name, the rest affixing their mark. On 11 May the borough assembly ordered that Charles II be proclaimed King.[45]

It remains to consider the legacy of the eleven years between the regicide and the restoration of the monarchy, and whether the promises made at Breda would be kept – and how the town of Shrewsbury, especially its churches, fared during the last decades of the seventeenth century.

Chapter 7
Restoration and Retribution

The return of Charles II to England was scheduled for the end of May 1660; in the interim he was feted at the Hague with banquets, receptions and entertainments, including fireworks. His sister Mary, the widowed princess of Orange, was in triumphant attendance on her brothers, Charles, James and Henry. Her nine-year-old son William was also there, aware of the implications for the royal Stuart succession, in which he had a place. On 29 May, his thirtieth birthday, Charles II entered London to rapturous acclaim. The celebrations were stage-managed, as they were a year later at the coronation. In the judgement of N.H. Keeble the 'assertive confidence of the celebratory pageantry ... disguised the fragility of the Restoration ... the uncertainty of its popular support ... the doubtfulness of the monarchy's durability'. During the autumn and winter of 1660 Stuart family circumstances changed: 20-year-old Henry duke of Gloucester died of smallpox and James duke of York admitted to being married to the heavily pregnant Anne Hyde (the baby, named Charles, died after a few months). The princess of Orange, visiting England, died of smallpox in December. She had named Charles II as her son's guardian but William was a Child of State in Holland, the States having rights as 'superior guardians'. Charles II and his queen, Catherine of Braganza, remained childless, so his brother James was his heir, and after him James's two daughters, Mary and Anne. In 1670 William was received in England, a declared Protestant and fourth in line to the English throne, after James and his daughters. In 1677 William married his first cousin Mary – the 15-year-old bride wept at the prospect. King Charles was suspected of Catholic sympathies and his brother and heir James had converted to Catholicism by 1673, by which time he was married to Maria Beatrice D'Este (Mary of Modena).[1] Leaving these royals in the background or the wings we can turn our attention to the subject of regime and religion, and to the local situation in north Shropshire and in particular Shrewsbury.

In 1660 the Royalists might look forward not only to restoration but to retribution against enemies. In Shropshire Royalists included members of the Newport family who had lost property and wealth as well as place in society. Andrew Newport returned with the King, for whom he had worked in exile. In March 1659 Charles had written to John Mordaunt, a leading member of the Action Party, one of the two Royalist groups in exile (not to be confused with subsequently better known but then rather inactive Sealed Knot): 'I desire that Andrew Newport, upon whose affection and ability to serve me I do very much depend, and know he will act in any commission he shall be desired, may be put in mind to do all he can for the possessing Shrewsbury at the time which shall be appointed.' Andrew played an active part in the rising of that summer, which failed; he was put in the Tower but released after four months on bail of £1,500. In June 1660 Andrew wrote from London to his uncle Sir Richard Leveson at Trentham: 'My brother is Lord Lieutenant of Shropshire.' Francis Lord Newport appointed as his deputy Sir Richard Ottley, son of Francis Ottley, Newport's colleague at the beginning of the Civil War and sometime governor of Shrewsbury. Richard Ottley had met the King and his party at Canterbury, as he reported excitedly to his mother Lady Lucy at Pitchford: he 'had the happinesse to be of the life guard since Fryday last'. On 30 June the House of Lords issued an order, upon information given to it that day, that Thomas Nicholls, Andrew Lloyd, Thomas Hunt and others 'Doe detaine divers goods, household stuffe, writings, and plate belonging to the Lord Newport which were taken from High Ercall, Shrewsbury and other places'. Newport's agents were given liberty to make a search for these goods. Following the search, conducted in July, Thomas Hunt presented a petition to the Commons, that his house had been ransacked 'contrary to the Rights and Liberties of the meanest Commoner': he prayed to receive 'such rights therein as to your wisdome shall seem meet'. An inventory lists goods totalling £1,377 18s 9d in value.[2] The old battle lines were being re-formed, with petitions and law as weapons.

Even as the King returned there were scares about plots. Events of the previous twenty years did not inspire confidence that there would be no more changes, no more turns in 'the maygame of fortune' (to quote the Royalist Sir Philip Warwick) or, as Richard Baxter complained, the setting up and putting down by fanatics of governments, 'as boldly as if they were making a Lord of May game'. This was not a restoration of the monarchy of Charles I. There were, Tim Harris writes, some republicans, and among the majority there were tensions between those who believed the authority of the crown should be limited and those who wanted it strengthened. Anglican Royalists 'tended to the view that the King had been restored by divine providence and that the Convention that succeeded the Long Parliament had simply acknowledged Charles's rightful position as King'.[3] The Convention was declared a legal Parliament in June 1660. In April 1661 the Savoy Conference was held to attempt a 'comprehension', a compromise settlement, between moderate Episcopals and Presbyterians, according to the promises of Breda. In his proclamation Charles declared his 'esteem of the liturgy of the Church of England, contained in the Book of Common Prayer' but he also advocated any alterations necessary to accommodate Presbyterians. Details of the Restoration settlement were worked out by the properly elected Cavalier Parliament which sat from May 1661 until January 1679: it was less inclined than the Convention to work for reconciliation between moderate Presbyterians and Episcopals within a national church. Outside that institution, the best the sects could hope for was toleration.[4]

We can view events through the comments of Andrew Newport. On 29 September 1660 he reported to his uncle Leveson that the proclamation concerning religion was expected any day: 'the presbiterian ministers, we hear, are very unreasonable'. On 23 October he wrote about the Worcester House conference between Presbyterian and Episcopal divines (Baxter was a leading figure at this conference): 'the Presbiterians agreed to an Episcopall government, but they would not have the Bishops have any power but joyntly with the presbiters and with their consent'. When Parliament reassembled, the Independents, resentful of Presbyterian tactics, voted with the Episcopals, and the much debated bill for comprehension was defeated by 26 votes. Andrew Newport sent the news to his uncle on 1 December: 'John [Presbyter] is very angry.' Another of Sir Richard Leveson's nephews, Thomas Gower, wrote that 'some of the old commonwealth party joined with the Cavaliers'. On 26 February Andrew Newport wrote to his uncle that writs for the new Parliament (that which became the Cavalier Parliament) would soon be ready and that he intended to stand for Shrewsbury, but in the event the borough elected Thomas Jones, the town clerk, and Robert Leighton who had not committed himself during the Civil War. Andrew Newport therefore continued his career at Court. In contrast to the continued adherence of Shrewsbury to Presbyterianism, the county gentry chose as Parliamentary representatives two men recommended by Lord Newport, Sir Richard Ottley and Sir Francis Lawley.[5]

Events in London in the winter of 1660-1661 have to be taken into consideration. Several regicides had been executed as traitors in the autumn, their heads and quarters being displayed as a dreadful warning. The same thing happened to leaders of the Fifth Monarchist rising led by Thomas Venner in January – this was easily put down but caused great alarm. Lord Newport was one of the lords lieutenant instructed by the Privy Council to order his deputies to be watchful 'and to observe the motions and Meetings of dangerous persons' and to arrest and imprison them. On 24 January Newport wrote to Ottley at Shrewsbury, sending on the letter from the Privy Council and advising:

> Though it may bee conceived a very ineffectual way for the securinge of persons to send warrants to a constable, yet if soldiers bringe the warrant to him, your ends may seem accomplishable. You see the letter speakes of leading men. Therefore you did ill in releasinge Waringe [Edmund Waring, former governor], and you need not have apprehended his ranting demand of a mittimus {an arrest warrant issued by and on behalf of the state], which will serve him for discourse in his two pot houses. I would advise you to send for him agen, though not as a criminal by proofe, yet as a dangerous person ...

This gives a telling insight into attitudes and procedures: the local constables, the bar room lawyer, the anxious deputy, and the argument for summary arrest. Waring was duly imprisoned in Shrewsbury Castle. Another Independent arrested early in 1660 and imprisoned in Shrewsbury was Vavasor Powell whose influence was feared. He was moved to London and spent most of the last decade of his life in prison. But Ottley went further and now compensated for his earlier lenity by over-zealousness, as we learn in another letter to Newport from the Privy Council, dated at Whitehall on 4 March 1661. Under the notion of dangerous persons, Ottley had arrested and imprisoned many Quakers. The Council approved the zeal but since the danger appeared to be over 'his Majestie is dayly troubled with Petitions for enlarging multitudes committed to prison'. The deputy lieutenant was free to discharge from prison all such persons arrested merely upon suspicion. The Council advised that 'only the ringleaders of faction' should be detained.[6]

Quakers had been victims of persecution in Shrewsbury before this date, their provoking and eccentric behaviour making them objects of attack. Three examples will suffice here: 'In the 9th month [September] 1659, William Griffith went into the steeple-house called St Mary's in Shrewsbury, where he spake a few words to the Priest, but was presently haled away and carried before the Mayor, who sent him to Prison for 6 Months.' In November, Daniel Baker 'went publicly proclaiming the Testimony of the Truth to the People in the Streets of Shrewsbury, which he performed with much Jeopardy to his Life, the People sorely abusing him with Stones, Dirt and Snowballs'.

Baker was attacked in this way several times. In December, Friends meeting in their own hired house were insulted and forced out by soldiers of the Irish Brigade.[7] Lord Newport's orders of February 1661 and Sir Richard Ottley's zeal have a context in the town. In contrast to the dissenters who were regarded as seditious, the Shropshire gentry declared in an address of 23 April 1661 (the date of the coronation) that they themselves were:

> wholly concerned in upholding that Just Power and Authority, with which the fundamental Constitutions of this nation have invested your Royal Progenetors, much less do we partake in the sins of those truly Superstitious Persons who make it part of their Religion to be disobedient, and to Separate from a Truly Apostolic Church in those different things, which decency Order and the necessary rules of Holy Polity have enforced her to enjoin, in both which capacities, either of civil or Christian Subjects as we do own your Majestie for our sole supream Head so we look upon your Laws of both kinds, as the rule to which we are bound to conform.

It was in this spirit that Lord Newport saw all nonconformists, even moderate Presbyterians, as factious and dangerous. From this point of view Shrewsbury was defying the authorities in adhering to the Presbyterian church order. The town provides an example of what Ronald Hutton refers to as 'the role of ideology in urban politics during the civil wars and Revolution'.[8]

In March 1661 John Bryan of St Chad's was accused of keeping in place as parish clerk one Samuel Beale, 'a stranger and one of the same [Presbyterian] faction', who had been appointed in the late Thomas Paget's time. The status of St Mary's as a royal peculiar meant that the town clerk and MP for the borough, Thomas Jones, along with the mayor Richard Bagot and headmaster Richard Pigot, was able to draw up a new deed of appointment for Francis Tallents, the Presbyterian minister at St Mary's, in October 1661. Tallents was not complacent; his sermon notes drew on texts such as 'Blessed are the peacemakers' and 'if ye suffer for R[ighteousness] sake, happy are you'. The opportunity to remove some nonconformists came with the passing of the Corporation Act of December 1661. Commissioners appointed by Parliament but chosen by the King were to purge the municipalities of former anti-Royalists; officers would be required to take an oath against the Solemn League and Covenant and against resistance to the King. The Shropshire commissioner was Lord Newport who urged Sir

Richard Ottley at Westminster to make the case against Thomas Jones. Jones went from London to Shrewsbury to solicit the mayor and his brethren the aldermen to fill up the places on the council with supporters; he made a long speech in the Town Hall which persuaded them to consent. Lord Newport commented of this plan:

> If it had taken effect the act of Parliament had been totally eluded as to the greatest part of the governors of that corporation and consequently that towne, which has been ever held of the most factious in England, had remained soe to posterity.

His deputy lieutenants forestalled Jones' plan by confining the mayor and aldermen to their houses. They were turned out of office for refusing to subscribe: Bagot was removed as mayor and Thomas Jones was replaced as town clerk by Adam Ottley, brother of Sir Richard; Robert Clive, Thomas and Rowland Hunt and Sir John Corbet were among burgesses removed. Thomas Jones was also said to have given encouragement to 'the factious ministers [in the town] to preach soe boldly and seditiously as they did, and to refuse all along to reade the common prayers'.[9] In suggesting faction and sedition the government 'could foster fear while it preached reconciliation' (to borrow Hutton's phrase). John Miller writes: 'Taken in conjunction with piecemeal removals and voluntary withdrawals since 1660, the changes carried out by the commissioners were the most sweeping of the century so far.'[10] This work was continued with the settlement of religion by the Cavalier Parliament.

The North Shropshire Presbyterian *classis* was in the Bradford Hundred, Lord Newport's domain; Thomas Porter was ejected from Whitchurch in 1660 and Andrew Parsons arrested at Wem in November 1661. Porter found refuge first with Robert Clive and his wife Mary at Styche, and then in Shrewsbury. Parsons was again arrested in May 1662; after some weeks in prison, he was tried before Lord Newport at Shrewsbury and returned to prison. Francis Tallents, John Bryan and Richard Pigot were imprisoned for some days in July 1662. The Act of Uniformity had been passed on 8 May, receiving royal assent on the 19th, but it was not due to come into effect until 24 August, Bartholomew's Day. Newport had in fact anticipated the new Act, as did Bishop John Hacket who wrote on 23 August from Lichfield to Chancellor Clarendon: 'I will be vigilant (as God shall give me understanding) to see that city [Coventry] well taught, and Shrewsbury also.'[11] Far from achieving a comprehension of Episcopals and Presbyterians, the Uniformity Act was aimed at complete conformity to the Book of Common Prayer, the culmination of the long-standing division in the established Church of England.[12]

The text of the Act begins with a reference to the reign of Elizabeth and to the 'late unhappy troubles' after which many people now 'wilfully and schismatically abstain or refuse to come to their parish churches', creating factions and schisms. The Book of Common Prayer had been reviewed by the Convocations of York and Canterbury and approved by the King – there were few changes, and no attempt to placate puritan objections. Ministers were to read publicly the morning and evening prayer and declare their assent to all things in the Prayer Book, renouncing the Solemn League and Covenant. Subscription was to be made before a bishop or his ordinary. Otherwise ministers would be deprived of their benefices. It was necessary for schoolmasters and preachers to be licensed by a bishop, and for ministers to have been episcopally ordained. No other form of service was to be conducted openly. Illicit preaching was subject to the penalty of three months in the common gaol. A copy of the Prayer Book was to be placed in every parish church (in Wales it would be in Welsh). On 1 September Bishop Hacket came to Shrewsbury with Lord Newport and Sir Edward Littleton, a Staffordshire JP. At St Mary's Francis Tallents was put out for not subscribing according to the Act of Parliament and refusing episcopal ordination. A regular visitation was held at St Chad's; John Bryan and Richard Heath were ejected, and Richard Pigot was removed as headmaster of Shrewsbury School. Philip Henry, a minister ordained by the fourth Shropshire *classis*, entered in his diary that Black Bartholomew Day was remarkable for the massacre of Protestants in Paris threescore years before, and now was 'fatal to the Dissenting ministers of England ... who were put to silence on that day, and forbidden to preach the gospel under severe penalties, because they would not, they durst not, sin against God'. Henry's son Matthew, a pupil of Francis Tallents, wrote that Tallents was forced to quit his place and his livelihood and, more grievously,

> his Work and Usefulness which were his Life. He hath sometimes observ'd, that before the Wars the Puritans generally made a shift to Conform and come into the Church ... to prevent which for the Future ... new Barriers or Fortifications were erected by the Act of Uniformity to keep them out.[13]

As yet, however, the parish was mixed, conformists and puritans both worshipping in their local church, with the latter avoiding the ceremonies rejected for the past century as too much akin to Roman Catholic worship.

'The stringency of the Act was unprecedented', writes N.H. Keeble, adding that although a substantial number of ministers felt unable to comply 'the great majority of parish ministers submitted and conformed', so that 'Puritan opinion was not excluded from the established church overnight'. Even the ejected Presbyterian ministers in Shrewsbury and members of their congregations attended church services, but Quakers and Baptists ('Anabaptists') did not. In 1662 ten of the members of these sects were presented to the ecclesiastical authorities for not attending church and not having their children baptised. Yet all these people were part of the same community, as Janice Cox observes in her study of Shrewsbury Dissenters: they might be related to conformists, they lived in every street in the town, and 'they met Anglicans and members of other dissenting churches every day when going about their business'.[14] Not that they constituted 'churches' as such, though they had meeting places, but the parish churches were official and there the majority worshipped according to the Prayer Book of 1662.

St Mary's vestry book reveals the satisfaction of the new curate, Richard Fowler (who was there by November), and presumably many of the congregation. A special entry reads: 'This year EPISCOPACY and the LITURGIE of the Church were restored. Gloria Deo. Amen'. The altar was railed in and a surplice bought. Roger Hayward replaced Bryan at St Chad's. Hayward, a young man educated at Shrewsbury and St John's College, Cambridge, married into the Shropshire gentry, his wife Anne being a daughter of Sir Thomas Eyton. James Logan, incumbent of Holy Cross in the early 1640s, returned, being succeeded by Timothy Hammond in 1663, when Logan resigned. St Julian's lacked

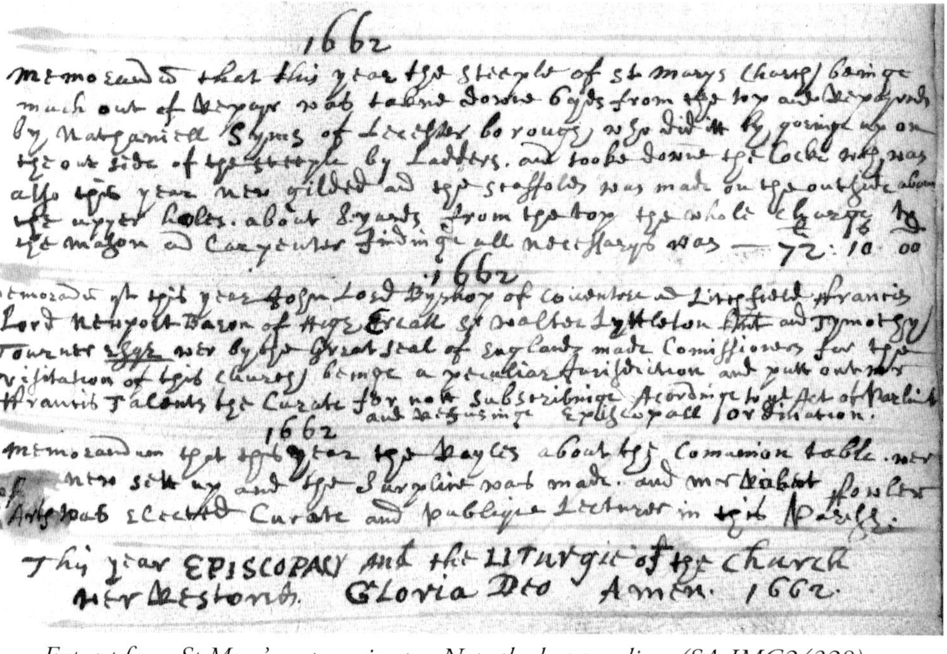
1662

1662

1662

This year EPISCOPACY and the LITURGIE of the Church
were Restored. Gloria Deo Amen. 1662.

Extract from St Mary's vestry minutes. Note the last two lines (SA-IMG24328)

a settled minister, as it had so often done, but in 1661-2 the parish spent money on mending the communion table, setting up rails, and buying a new surplice and two copies of the Prayer Book. Although there was no Laudian revival in the restored Church, some of those ideas were influential: 'the recreation of sacred space and the seemly reception of holy communion embodied in the erection of railed altars'. The process took a long time in some places but became general by 1700.[15] Shrewsbury's alacrity in restoring former ceremony was perhaps a reaction against the severity of Interregnum church life. The Prayer Book has been described as 'conservative, middle-of-the way, safe', rejecting 'high' Church tendencies and Presbyterian plainness of worship. One of the 'modest' changes noted by Horton Davies was provision for greater participation by the congregation through some versicles and responses. An example of this is found in the account by a French gentleman visiting the town in the later 1660s was taken by his host to a funeral, than which 'nothing was more pleasing' to the visitor. After the ceremony at home, the minister's oration and the drinking of toasts in wine to the deceased, he followed the silent procession to the church where the minister ascended the pulpit to read 'a portion of the holy scripture, concerning the resurrection of the dead, and afterwards sang some psalms; - to which all the company answered'. At the funeral itself the boughs they all carried were thrown into the grave.[16]

Some of the former Presbyterian congregations in the area maintained contact, their meetings arousing the suspicions of the authorities. Thomas and Elizabeth Hunt held to their puritanism but attended public services. By 1662 they had, in addition to their houses in Shrewsbury and London, the estate of Boreatton in the parish of Baschurch: 'there were several Families of Distinction that held fast their Profession, and gladly entertain'd the ejected Ministers', Philip Henry recalled. But the young Anglican minister who replaced Edward Lawrence, George Hudson, a graduate of Magdalene College, Cambridge, was also acceptable to the Hunts as 'a sober, judicious and peaceable Minister'. Mr Hudson and his family even attended some of the nonconformist preaching held in the Hunts' home, 'sometimes on Weekdays, sometimes on the Lord's Day out of the time of publick Worship'. The same situation pertained in Shrewsbury where Francis Tallents, like the Hunts, continued to attend 'the Liturgy both Morning and Afternoon, and Preach'd only in the Evening, and on Weekdays, as he had opportunity'. He and other puritans would stand instead of kneeling and afterwards conduct repetitions of sermons as in Laudian times. The influence of Tallents and John Bryan was to continue for decades.[17]

Such amiable and admirable reciprocity was perhaps rare, while the attitude to sects was often harsh, especially towards Quakers. Richard Baxter condemned them for their belief in the inner light and their neglect of the doctrines of justification, the pardon of sin and reconciliation with God through Christ:

> They will not have the Scripture called the Word of God: Their principal Zeal lyeth in railing at the Ministers as Hirelings, Deceivers, False Prophets &c. and in refusing to Swear before a Magistrate, or to put off their Hat to any, or to say [*You*] instead of [*Thou*] or [*Thee*] which are their words to all.

Persecution did continue in Shrewsbury. There were fines for refusing to pay tithes and imprisonment 'for Meeting together to worship God, and for not Swearing [Oaths]'. In December 1660 a lieutenant brought into the Quaker meeting in the town several files of soldiers, 'with Swords drawn, and Matches lighted', who first put out the women and then escorted the men to the Town Hall. 23 men were committed to prison for 15 weeks; others were made to join them, including friends from outside the town who came to visit the prisoners. One, 'a poor labouring Man, having a Wife and five small Children depending on him', was put in a dungeon. One heavily pregnant woman who walked 40 miles to see her husband was treated roughly, kept in the cold overnight, then turned out. In December 1663 several Friends were taken from the meeting and committed to prison. In 1665 Constantine Overton and Abraham Poyner, freemen of the corporation of Shrewsbury, were disenfranchised 'because they refused to Swear, and had Meetings at their Houses'. Ronald Hutton points out that Quaker leaders could still draw gatherings of their followers in parts of the country, but the experience of persecution brought a turning-point: 'The energy of the evangelists was turning inward, upon the task of maintaining the spirits and numbers of existing converts.' Safety lay in moderation.[18]

During 1663 there were risings and rumours of risings, beginning in the north of England. Some risings planned for March were postponed until May in which month Lord Newport wrote to Ottley about a supposed scheme for capturing Chester Castle; he believed there might also be a design against Shrewsbury. He had heard of 'factious meetings' of ministers in the town (the ejected men) and instructed Ottley 'to employ, if possible, one of the brotherhood to give an account of their designs: otherwise to find out their next meeting, and when they are assembled, to go into them, and enquire their motives, and take down their names'. There were certainly meetings of Presbyterians and of Independents, such as James Quarrel, formerly an itinerant preacher, now living in Shrewsbury, but these were of a religious nature. In March 1663 Philip Henry attended a day of prayer and preaching at the home of the ejected John Adams of Stoke-upon-Tern, who now lived at Ellesmere. At the meeting 'were present several of the Congregational way wholly unsatisfy'd about coming to hear the service book or any that read it'. Lord Newport also feared contacts with Ireland: on 11 July he wrote to Ottley at Shrewsbury to thank him for news of 'the Meetings of those factious Ministers ... at this time, when we have been so freshly alarmed out of Ireland'. He advised Ottley to 'employ some Person that has been formerly of the Brotherhood' to spy at the meetings and to make arrests if necessary, following this on 24 October with a direction to arrest 'the Ejected Ministers still residing in Shrewsbury': Mr Bryan, Mr Tallents and Mr Lawrence. They and others, including a Captain Doughty, were to be questioned separately about any conspiracy. Spies were also active in London: an Edmund Potter reported in 1664 that seditious meetings were taking place at the house of Thomas Hunt who held a dinner for ministers every Tuesday. Great persons were said to attend and collections were made for ejected ministers. Tallents and Parsons were among those preaching at 'conventicles'.[19]

The church authorities were also active. Bishop John Hacket, reporting regularly to Archbishop Sheldon, informed him in November 1664 that since the summer he had visited 26 churches 'to take order that the communion table and font be well placed (beside other reformations)'. He was concerned that ministers should be 'virtuous and orthodox', that they should read the full service of the Common Prayer at least once a month, wearing a surplice, and that parishioners should behave reverently in church. In 1665 he made a tour of the archdeaconry of Shrewsbury:

> I began my journey on the last day of May and returned to my home on the 16th of this June. I began at Bridgnorth, so to Salop, to Elsmere, to Wem, to Whitchurch, to Drayton in Hales, to Hodnet and to Stafford ... God gave me strength to preach in all these eight market towns ... I was marvellously resorted to everywhere, and in those several places I confirmed 5,384.[20]

In the autumn the borough assembly of Shrewsbury ordered 'that the Public Sermons be held in St Chad's and St Mary's as formerly and aldermen etc. attend the mayor on Sabbaths'.[21]

To further the success of the re-established Church of England and to hinder the progress of Nonconformity a series of Acts was passed: *to Prevent and Suppress Seditious Conventicles*, in 1664, and that *for Restraining Non-Conformists from inhabiting in Corporations* in 1665. The latter, known as the Five Mile Act, forced Presbyterian ministers away from their congregations. Francis Tallents moved to his native

Derbyshire to live with the Gell family, a devout puritan household near Wirksworth. John Bryan made a shorter move, from Shrewsbury to Shifnal; he was into his second marriage, to a niece of Benjamin Whichcote. Despite the dangers, Bryan continued to visit Shrewsbury, making his journeys at night. Richard Heath moved to Wellington in Shropshire in March 1666 but he died there in May. Edward Lawrence attended Heath to the end; when asked about his nonconformity Heath affirmed 'hee would not but have done as hee did for a thousand worlds'. Tallents hoped that the ejected ministers would be purified, 'our Hearts made better by our Sadness'. He believed that God could carry on his work another way 'and make even the Sufferings of his Ministers to turn to the Furtherance of the Gospel of Christ'.[22]

Nonconformist groups met as before, at homes such as the Hunts' at Boreatton, where Philip Henry continued to attend them as pastor. Henry recorded: 'At Lady Day, 1666, the Five-mile Act commenced, by which all Nonconformist ministers were forbidden, upon pain of six months' imprisonment, to come or be within five miles of any corporation, or of any place where they had been ministers, unless they would take an oath ... not to endeavour, at any time, to alter the government in church or state.' This he regarded as an oath to the bishops. Like others, including Tallents, he refused to take it. Lady Day, on which the Five-mile Act took effect, was another sad day for nonconformist ministers: 'The Lord be a little sanctuary to them, and a place of refuge from the storm.' Henry moved with his family from Broad Oak in Flint to Whitchurch in Shropshire; he returned in 1668. In London the Hunts continued to entertain preachers, as did their neighbour the countess of Exeter in Little Britain, London, and their kinsman Richard Hampden (son of the patriot, John) outside the capital. Hampden's wife Letitia was sister to William Lord Paget whose daughter Frances married the Hunts' son Rowland in 1665. Hampden's son John went abroad, with Francis Tallents as his tutor.[23] The first Conventicle Act lapsed on 1 March 1669 but its 1670 successor 'was more stringent in its penalties, more determined to ensure its enforcement and prepared to allocate a still more prominent role to informers'. The Second Conventicle Act empowered any one justice of the peace to act on the testimony of two witnesses or merely by 'notorious evidence', denying the rights of Magna Carta.[24]

Charles II was ready to grant Presbyterians a place in the national Church – as we saw, this was not achieved. Nor could his lenience to Quakers prevent their persecution. He did, however, confirm for the London Jewish community the privileges granted by Cromwell, by endorsing their petition for protection in 1664: 'They may enjoy the same favour as before, as long as they demean themselves peaceably and obey the laws.' This has been called the simplest charter of settlement in Jewish history.[25] In 1676 a religious census was taken, named after Bishop Compton of London. There are statistics for the Shrewsbury parishes, except for St Mary's which made no returns (Janice Cox has made calculations for this parish). The total number of conformists in all five parishes was about 4,300 out of a population of some 7,000; those under sixteen were not counted. The overwhelming majority of the parishioners were Anglican, but Presbyterians were included among the conformists: this important fact has to be borne in mind in interpreting the census figures. The wording of the question in the census in Shrewsbury meant that only 'obstinate refusers' were regarded as nonconformist; they numbered eighty in all. Janice Cox's research shows that the nonconformists were Independents, Baptists and Quakers. Only twelve known papists are listed in addition, with none from Holy Cross, which is surprising.[26] In March 1672 the King issued, as he had done a decade earlier, a Declaration of Indulgence, suspending the penal laws against nonconformists, essentially to help the Roman Catholics with whom he sympathised. Francis Tallents returned from his travels in France and Switzerland at the time of this Indulgence:

> he found the Dissenters in England bless'd with some Breathing-time from the extreme Persecutions with which for many Years they had been harrass'd, and their Assemblies tolerated. This soon brought him back to *Shrewsbury*; for no Employment, no Entertainment was in his account comparable to that of Preaching the Gospel, for the Honour of CHRIST, and the Salvation of precious Souls.

So he joined with John Bryan to set up a meeting in the house of 'that Eminent Christian, Mrs Hunt', widow of Thomas Hunt. Matthew Henry comments: 'Much Good was now done in [Shrewsbury] by the Ministry of these two worthy Men', Bryan and Tallents. It was now possible to obtain a licence for a meeting-place. Mrs Hunt's house was one of five in Shrewsbury licensed for Presbyterian worship, and there were other ministers in the town besides Tallents and Bryan. The Independents licensed a room at the King's Head (a parish register entry for one minister calls him an Inn-dependent). Neither the Quakers nor the Baptists took out licences in Shrewsbury.[27]

This breathing-time was short-lived. Parliament forced the King to withdraw the Indulgence, bringing in the Test Act in 1673: 'For preventing dangers which may happen from popish recusants'. This required holders of civil or military offices to take, before 1 August, oaths of supremacy and allegiance, and to receive the sacrament according to the usage of the Church of England, signing a declaration against the doctrine of transubstantiation. There was to be a register of the names of those taking the oaths. There was specific mention of popish recusants being disabled from taking office; children were not to be instructed in the Catholic religion. There were special provisions for the peerage, including Catholics at Court. According to John Evelyn, James duke of York, heir to the throne, had ceased to receive communion in the chapel royal a year earlier. The Test Act was not repealed until 1828. It was, however, modified in 1678: the first Act had not applied to MPs – this was now remedied but was directed only against Catholics.[28] Persecution of Catholics increased during the years 1678 to 1681, inflamed by alleged conspiracies to murder the King and replace him with his Catholic brother James. The infamous Titus Oates was an instigator, but politicking at the highest level resulted in deliberate perversion of justice, Samuel Pepys being one of those accused of conspiracy: as Secretary to the Admiralty he was a servant of the duke of York, now in temporary exile.[29] In Shrewsbury equally spurious rumours were attached to Francis Tallents: of Huguenot descent, he was fluent in French and had travelled in France, and was consequently accused of being a French Jesuit, one part of the propaganda being that Jesuits disguised as Presbyterians would provoke revolt.[30]

Between the dissolution of the Cavalier Parliament in 1679 and 1681 Charles called three Parliaments, which he dissolved when they tried to pass bills excluding James from the succession to the throne. One of the many tracts published to support the case against exclusion was a sermon *Concerning the Deposition of Princes* – preached by Thomas Merk, bishop of Carlisle, against the deposition of Richard II in 1399. Events in 1680 echoed those of the years leading to the Civil War, but Charles was wiser than his father and the situation was turned around in surprising fashion. 'Charles II maintained control of London and of most of the machinery of government, and took advantage of the Tories' fear and anger to wreak revenge on the Whigs and their allies, the Protestant Dissenters, raising the Stuart monarchy to the zenith of its power.'[31] In fact the Protestant nonconformists constituted less than five per cent of the population. As for Catholics, while they remained numerous among the peers and gentry, their total number by this time was nearer one per cent of the population. There were concentrations of Catholics along the Welsh border: the highest percentage of Catholic recusants in the Kingdom was to be found in Monmouthshire, where there was a Jesuit centre and a Catholic shrine which drew many pilgrims. There was also an important concentration in Denbighshire and Flint with another Jesuit centre and the famous shrine of Holywell. In 1679 a Jesuit from north Wales wrote that the centre in south Wales was 'totally rooted up. We in the north fared a little better, thus far', but they lived in fear and only three priests remained. In Montgomeryshire Lord Powis sheltered Jesuits; he also intervened successfully in 1675, 1677 and 1685 to help Quakers.[32]

In Shrewsbury, Dr Roger Haywood of St Chad's died in November 1680, to be succeeded by William Bennett. It was to Bennett that John Bryan wrote from Wolverhampton in May 1684 on behalf of some of his former parishioners who had conscientious objections to kneeling to take communion. At that time the meetings were again suppressed and the Five-mile Act in force. Bryan asked indulgence for the objectors, citing the Declaration of Breda and speeches made by the King since then.

> What my judgment is as to the gesture, you know: yet you cannot forgett, that in the Times of Great disturbance, and Rebellion, when Authority commanded sitting (and few, if any gave it otherwise) yet I durst not deny the sacrament to those that could not sitt, but ventured, and gave itt them kneeling. I am sure when we come to Heaven we shal not repent of any good deed done by us on Earth.

Like Tallents, he wanted concord with his fellow ministers, arguing that 'true unity lies in the profession of one God, one Lord Jesus Christ, One Spirit, and not in one ceremonye, and our love will be the more eminent'. In a letter to the Recorder, Thomas Baldwin, Bryan wrote that 'The Reverend Dr. Haywood ... never prosecuted any that lived peaceable, and went to church.' He begged the Recorder to save the poor men from ruin: 'You will never repent of your moderation.' At St Mary's there was change too: Robert Fowler died and was buried there in January 1679. He was succeeded by Thomas Dawes of Queens' College, Cambridge, a burgess's son, educated at Shrewsbury School; he was to remain at St Mary's until his death, aged 63, in January 1715. Tallents argued that it would be good sometimes for dissenters and conformists to worship together, although he rejected occasional conformity as hypocritical.

> It's much to be desir'd, that all in the World that fear God, and all in this Nation should heartily worship God together always, without any differences; But since this <u>is</u> not, nor is <u>like to be</u>, as things stand, 'tis the Duty of every one in his place, to do what he <u>can do</u>, and <u>ought to do</u>, as most pleasing to God.

Dawes is likely to have been of the same opinion as his Anglican colleague, Bennett, the issues of kneeling at communion and railing in the altar creating outward signs of the Church's liturgy and theology in many Restoration churches. Tallents thought that most people were indifferent: 'the Generality little mind Religion' but take up what is 'most for their Ease, and keeps them from Trouble'. Philip Henry, a long-time friend of the Shrewsbury preachers, shared their views. He regarded his preaching 'as an assistant to the parish ministers' who were too few in number. He was greatly pleased, when preaching at Oswestry, that the minister there, Mr Edwards, answered 'That's well, the Lord prosper your seed and mine too, there is need enough of both.' When he worshipped at Whitchurch, however, he found Matthew Fowler to be an opponent, arguing with him over the rites and ceremonies in church services. Fowler excommunicated a group of nonconformist parishioners for showing contumacy in not taking communion, and refused baptism without the sign of the cross and godparents. Fowler preached at the assizes in Shrewsbury in 1682, the year before his death. In that year there was also an episcopal visitation after which it was reported that several gentlemen pretended to come for the Anglican service but were attended by 'Fanatics', an abusive term for radical dissenters. It was also reported that although the loyal gentry outnumbered the disaffected Shrewsbury was 'full of faction, and conventicles kept there without any opposition of the magistrates'. We have already noted the Presbyterian meetings; the Quakers met too.[33]

In February 1685 Charles II died. He became a Catholic on his deathbed, ministered to by Father John Huddleston, who had helped him escape after the defeat at Worcester in 1651; he confessed and received the eucharist and extreme unction, refusing Anglican communion. His Catholic brother was with him, succeeding as James II. Despite their religious tendencies, both brothers were popular at this time. Catholics and Dissenters both hoped for improved conditions under the new King. Tim Harris writes: 'As it turned out, James's reign began better than anyone could have expected. There was no immediate challenge to the accession of a Catholic ruler, as had been feared; indeed there is considerable evidence of support for the new monarch across all three of his Kingdoms [England with Wales, Scotland and Ireland].' But in reality the support was conditional upon his keeping the promise made as soon as he became King, 'to observe the rule of law and uphold the existing establishment in the Church'. Enthusiasm waned when it was realised that he would not keep his promises.[34] Shrewsbury was one of the corporations which sent a loyal address expressing their thanks to James 'for his gracious declaration in preferring the protestant religion'. Popular sentiment (and a tendency to use violence) is reflected in an anecdote concerning Richard Clarke of Myddle (who had long ago carried messages from Wem):

> At that tyme a limner [whitewasher with lime] was imployed to beautify the Parish church at Ellesmeare. This Clarke went to see his worke, and said, 'You doe well to leave the Churche in good repaire for us; for you had it from us in good order.' The limner (knowing him to be a Papist) said, 'What, doe you thinke the Papists must have the Church? ... What doe you think shall become of us Protestants?' Then Clarke answered, 'I hope to see all Protestants fry in their owne grease ...'

The limner reported Clarke to the JP Edward Kynaston, who committed him to prison. At the assizes he was sentenced to be put in the pillory on three market days, first at Shrewsbury, where the people pelted him so fiercely with eggs, turnips, carrots, stones and dirt that the under-sheriff had to rescue him before he was killed. He met similar treatment at Ellesmere, but the sentence was not carried out at Oswestry for fear of the ferocity of the Welshmen.[35]

Shrewsbury was on the King's itinerary in the summer of 1687 when he also visited the shrine of St Winifred at Holywell. The visit was part of a pre-election tour before the King called a Parliament which he hoped would repeal the penal laws to help Catholics as well as Protestant Dissenters. In fact James II (and VII of Scotland) had stirred up conflict in his three Kingdoms by promoting his own religion. His Declaration of Indulgence of April 1687 openly stated:

> We cannot but heartily wish ... that all the people of our dominions were members of the Catholic Church; yet we humbly thank Almighty God, it is and has of long time been our constant sense and opinion ... that conscience ought not to be constrained nor people forced in matters of mere religion ... We do likewise declare, that it is our royal will and pleasure that from henceforth the execution of all and all manner of penal laws in matters ecclesiastical, for not coming to church, or not receiving the Sacrament, or for any other nonconformity to the religion established ... be immediately suspended.

Nonconformists welcomed this Indulgence, but the King was alienating the Tory-Anglican majority, who therefore gave a cool welcome to the royal progress. James arrived in Shrewsbury at about five o'clock on 24 August (a fateful date, being both St Bartholomew's Day and the day on which the Act of Uniformity had come into effect 25 years earlier), taking up residence at the Council House, where he had stayed with his father and brother in September 1642. The corporation presented him with a purse of gold coins, value 100 guineas. The next day he touched for the King's Evil, scrofula, a gift of healing attesting his divine right to rule. One sufferer, a woman from Myddle, was touched, 'which did her noe good'. Another source tells us that the Presbyterian preachers, John Bryan and Francis Tallents, with Rowland Hunt and others, presented the King with a purse of gold; this was accepted but they were reminded to elect suitable men at the next Parliament. William Penn, chief of the Quakers and an adviser to the King, began to address the crowd at Mardol Head but 'the mob gave a shoutt and over Bawled him, so he desisted'. At this time of religious freedom Mass was said in the town 'in a house of Mr Jevons, which is betwixt the high cross and the high Conduitt, sang openly'; 'Judge Alibond', Sir Richard Allibone who presided over the northern assizes, attended.[36]

Of the towns visited by James II eight were never to present a loyal address – Shrewsbury was one of these. In 1688 anti-Catholic demonstrations increased, with attacks on Roman Catholic chapels and houses; Shrewsbury was one of the urban centres where this happened. The hopes of Anglicans were centred in the fact that James's heir was his Protestant daughter Mary, the princess of Orange, but the situation changed dramatically when a son was born to the Catholic queen on 10 June 1688. On 30 June six lords and a bishop wrote to William of Orange asking him to intervene in English affairs; the way had been prepared by propaganda issued at the Hague by English and Scottish supporters of William. William landed at Tor Bay on 5 November; the number of his supporters increased and the new song, 'Lillibulero', was the anthem of the Williamites. Addresses for a free Parliament were sent from all over the country. On 4 December a spurious 'Declaration' warned of armed papists; this terrified Catholics and put Protestants on their guard. The Whig Richard More of Linley (son of Samuel) summoned Shrewsbury to let Lord Herbert of Chirbury and Sir John Morgan take possession of the town. Herbert had taken up arms for William and with Sir Edward Harley raised support in the Welsh marches; they had occupied Ludlow Castle. On 8 December an unsigned reply from a member of Shrewsbury corporation was addressed to 'My Lord': the letter had been received and passed to the Recorder and Council. The mayor at the time was John Hill, brewer. The town was 'open and ungarrisoned' so his Lordship might enter without any opposition. With support ebbing from him, James II fled to France; William entered London on 18 December. Lord Newport had been deprived of his offices in 1687 but was restored by William III and elevated to the peerage as earl of Bradford in 1694. In Shrewsbury the earl built himself Newport House, moving the old timbered house nearer the castle so that the new house could occupy this central site; of brick, with stone portico, it is imposing but restrained.[37]

After much debate, the Convention Parliament declared William and Mary king and queen on 13 February 1689. A Declaration of Rights recited the charges against James II – as with the deposition of Richard II 300 years earlier, 'evil counsellors' were blamed. James was said to have 'abdicated the government' leaving the throne vacant, to be replaced by the Prince of Orange, 'whom it hath pleased Almighty God to make the glorious instrument of delivering this Kingdom from popery and arbitrary power'. If Mary had no heir of her body her sister Anne, princess of Denmark, should succeed. Both sisters were attached to the Anglican faith, while William was a tolerant Protestant. The declaration petitioned that no Catholic or anyone married to a Catholic should inherit the throne. William would have granted toleration to Catholics but this leniency came up against English Protestantism. Anglican prejudice meant that a proposed Comprehension Bill to incorporate Dissenters into the Church of England was defeated. A compromise was the Indulgence Bill of May 1689, the famous Toleration Act, though this was not its official title, nor was toleration mentioned in it. The Act maintained all earlier acts of uniformity but dissenters who had scruples against taking oaths could subscribe a declaration of loyalty, professing their Christian belief. It applied only to Dissenters who believed in the Trinity, and not of course to Catholics. Congregations or assemblies for religious worship were to be certified by a bishop or archdeacon, or by justices of the peace, and registered. Freedom to worship publicly was granted, but doors were to be left open. Nonconforming Protestants could still be penalised, and the Act did not put an end to intolerance. Nevertheless its practical achievement has been described as remarkable: 'Presbyterians, Independents, Baptists and Quakers all gained the right, by law, to worship freely. Paradoxically fear of Popery had proved necessary to break the monopoly of the Church of England, and Catholics were the losers.'[38] From another point of view the Act might be seen to undermine the established Church, which was not the national Church. Dissenters were, however, in the minority. For Shrewsbury, figures have to be borrowed from 1715 when 'hearers' or attenders at services are numbered: 440 Presbyterians, 150 Independents, 50 Baptists. To these must be added Quakers.[39]

After the Toleration Act, Francis Tallents published *Sure and Large Foundations*, 'a small Tract of two or three Sheets', arguing for 'Catholick Christianity, and Catholick Charity' as healing methods in the Church of England. In October 1690 Mrs Hunt died, so the Presbyterian meeting moved to Tallents' house 'while they were building and fitting up a very decent Place for the purpose'. It was ready by 25 October 1691: written on the walls was the testimony that it was built 'not for a Faction or a Party; but for promoting Repentance and Faith, in Communion with all that love our Lord

A

SERMON

Preach'd at the

PARISH-CHURCH

OF

St. *Chad's* in *SHREWSBURY*,

March 5. 169$\frac{4}{5}$

BEING THE

Funeral Day *of our Most Gracious Sovereign*

Queen Mary.

By *THOMAS DAWES*, B.D

Minister of the Church of St. *MARY*

in the said Town.

LONDON:

Printed by *F.C.* for *Gabriel Rogers* in *Shrewsbury*; and are to be Sold by *John Whitlock* near *Stationers-Hall*. 1695.

Title page of sermon by Thomas Dawes, 1695 (SA-IMG24329)

Jesus Christ in sincerity. Our Help stands in the Name of the Lord, who made Heaven and Earth.' This meeting place was in High Street, near St Mary's church, where the established liturgy was celebrated. On 5 March 1695, the day of the funeral of the much-loved Queen Mary, a sermon was preached at St Chad's by Thomas Dawes, minister of St Mary's and public preacher. In the congregation were the mayor and other members of the corporation together with gentry of the town. The grief is expressed in hyperbole, as we might expect, but Dawes also expatiates on Old Testament history, idolatry, heathen altars and religious Kings, such as Hezekiah and Josiah. As for the late Queen Mary:

> She found the Nation, & that She lov'd the most in it (the Church of England) a'entring, in melancholy plight, the Plague of an Aegptian Darkness, the Land, from one corner to another, a swarming with Popish Emissaries ... I think, 'tis own'd on all sides, that Popery (especially as 'tis of late years refin'd by new Jesuitical Morals) is a Terror to all Protestant Kingdoms.

The truth of 'our religion', that of the Church of England, is asserted, associated with the 'honest, good, peaceable, Loyal Subject': 'our Reform'd Religion' has been vindicated and saved; 'we of this National Church are happily restor'd to our Religion'. Mary, like Queen Elizabeth 'of ever Blessed Memory', was a nursing mother of the Church of England. Dawes is now forgotten but a more obscure seventeenth-century clergyman is still revered: the poet George Herbert, son of Richard Herbert of Montgomery and Magdalene Newport of north Shropshire. He died before the Civil War and before the invention of the term Anglican, but his sacred poems and his prose work *The Country Parson,* published in 1652, epitomise the Church of England as a *via media*. In the significantly titled poem 'The British Church' he indicates a history pre-dating Rome for the Church which avoids the excesses of both Rome and Geneva:

> A fine aspect in fit array,
> Neither too mean, nor yet too gay,
> Shows who is best.

In the Church of England, 'Beauty ... takes up her place', and God 'double-moats' her with his grace, 'And none but thee'.[40]

From the Catholic hegemony at the start of our story we have reached Anglican ascendancy, alongside the open practice of Nonconformity. Having a town such as

Shrewsbury to study makes it easier to understand how national developments affected a particular community, especially when we have such useful archives, letters and diaries to give us the immediacy of local evidence. Furthermore, there are individuals who make the narrative a human story, not just the preserve of theologians and historians. One particular strain in this narrative is the transition from the town's compliance with the beliefs and practices of the Catholic Church, through the dedication of an elite Protestant minority at the Reformation, to a struggle within Protestantism between Catholic and Reformed tendencies. It is striking also that post-Reformation Shrewsbury exhibited considerable independence in its religious affairs, instituting puritan preachers and then Presbyterian ministers without waiting from instructions from above. After the Restoration, however, such efforts met with establishment resolution. By the end of our story Anglicanism had prevailed, but Nonconformity was firmly rooted.

References

Introduction

1 John Chandler, *John Leland's Itinerary. Travels in Tudor England* (Stroud, 1993), 388-90.

Chapter 1

1 C. Given-Wilson (ed.), *The Chronicle of Adam Usk 1377-1421* (Oxford, 1997), 37-77; Ian Mortimer, *The Fears of Henry IV. The Life of England's Self-Made King* (London, 2007).

2 *Calendar of Patent Rolls. Henry IV*, vol. 1, 359.

3 H. Owen and J. B. Blakeway, *A History of Shrewsbury* (2 vols, 1825), I, 172-4; *Calendar of Patent Rolls. Henry IV*, vol. 2, 1401-1405, 48-9. Thornes and Gerard were wealthy borough officials.

4 J.S. Roskell (ed.), *The History of Parliament. The House of Commons 1386-1421* (London, 1992), vol. 1, 580-5; Mortimer, *Fears of Henry IV*, chapter 14 (battle of Shrewsbury) and p. 325.

5 J.C. Dickinson, *The Origins of the Austin Canons and their Introduction into England* (London, 1950); *Victoria County History* [*V.C.H.*] *Shropshire*, II, 59-83. There were also canonesses.

6 *V.C.H. Shropshire,* II, 70-79. The abbot of Lilleshall 1398-1432 was William de Lye.

7 *Mirk's Festial*, ed. Theodor Erbe (Early English Text Society, extra series, 96, 1905); *John Mirk's Instructions for Parish Priests*, ed. Gillis Kristensson (Lund, 1974); Martyn F. Wakelin, 'The Manuscripts of John Mirk's *Festial* ', *Leeds Studies in English*, new series, I (1967), 93-118.

8 G.R. Owst, *Preaching in Medieval England* (Cambridge, 1926), 243.

9 L.E. Boyle, 'The *Oculus Sacerdotis* and some other works of William of Pagula', *Transactions of the Royal Historical Society*, fifth series, V (1955), 81-106; Kristensson, *Instructions*, 9.

10 Miri Rubin, *Corpus Christi. The Eucharist in Late Medieval Culture (*Cambridge, 1991), 78; David L. Edwards, *Christian England,* I (London, 1981), 111-2, 132.

11 J.A.B. Somerset (ed.), *Records of Early English Drama* [*R.E.E.D.*] *Shropshire* (two vols, Toronto, 1994), II, 563-4.

12 *Mirk's Festial*, 168-75; *Oxford Dictionary of National Biography [O.D.N.B.*], Mirk; J.A.F. Thomson, 'Orthodox Religion and the Origins of Lollardy', *History,* 74 (1989), 39-55.

13 Wendy Scase, 'Lollardy', in David Bagchi and David C. Steinmetz (eds), *Reformation Theology* (Cambridge, 2004), 15-21; bibliography 257-8.

14 Peter McNiven, *Heresy and Politics in the Reign of Henry IV* (Woodbridge, 1987), 59

15 Anne Hudson (ed.), *Two Wycliffite Texts: the Sermon of William Taylor 1406; The Testimony of William Thorpe 1407* (Early English Text Society, Oxford, 1993), 24-123: lines 936-45.

16 Claire Cross, *Church and People 1450-1650* (Fontana, 1976), 16. The Langland quotation is from the modern verse translation of *Piers Plowman* by Terence Tiller (1981), 16.

17 Maureen Jurkowski. 'The arrest of William Thorpe in Shrewsbury and the anti-Lollard statute of 1406', *Historical Research*, 2002, 273-95.

18 Ritchie D. Kendall, *The Drama of Dissent. The Radical Poetics of Nonconformity, 1380-1590* (University of North Carolina Press, Chapel Hill and London, 1986),58.
19 Jurkowski, 282, 292; *R.E.E.D. Shropshire,* II, 564-5.
20 *O.D.N.B.,* Thomas Arundel; Anne Hudson, *The Premature Reformation. Wycliffite Texts and Lollard History* (Oxford, 1988), 62, 117.
21 David Aers, 'Walter Brut's Theology of the Sacrament of the Altar', in *Lollards and their Influence in Late Medieval England,* ed. Fiona Somerset, Jill C. Havens and Derrick G. Pitard (Woodbridge, 2003), 115-26; Hudson, *Premature Reformation,* 179; Eamon Duffy, *Saints and Sinners. A History of the Popes* (3rd ed., New Haven, 2006), 168-9.
22 Edward Powell, *Kingship, Law and Society. Criminal Justice in the Reign of Henry* V (Oxford, 1989), 37; *Calendar of Patent Rolls. Henry IV,* vol. 3, 1405-1408, 352, 476; McNiven, 114.
23 Mortimer, *The Fears of Henry IV,* 236.
24 *O.D.N.B.,* Oldcastle.
25 A.J. Pollard, *Late Medieval England 1399-1509* (Harlow, 2000), 73. Henry V became king on 21 March 1413: he buried his father at Canterbury and re-buried Richard II at Westminster.
26 Powell, *Kingship, Law and Society,* 64, 163, and chapter 7; G. O. Sayles (ed.), *Select Cases in the Court of King's Bench,* vol. VII (Selden Society, London, 1971), 226-9. Edward duke of York died at Agincourt in 1415.
27 J.R. Lander, *Conflict and Stability in Fifteenth Century England* (3rd ed., London, 1977),55.
28 Eamon Duffy, *Saints and Sinners. A History of the Popes,* 170.
29 K.B. McFarlane, *England in the Fifteenth Century* (London, 1981), 102.
30 Adam Usk, *Chronicle,* 263; R.R. Davies, *The Age of Conquest,* 447-59.
31 *Historical Manuscripts Commission, 15th Report, Appendix, Part X,* 28; *Calendar Patent Rolls. Henry V,* vol. 2, 335.
32 *Mirk's Festial.* 1-5; Norman Davies, ed., *Non-Cycle Plays and Fragments* (Early English Text Society, Supplementary Text no. 1, Oxford, 1970), xiv-xxii, 124-33; Marianne G. Briscoe and John C. Coldewey (eds), *Contexts for Early English Drama* (Indiana, 1989), 198, 214 n. 9. The fragments have no real connection with Shrewsbury: the school bought them from Lichfield Cathedral in 1606 along with about 20 other manuscripts: I am indebted to Mike Morrogh, archivist of Shrewsbury School, for this information.
33 *Mirk's Festial,* 238; Owst, *Preaching in Medieval England, 338.*
34 Henry Pidgeon, 'Ancient Gilds of Shrewsbury', *Transactions of the Shropshire Archaeological Society* [*T.S.A.S.*], vol. VI (1883), 183-204; Irene Mary Rope, 'The Earliest Book of the Drapers' Company, Shrewsbury', *T.S.A.S.*, 4th series, vol. III, 135-262: the date of the Drapers' Company foundation was 1461. For Coventry, Hardin Craig, *Two Coventry Corpus Christi Plays* (Early English Text Society, extra series, LXXXVII, 1957).
35 Rubin, *Corpus Christi,* 261: the Corpus Christi cycle-plays 'were usually later'. This view is contested by evidence from York where the procession and the plays were contemporary and distinct: A. F. Johnston, 'The Procession and Play of Corpus Christi in York after 1426', *Leeds Studies in English,* new series, vol. VII (1974), 55-9; J. F. Hoy, 'On the Relationship of the Corpus Christi Plays to the Corpus Christi Procession at York', *Modern Philology,* 71 (1973-4), 166-8.
36 Owen and Blakeway, I, 206-9.
37 *R.E.E.D. Shropshire* II, 567-9; K. B. McFarlane, *England in the Fifteenth Century,* 149. For the career of Talbot, A. J. Pollard, *John Talbot and the War in France 1421-53* (London, 1983). For the younger John Talbot see *O.D.N.B.*

38 *R.E.E.D. Shropshire,* II, 571-3, and passim; John Southworth, *Fools and Jesters at the English Court* (Stroud, 2003), 114-20, 154-5; M.C. Bradbrooke, *The Rise of the Common Player* (Cambridge, 1962), 23-5.
39 'Early Chronicles of Shrewsbury', *T.S.A.S.*, vol. III (1880), 246 the manuscript is in Shrewsbury School library: 'Dr Taylor's MS'; Anne Crawford, *The Yorkists. The History of a Dynasty* (London, 2007), 10-11.
40 Crawford, *The Yorkists*, 15.
41 *H.M.C. 15th Report. Appendix. Part X*, 29.
42 Owen and Blakeway, I, 248: petition of Sir Richard Corbet to Henry VII. For an account of the battles and exile see Ralph A. Griffiths and Roger S. Thomas, *The making of the Tudor Dynasty* (rev. ed., Stroud, 2005), chs 5-9.
43 *T.S.A.S.*, 4th series, vol. III, 135; *R.E.E.D. Shropshire,* II, 576-7; Trevor Royle, *The Road to Bosworth Field* (2009), 289-92
44 'Early Chronicles', *T.S.A.S.* III, 246; Owen and Blakeway, I, 232-3.
45 'Early Chronicles', 248; Owen and Blakeway, II, 234
46 *R.E.E.D. Shropshire,* II, 583; Owen and Blakeway, I, 233.
47 Crawford, *The Yorkists*, 120-2.
48 Crawford, *The Yorkists*, 132-3, 150.
49 George Glazebrook, 'An Unpublished Letter by Henry, Earl of Richmond', *Miscellanea Genealogica et Heraldica,* 4th series, vol. 4 (1914), 30-9.
50 'Early Chronicles', 249-50: Mytton and his company visited Tudor at his camp at Forton, three miles from Shrewsbury; next day ambassadors came to speak with the bailiffs requesting to pass quietly – they did not mean to hurt the town. To save his oath, this story goes, Mytton lay on the ground 'and so the said Erle stepped over him and savyd hys othe'.
51 R.A. Griffiths and R. S. Thomas, *The Making of the Tudor Dynasty*, 150-207.
52 D.R. Walker, 'An Urban Community in the Welsh Borderland: Shrewsbury in the Fifteenth Century', Ph. D. thesis, University of Swansea, 1981, 147-264.
53 Hudson, *Premature Reformation*, 455.
54 Alexandra Walsham, *Charitable hatred* (Manchester, 2006), 21.
55 Penry Williams, *The Tudor Regime* (Oxford, 1979), 253; M.K. Jones and M.G. Underwood, *The King's Mother* (Cambridge, 1992).

Chapter 2

1 Henry Pidgeon, 'Ancient Gilds of Shrewsbury', 183-204; *V.C.H. Shropshire*, vol. II, 33-5; *Cal. Patent Rolls. Henry VII* , vol. I, 158. Thomas Mynde was abbot from 1460 to 1498.
2 C. S. Watkins, *History and the Supernatural in Medieval England* (Cambridge, 2007), 21.
3 Anne Hudson, *Premature Reformation* 449, 455; Shannon McSheffrey and Norman Tanner (eds), *Lollards of Coventry, 1486-1522* (Camden Society, 5th series, vol. 23, 2003), introduction.
4 *R.E.E.D. Shropshire,* II, 585; Sydney Anglo, *Spectacle, Pageantry* and *Early Tudor Policy* (Oxford, 1969), 21-56; W. R. B. Robinson, 'Prince Arthur in the Marches of Wales 1493-1502', *Studia Celtica*, XXXVI (2002), 89-97.
5 'Early Chronicles of Shrewsbury', 250-1; *R.E.E.D. Shropshire,* II, 586-7; M. K. Jones and M. G. Underwood, *The King's Mother* , 150.
6 G. W. Bernard and S. J. Gunn (eds), *Authority and Consent in Tudor England* (Aldershot, 2002), 142: this marriage did not in fact take place. See also David Starkey, *Henry. Virtuous Prince* (Harper, 2008; paperback 2009): this covers the early life of Henry.

7 *O.D.N.B.*, John Wyclif (article by Anne Hudson and Anthony Kenny).
8 *V.C.H. Shropshire* II, 36, 96; *H.M.C. 15th Report, Appendix Part X,* 31.
9 *R.E.E.D. Shropshire,* II, 593-5; David Mills (ed.), *The Chester Mystery Cycle* (1992), 150-75.
10 Roy Palmer, *The Folklore of the Black Country* (Logaston Press, 2007), 205; *R.E.E.D. Shropshire,* II, 595-607; Ronald Hutton, *The Rise and Fall of Merry England* (Oxford, 1994), 90; Chris Humphrey, *The Politics of Carnival* (Manchester, 2001), 56; 'Early Chronicles', 255..
11 *H.M.C. 15th Report, Appendix Part X,* 47-8.
12 Michael A. Mullett, *Martin Luther* (London, 2004, reprinted 2005), 50-76.
13 Christopher Harper-Bill, 'Dean Colet's Convocation Sermon and the Pre-Reformation Church in England', *History,* vol. 73 (1988), 191-210; Susan Brigden, *London and the Reformation* (Oxford, 1989), 121, 157-9.
14 Mullett, *Martin Luther*, 74; Patrick Collinson, chapter 9 in Peter Marshall and Alec Ryrie (eds), *The Beginnings of English Protestantism* (Cambridge, 2002); Robert Lutton, *Lollardy and Orthodox Religion in Pre-Reformation England* (Woodbridge, 2006), 3-4.
15 *R.E.E.D. Shropshire*, II, 595-6.
16 *O.D.N.B.,*Tyndale; A. G. Dickens, *Late Monasticism and the Reformation* (London, 1994), 119.
17 Owen and Blakeway, *History*, I, 309; Brigden, *London and the Reformation*, 121.
18 *R.E.E.D. Shropshire,* II, 598-9; W. R. B. Robinson, 'Princess Mary's Itinerary, 1525-7', *Historical Research,* vol. 71 (1998), 233-52.
19 *Letters of Henry VIII, 1526-29. Extracts from the Calendar of State Papers of Henry VIII* (London, 2001): quotations on p. 229.
20 Janette Dillon, *Performance and Spectacle in Hall's Chronicle* (London, 2002), 134.
21 G.W. Bernard, *The King's Reformation. Henry VIII and the Remaking of the English Church* (New Haven and London, 2005), 38-50; *Hall's Chronicle*, 134.
22 Bernard, *The King's Reformation*, 236-7; Diarmaid MacCulloch, 'Henry VIII and the Reform of the Church', in idem. ed. *The Reign of Henry VIII. Politics, Policy and Piety* (Basingstoke, 1995), 162-70.
23 Stanford E. Lehmberg, *The Reformation Parliament 1529-1536* (Cambridge, 1970).
24 'Early Chronicles', 255; Bernard, *King's Reformation*, 247-76; *V.C.H. Shropshire,* II, 37.
25 William Rees, 'The Union of England and Wales', *Transactions of the Honourable Society of Cymmrodorion* (1937), 27-100; Michael Anthony Jones, ' "An Earthly Beast, a Mole and an Enemy to all Godly Learning": The Life and Career of Rowland Lee, Bishop of Coventry and Lichfield, and Lord President of the Council in the Marches of Wales, c. 1487-1543', M.Phil. thesis, University of Wales (Cardiff), 1997.
26 Jones, thesis, 17-51: the bishop married nieces into local gentry families such as Onslow and Thornes, Jane Fowler marrying a son of the Shrewsbury bailiff Humphrey Onslow who secured for himself a large part of the rents and privileges of St Chad's from its dean and chapter. For Lee's burial before the high altar, Owen and Blakeway, *History*, I, 340.
27 Jessie Childs, *Henry VIII's Last Victim. The Life and Times of Henry Howard, Earl of Surrey* (London, 2006), 52-113; *O.D.N.B.* Henry Fitzroy.
28 *Tudor Royal Proclamations I (1485-1553)* , 251-2; Owen and Blakeway, I, 317.
29 Dillon, *Hall's Chronicle,* 153-4; Greg Walker, 'Rethinking the Fall of Anne Boleyn', *The Historical Journal*, 45 (2002), 1-29; *O.D.N.B.* Henry was buried at Thetford and later at Framlingham.
30 Bernard, *King's Reformation*, 446-7, 490-1, 290-2; MacCulloch, *Cranmer*, 161-6. For John Bale and his troupe see Paul Whitfield White, *Theatre and Reformation* (Cambridge, 1993), 22-7.

31 'Early Chronicles', 256; Owen and Blakeway, *History*, I, 316; *H.M.C. Fifteenth Report*, 12.
32 *The Sword and the Book*: booklet accompanying an exhibition of Bibles in English, John Rylands Library, Deansgate, Manchester, 2007-8.
33 Richard Rex, *Henry VIII and the English Reformation* (Basingstoke, 1993), 165; C. John Sommerville, *The Secularization of Early Modern England. From Religious Culture to Religious Faith* (Oxford, 1992), 56, 20.
34 *H.M.C. 15th Report*, 12; Owen and Blakeway, *History*, I, 322, 388; William Rees, 'The Union of England and Wales', 60-63; *R.E.E.D. Shropshire*, II, 610.
35 B. Coulton, 'The Establishment of Protestantism ... in Shrewsbury', *Sixteenth Century Journal*, 27 (1996), 309-12; G. W. Bernard, *The Power of the Early Tudor Nobility. A study of the Fourth and Fifth Earls of Shrewsbury* (Brighton, 1985), 11.
36 'Early Chronicles', 258-9; MacCulloch, *Cranmer*, 365, 372-84.
37 S. Bindoff, (ed.), *History of Parliament. The House of Commons 1509-1558* (1982), I, 178-9, 508-10, 700; 'Early Chronicles', 259-60; Coulton, 'Establishment of Protestantism', 310-1: I am grateful to Bill Champion for the information about the wills mentioned.
38 G.W. Fisher, *Annals of Shrewsbury School* (London, 1899), 1-2.
39 R.T. Beckwith, 'Thomas Cranmer and the Prayer Book' in *The Study of Liturgy* ed. Cheslyn Jones, Geoffrey Wainwright, Edward Yarnold SJ and Paul Bradshaw (rev. ed. London, 1992), 105; Diarmaid MacCulloch, *Tudor Church Militant* (Penguin, 1999), 11.
40 'Early Chronicles', 258; for property information, I am grateful to Bill Champion.

Chapter 3

1 David Starkey, *Elizabeth. Apprenticeship* (2nd rev. ed., London, 2001), 50, 82.
2 David Loades, 'The Personal Religion of Mary I', in *The Church of Mary Tudor* ed. Eamon Duffy and David Loades (Aldershot, 2006), 12-15.
3 Thomas S Freeman, ' "As True a Subiect being Prysoner": John Foxe's Notes on the Imprisonment of Princess Elizabeth, 1554-5', *English Historical Review* 117 (2002), 104-16, and idem. 'Providence and Prescription: The Account of Elizabeth in Foxe's "Book of Martyrs"', in *The Myth of Elizabeth*, ed. Susan Doran and Thomas S. Freeman (Basingstoke, 2003), 27-55.
4 Rex, *The Tudors,* 147; David Loades, 'The Personal Religion of Mary I', in *The Church of Mary Tudor,* 19; 'Early Chronicles',
5 MacCulloch, *Cranmer*, 552-6; Margaret Cranmer remarried at an unknown date, 611.
6 David Loades, 'The Marian Episcopate', in *The Church of Mary Tudor*, 35-50.
7 David Edwards, *Christian England*, vol. 2, 64-8. For the Council of Trent see Michael A. Mullett, *The Catholic Reformation* (1999).
8 Ritchie Kendall, *The Drama of Dissent*, chapter 3, 90-131.
9 *O.D.N.B.*, article by John King. Bale returned to England and died in late 1563.
10 *Church of Mary Tudor*, editors' introduction, xv; Loades, *The Reign of Mary Tudor* (second edition, London, 1991), 299-302.
11 Owen and Blakeway, II, 340-1; Archdeacon Lloyd, *Notes on St Mary's* (Shrewsbury, 1900), 26.
12 Loades, *Reign of Mary Tudor*, 273-4. Cranmer, Latimer and Ridley were burned at Oxford.
13 *O.D.N.B.*, Baynes; Susan Wabuda, 'Shunamites and Nurses of the English Reformation: The Activities of Mary Glover, Niece of Hugh Latimer', in *Women in the Church* ed. W. J. Shiels and Diana Wood, Studies in Church History 27 (Oxford, 1990), 335-44.
14 *O.D.N.B.*; A. G. Dickens, 'The Early Expansion of Protestantism in England 1520-1558', in *Reformation to Revolution* ed. Margo Todd (London, 1995), 167-8.

15 *T.S.A.S.* vol. V ((1882), 298, and 2nd series, vol. VI (1894), 372, 391-3: Foxe has the account, slightly inaccurate but true in substance. After 56 years the first memorial stone became illegible, and the tomb in disrepair, so Andrew Corbet, then lord lieutenant of Shropshire, advised repairs; he wrote verses (anti-popish) celebrating Burton as 'Truly professing Christianity' and, like Christ, laid in a garden, where he would rest in peace. Further repairs were made in the early 19th century, when bones were found and covered up again.

16 Duffy, 'Cardinal Pole Preaching: St Andrew's Day 1557', in *The Church of Mary Tudor*, 176-200: this is a most important study of Pole, addressing misunderstandings by other historians. For comparison see Thomas Lever, *Sermons 1550* (London, 1870).

17 Duffy, *Saints and Sinners*, 215-6; Loades, 'The Personal Religion of Mary I', *The Church of Mary Tudor*, 25-8.

18 Brett Usher, ' "In a Time of Persecution": New Light on the Secret Protestant Congregation in Marian London', in *John Foxe and the English Reformation,* ed. David Loades (Aldershot, 1997), 233-251; B. Coulton, 'Implementing the Reformation in the Urban Community: Coventry and Shrewsbury 1559-1603', *Midland History* XXV (2000), 43-60. Entries on Bentham and Lever in *O.D.N.B.*

19 For Emden see Andrew Pettegree, *Marian Protestantism* (Aldershot, 1996), chapter 1, and p. 188 for the publication at Emden (Ashton's copy is at Shrewsbury School).

20 Pettegree, *Marian Protestantism*, 101-5, 108-10; B. W. Beckingsale, *Burghley: Tudor Statesman 1520-1598* (London,, 1967, chapter V: 'In the Wilderness'.

21 Nicholas Tyacke, *Aspects of English Protestantism c. 1530-1700* (Manchester, 2001), 40-43, 178; Ian Hazlett, 'Bucer', *Reformation Theology*, ed. Bagchi and Steinmetz, 102-3.

22 Pettegree, 'Nicodemism and the English Reformation' in *Marian Protestantism*, 109-10.

23 Starkey, *Elizabeth. Apprenticeship*, 238-64.

24 Roger Bowers, 'The Chapel Royal, the First Edwardian Prayer Book, and Elizabeth's Settlement of Religion, 1559', *Historical Journal* 43 (2000),317-44.

25 *The Zurich Letters, I* (Parker Society, Cambridge, 1842), 84-88. For the proclamation against preaching and the royal injunctions of 1559 see *Documents Illustrative of English Church History*, ed. Henry Gee and William John Hardy (London, 1921), 416-42.

26 'The Letter-Book of Thomas Bentham, Bishop of Coventry and Lichfield', ed. R. O'Day and J. Berlatsky, *Camden Miscellany XXVII* (Camden Society, 4th series, 22, 1979), 144, 152, 162, 168.

27 G.W. Fisher, *Annals of Shrewsbury School* (London, 1899), 3-4; Henry Gee, *The Elizabethan Clergy and the Settlement of Religion* (Oxford, 1898), 59, 122; *H.M.C. Fifteenth Report,* 13-14.

28 *The Writings of John Bradford I* (Parker Society, Cambridge, 1848), 137; *Original Letters relative the English Reformation*, I (Parker Society, Cambridge, 1846), 155.

29 Pettegree, 'The Marian Exiles and the Elizabethan Settlement', *Marian Protestantism*, 143.

30 Coulton, 'Establishment', 314; Bentham, 'Letter-Book', 210-1; Fisher, *Annals*, 4.

31 H.F. Howard, *An Account of the Finances of the College of St John Cambridge 1511-1926* (Cambridge, 1935), 16, 41, 282; E. Calvert (ed.), *Shrewsbury School Regestum Scholarium 1562-1635* (Shrewsbury, 1892), 1-17.

32 Coulton, 'Establishment of Protestantism', 314-5; Fisher, *Annals*, 41-3; F. S. Boas, *University Drama in the Tudor Age* (Oxford, 1914; reprinted New York, 1978), 140; for the Corbet family, see Coulton, 'Moreton Corbet', *T.S.A.S.* LXX (1995), 184-90.

33 *R.E.E.D. Shropshire* I, 207-8, II, 378-9; 'Early Chronicles', 268; Thomas Churchyard, *The Worthines of Wales* (1587), 97.

34 Glynne Wickham, *Early English Stage* vol. 2, part 1 (London, 1963), 329; Constantin Hopf, *Martin Bucer and the English Reformation* (Oxford, 1946), 102-4.

35 Fisher, *Annals of Shrewsbury School*, 428.
36 'Letter-Book of Thomas *Bentham', Camden Miscellany XXVII*, 211-2, 236.
37 W.A. Leighton, 'The Guilds of Shrewsbury', *T.S.A.S.* VIII (1885), 317, 402.
38 'A Collection of Original Letters from the Bishops to the Privy Council', ed. Mary Bateson, *Camden Miscellany* 9 (1895), 39-47.
39 David Loades, *The Cecils. Privilege and power behind the throne* (National Archives, Kew, 2007), 68; Penry Williams, *The Tudor Regime* (Oxford, 1991 ed.), 446, 349-50; Coulton, 'Moreton Corbet', 186; Fisher, *Annals*, 429-30; Robert Hutchinson, *Elizabeth's Spy Master* (London, 2007), 36-45. Fisher reads the subscription to Ashton's letter 'At Charlecote' but it is more likely to have been written from Chartley in Staffordshire, the Devereux home where he was about to take up his duties as tutor to six-year-old Robert. Norfolk was executed for high treason in June 1572. Another Dacre plot, reported in 1572, aimed at making Cumberland, Westmorland, Northumberland, Durham, Yorkshire and Lancashire 'a realm free and independent' for English Catholics to repair to: Hutchinson, *Spy Master*, 65.
40 *H.M.C. 15th Report*, 17; Owen and Blakeway I, 360, 370; II, 212; Fisher, Annals, 427-8.
41 W.P. Stephens, *Zwingli. An Introduction to His Thought* (Oxford, 1999, rev. ed.), 25-6, 31.
42 'Early Chronicles', 35; *Documents Illustrative of the History of the English Church,* 432.
43 Coulton, 'Establishment', 319-20. The School's statutes are printed in Thomas Baker's *History of St John's College, Cambridge*, ed. J.E.B. Mayor, part 1 (Cambridge, 1869), 405-13. The indenture was signed at Keiston in Huntingdonshire, a manor of the young earl of Essex. For the first performances of *Richardus Tertius* and its plausibility as a source for Shakespeare's play, see Boas, *University Drama*, 112-32; and Appendix V for list of performers, 394-7.
44 Irvonwy Morgan, *The Godly Preachers of the Elizabethan Church* (London, 1965), 205; Daniel Neal, *History of the Puritans* (London, 1822), vol. 1, 283-9.
45 Owen and Blakeway, *History*, II, ; Fisher, *Annals*, 431-2; 'Early Chronicles', 288; *H.M.C. 15th Report*, 19-22. Letters of Bulkeley to the lawyer George Bromley, S.A. 3365/2699.
46 Penry Williams, *Tudor Regime*, 275-7; E. Gwynne Jones, 'Catholic Recusancy in the Counties of Denbigh, Flint and Montgomery', *Cymmrodorion Transactions*, 1945, 117.
47 Coulton, 'Establishment', 325-7; S.A. P257/B/3/1, fos 170-81; 'Early Chronicles', 315.
48 Camden, *Britannia* (1610 trans.), 596; Eric Mercer, 'The Town of Shrewsbury' in *Sixteenth Century Britain*, ed. Boris Ford (Cambridge, 1992), 158-68; 'Early Chronicles', 384-6.
49 'Early Chronicles', 296; *A Sermon preached in Shrewsburie ... by John Tomkys* (1585).
50 'Early Chronicles', 297; Penry Williams, *Tudor Regime,* 201-2; F. E. Halliday, *Shakespeare in his Age* (London, 1971 ed.), 65; E. K. Chambers, *The Elizabethan Stage* II (Oxford, 1951), 102-3. In 1593 Lord Strange's Men with Edward Alleyn visited Shrewsbury: Chambers, op. cit. 124.
51 'Early Chronicles', 306-7, 313; David Loades, *The Cecils.*, 156-160.
52 'Early Chronicles', 315, 295; *R.E.E.D. Shropshire,* I, 225.
53 S.R.R.C. 3365/1113 (court rolls).
54 Coulton, 'Establishment', 328-9; J. Morris, 'The Provosts and Bailiffs of Shrewsbury', *T.S.A.S.* 3rd series, V (1905), passim; 'Early Chronicles', 322, 324. Compare Thomas Owen's decision to an order of the Privy Council over a similar affair at Banbury: Hutton, *Merry England*, 139-40
55 Collinson, 'The Shearmen's Tree and the Preacher ...', in *The Reformation in English Towns 1500-1640,* ed. Patrick Collinson and John Craig (Basingstoke, 1998), 205-20.
56 Fisher, *Annals*, 426-7; S.A. 3365/2699, 3365/2590, 6001/290, 3365/2594. Lady Margaret Newport, who died in 1598, was mourned in Shrewsbury as 'a verteous lady in all hyr lyfe tyme and verey good to the poore in towne and countrey': 'Early Chronicles', 339.

57 The appointment was made by Lord Keeper Thomas Egerton, on behalf of the Crown. Leech was an alumnus of Shrewsbury School and a graduate of Emmanuel College, Cambridge.
58 Patrick Collinson, 'Windows in a Woman's Soul', *Elizabethans* (London, 2003), 114-5.
59 Andrew Foster, 'The function of a bishop', in *Continuity and change* ed. Rosemary O'Day and Felicity Heal (Leicester, 1976), 37. For the various articles and acts, *Documents Illustrative.*
60 Alexandra Walsham, 'A Very Deborah? The Myth of Elizabeth I as a Providential Monarch', in *The Myth of Elizabeth,* ed. Susan Doran and Thomas S. Freeman, 143-68.

Chapter 4

1 *O.D.N.B.* vol. 58, 717-28: 'John Whitgift, 1530/31?-1604', by William Joseph Sheils.
2 Elizabeth Gilliam and W. J. Tighe, 'To "Run with the Time". Archbishop Whitgift, the Lambeth Articles, and the Politics of Theological Ambiguity in Late Elizabethan England', *Sixteenth Century Journal*, XXIII (1992), 325-40: they discuss various interpretations of the affair.
3 Coulton, 'Establishment of Protestantism', 332-3; Leech, *A Triumph of Truth* (1609), 27.
4 E.H. Browne, *An Exposition of the Thirty-Nine Articles* (London, 1887), 444-68, 492-540.
5 Philip Benedict, *Christ's Churches Purely Reformed. A Social History of Calvinism* (New Haven and London, 2002), xxiii.
6 D.H. Cranage, *An Architectural Account of the Churches of Shropshire* (Wellington, 1905), 655. Newport, son of the Lady Newport who was so highly regarded in Shrewsbury, was MP for the town in 1589; he died in 1610. His sister Magdalen was mother of the poet George Herbert.
7 Frederick Shriver, 'Hampton Court Revisited: James I and the Puritans', *Journal of Ecclesiastical History*, 33 (1982), 48-71.
8 J. C. Cox, 'An Elizabethan Clergy List of the Diocese of Lichfield', *Journal of the Derbyshire Archaeological Society* 6 (1884), 157-180.
9 Antonia Fraser, *The Gunpowder Plot. Terror & Faith in 1605* (London, 1999 ed.), 134-5.
10 Nicholas Tyacke, 'Religious Controversy', chapter 10 of *The History of the University of Oxford*, vol. IV, ed. Tyacke (Oxford, 1997), 569: note the careful use of the term Calvinist.
11 Kenneth Fincham, 'Oxford and Early Stuart Polity', in *History of the University of Oxford*, vol. 4, 187. For Leech, B. Coulton. ' "Casting Anchor in the Harbour of Religion": The Peregrination of Humfrey Leech (1571-1629), *Recusant History* 28 (2006-7), 55-74.
12 Andrew Foster, 'The function of a bishop: the career of Richard Neile, 1562-1640', in *Continuity and change*, ed. O'Day and Heal, 38; see too the note on p. 54.
13 Diarmaid McCulloch describes the Abbey as 'a liturgical showcase', with Andrewes as dean and then Neile, who had been at Westminster School, dean from 1605-8: *Reformation*, 512.
14 B. Coulton, 'Rivalry and Religion: The Borough of Shrewsbury in the Early Stuart Period', *Midland History* XXVIII (2003), 29-31: other details in this paragraph are from this source.
15 For Abbot, Kenneth Fincham's article, *O.D.N.B.*
16 Price, *The defence of truth,* preface; *O.D.N.B.* Bancroft; Lichfield Record Office, B/A/4/17; Samuel Clarke, *A Generall Martyrologie* (1651), 462-5.
17 *O.D.N.B.* Daniel and Sampson Price.
18 Price's sermon was printed in London in 1618 by John Meighen, son of headmaster Richard Meighen. I am grateful to James Lawson, archivist emeritus of the School, for a copy.
19 B. Coulton, 'Rivalry and Religion'. 31-2. For the Elizabethan presbyterian movement, Patrick Collinson, *The Elizabethan Puritan Movement* (London, 1967).
20 S.A. 6001/290, transcript of borough council minutes, 9 April 1621, 6 May 1622.

21 Owen and Blakeway, *History*, II, 214. Sir Roger was patron of Pontesbury, Shropshire.
22 Kenneth Fincham, 'Episcopal Government 1603-1640' in *The Early Stuart Church, 1603-1642* (Basingstoke, 1993), 78.
23 Hugh Trevor-Roper, *Catholics, Anglicans & Puritans* (Fontana, 1989), 47, 56.
24 Kenneth Fincham and Peter Lake, 'The Ecclesiastical Policies of James I and Charles I', in *The Early Stuart Church*, ed Fincham, 31-2.
25 Overall was elected to the see of Norwich but died in May 1619; vol. 39, 433-40: Morton had been bishop of Chester from 1616: *Handbook of British Chronology* (3rd ed., Cambridge, 1996), 254 (bishops of Lichfield).
26 Collinson, *Elizabethan Puritan Movement*, 125-6, for Bright: Emmanuel College Archives, Box 1, NOM 3.
27 *H.M.C. 15th Report*, Municipal records, Shrewsbury, 37-8.
28 *The Beauty of Holinesse,* 35, and notes in margin; Samuel Clarke, *Generall Martyrologie,* 'Life of Doctor Preston', 480; Coulton, 'Rivalry and Religion', 33.
29 S.A. 6001/290, 24 March 1619; 1831/6, fo. 29r (lease to Drapers Hall); Clarke, *Generall Martyrologie*, 464-5; Robert Halley, *Lancashire: Its Puritanism and Nonconformity* (Manchester, 1872), 129-32.
30 Lichfield Record Office, B/V/1/37, 1620, fo. 110: St Chad's: Sampson Preece, curatus; S.R.R.C. 6001/290, transcript of borough council minutes, 9 April 1621, 6 May 1622.
31 Fisher, *Annals*, 149 n. 2. I am grateful to Bill Champion for correcting this information.
32 Christopher Hill, 'The Political Sermons of John Preston', in *Puritanism and Revolution* (Penguin, 1990), 234-266; *O.D.N.B.* Sibbes; E. W. Kirby, 'The Lay Feoffees: A Study in Militant Puritanism', *Journal* of *Modern History*, XIV (1942); I. M. Calder, *The Activities of the Puritan Faction in the Church of England 1625-33* (London, 1957); *Calendar of State Papers. Domestic*, *1634*, 337.
33 Fincham and Lake, 'Ecclesiastical Policies' in Fincham, *Early Stuart Church*, 37.
34 *O.D.N.B.* vol. 39, 436 (Morton); Lichfield Record Office, B/V/1/48, 1626 Salop, fos 14-24.
35 Clarke, *Generall Martyrologie*, 465; *Shropshire Parish Registers*, Lichfield Diocese.
36 Keith Thomas, *Religion and the Decline of Magic (*Penguin, 1991), 68-9; Katherine Chidley, *The Justification of the Independent Churches of God* (London, 1641), 2.
37 Coulton, 'Rivalry and Religion', 34-6.
38 Clarke, *Generall Martyrologie*, 464. Clarke mentions 'Master Pierson, Master Nicols &': Thomas Pierson (died 1633) had as patron Sir Robert Harley of Brampton Bryan in Herefordshire; Robert Nichols of Wrenbury in Cheshire was a brother-in-law of Hering. Ball had been ordained with Hering in 1610.
39 *The Works of the Most Reverend Father in God, William Laud D.D.,* ed. William Scott and James Bliss, vol. I (1847), 152-82; *Documents Illustrative of English Church History*, 518-20.
40 Tyacke, 'Religious Controversy', *History of the University of Oxford*, IV, 585; G. E. Gorman, 'A Laudian Attempt to "Tune the Pulpit": Peter Heylyn and his Sermon against the Feoffees', *Journal of Religious History*, VIII, 333-49; S.A. 6000/17448 (will, proved 1632).
41 *O.D.N.B.* Sir Robert Wright and Bishop Robert Wright.
42 Lichfield Record Office B/V/1/53, fos 9-21; *Looking-Glasse*, 279-83; Keith Thomas, *Religion and the Decline of Magic* (Penguin, 1999), 71-4.
43 Lichfield Record Office B/A/4/18, and *T.S.A.S.* 3rd ser. 1, 266. Fisher is described in the subscription book as a lecturer of Birmingham – he was not the Samuel Fisher of Stratford with whom he is sometimes confused. In July 1635 he was presented to the rectory of Upton Magna by another of the godly patrons in the area, Walter Barker of Haughmond.

44 Bodley Bankes MS 64/8 (I am grateful to Kenneth Fincham for this reference); Bodley Gough Shropshire, 12, fo. 204v, 14 Jan. 1634/5; Esther S. Cope, 'Politics without Parliament: The Dispute in Shropshire in the 1630s', *Huntingdon Library Quarterly* 45 (1982), 271-8.
45 *Anglicanism*, ed. P. E. More and F. L. Cross (London, 1962), 702-18 (Laud's Articles); *C.S.P.D. 1635*, xxxvi-xxxvii (Brent's visitation).
46 William Brereton, *Travels in the United Provinces, England, Scotland and Ireland* (Chetham Society, I, 1844), 186-7. St Chad's churchwardens accounts do not survive.
47 For these events see Coulton, 'Rivalry and Religion'.
48 Coulton, 'Rivalry and Religion', 44-6.
49 *Reliquiae Baxterianae* ed. Matthew Sylvester (London, 1696), 1-18; *Documents Illustrative of the History of the English Church*, 535-51; Hugh Trevor-Roper, *Archbishop Laud* (2000), 390-406.
50 Coulton, 'Rivalry and Religion', 46-7; Clarke, *Generall Martyrologie*, 470-1; S.A. 6001/290, 30 August 1642; Edward Hyde, Earl of Clarendon, *The History of the great Rebellion,* ed. Roger Lockyer (Oxford, 1967), 38.

Chapter 5

1 Austin Woolrych, *Britain in Revolution* (Oxford, 2002), 219-36; *H.M.C. Fifth Report* Part 1, App., 30; *H.M.C. Thirteenth Report* I, 144-5; H. Beaumont, 'Events in Shropshire at the Commencement of the Great Civil War', *T.S.A.S.* LI (1941-43; *'Ottley Papers', T.S.A.S.* 2nd ser., VI, 27-38.
2 Charles Spencer, *Prince Rupert. The Last Cavalier* (London, 2007).
3 *H.M.C. Fifth Report*, Part 1, App., 30; *H.M.C. Thirteenth Report,* I, 144-5; 'Ottley Papers', *T.S.A.S.* 2nd series, VI, 27-38.
4 Ronald Hutton, *The Royalist War Effort 1642-46* (Harlow, 1986); Richard Gough, *The History of Myddle* (Penguin, 1981), 72.
5 *H.M.C. Thirteenth Report,* Part I, 144-5; *Fifth Report,* 49; J.R. Phillips, *Memoirs of the Civil War in Wales and the Marches, 1642-1649* (2 vols, London, 1874), I, 109-15, II. 16-19, 30-31, 42-3; S.A. 6001/290, 17 October 1642.
6 'Sheriffs of Montgomeryshire', *Montgomeryshire Collections* XXVII, 156-7; P.R.O. SP28: I am grateful for the latter reference to Dr Alan Thomson of the University of Hertfordshire.
7 John Morrill (ed.), *Reactions to the English Civil War 1642-1649* (Basingstoke, 1982), 31, 37.
8 *Tracts Relating to Military Proceedings in Lancashire,* Chetham Society 2 (1844), 210.
9 Phillips, *Memoirs of the Civil War*, II, 42-3.
10 John Morrill, *Cheshire 1630-1660: County Government and Society during the English Revolution* (Oxford, 1974), 129.
11 'Ottley Papers', *T.S.A.S. 2nd ser.* , 269-73, 279.
12 *H.M.C. Fifth Report,* 104; *O.D.N.B.* earl of Denbigh.
13 *H.M.C. Fourth Report,* part I, 267-76 (Civil War letters); W.J. Farrow, *The Great Civil War in Shropshire* (Shrewsbury, 1926): list of Shropshire Parliamentary Committee.
14 Roy Sherwood, *The Civil War in the Midlands 1642-1651* (Stroud, 1997), 27-29.
15 ibid, 37-9; Martin Bennett, *The Civil Wars Experienced* (London, 2000), 94-5.
16 *V.C.H. Shropshire* III, 112; Thomas Malbon, *Memorials of the Civil War in Cheshire,* Record Society of Lancashire and Cheshire, XIX (1889), 75-83.
17 *Documents Illustrative of the History of the English Church,* 569-74. For Scotland, Bennett, *The Civil Wars Experienced,* chapter 4.

18 *H.M.C. Fourth Report,* Part I (Denbigh correspondence), 262-3; *Reliquiae Baxterianae,* 43-5; *O.D.N.B.* for Parsons; A.G. Matthews, *Walker Revised* (Oxford, 1943), 303-4.
19 Ronald Hutton, *The Royalist War Effort 1642-1646* (Harlow, 1986), 135-41.
20 Phillips, *Memoirs of the Civil War,* I, 183-219, II, 134-5; *H.M.C. Fourth Report,* 263-5.
21 Gough, *History of Myddle,* 74-5; B. Coulton, 'Moreton Corbet', 188.
22 Morrill, *Reactions to the English Civil War,* Introduction, 8.
23 Malbon, *Memorials,* 130-40.
24 ibid; *Reliquiae Baxt.,* 45.
25 *H.M.C. Fourth Report,* 268-70; *O.D.N.B.* Newport.
26 D.C. Gilbert, 'Clubmen in South West Shropshire 1644-45', *T.S.A.S.* 68 (1993), 93-8.
27 Gough, *History of Myddle,* 171; R.N. Dore (ed.), *The Letter Books of Sir William Brereton,* I, Record Society of Lancashire and Cheshire, 123 (1984).
28 *Brereton Letter Books,* I, 45-7; *A More Exact and Particular Relation of the taking of Shrewsbury ...by Lieutenant Collonel William Reinking Commander in chief in that Design,* published by Authority, London, 1645; Mytton's reply, Thomason Tract 284, 10.
29 *Brereton Letter Books,* I, 45-7; Phillips, *Memoirs of the Civil Wars,* I, 289-328.
30 Bodley, Tanner MSS, 60, fo. 11; *Dictionary of Welsh Biography* (Oxford, 1959), 679 (Mytton): Mytton's new command was made on Mackworth's advice.
31 S.A. 6001/290 (unpaginated); *Register of St Chad's,* 171.
32 B. Coulton, 'Thomas Hunt of Shrewsbury and Boreatton', *T.S.A.S.* LXXIV (1999), 33-42; *Reliquiae Baxterianae,* 46.
33 Owen and Blakeway, II, 147, 261, 281; J.E. Auden, 'Ecclesiastical History of Salop', *T.S.A.S.* 3rd ser., VII, 257, 260; Fisher, *Annals of Shrewsbury School,* 173-6.
34 James Hall, *A History of Nantwich* (1883), 295-479; *St Chad's Register,* xviii, 179, 191.
35 Charles Carlton, *Charles I. The Personal Monarch* (2nd ed., London, 1995), 294, 308-9.
36 Morrill, 'The Church in England, 1642-49', in *Reactions to the English Civil War,* 89-114; William Shaw, *History of the English Church,* I, 406-12; J.E. Auden, 'Ecclesiastical History of Shropshire during the Civil War, Commonwealth and Restoration', *T.S.A.S.* 3rd ser., VII (1907), 263-72; B. Coulton, 'The North Shropshire Presbyterian Classis', *T.S.A.S.* LXXIII (1998), 33-43.
37 Philip Benedict, *Christ's Churches Purely Reformed* (Yale, 2002), 398; Robert Halley, *Lancashire: Its Puritanism and Nonconformity* (Manchester, 1872), 284; Geoffrey Robertson, *The Tyrannicide Brief* (London, 2006), 31.
38 G.E. Aylmer, *Rebellion or Revolution? England from the Civil War to the Restoration* Oxford, 1986), 92-100; Owen and Blakeway, I, 468; J.E. Auden, 'Shropshire and the Royalist Conspiracies, 1648-1666', *T.S.A.S.* 3rd ser., X (1910), 87-103. Fairfax and Cromwell put down various risings; Cromwell's victory at Preston, Lancashire, in August ended the Scottish threat. Many Scots prisoners were housed in churches, including those in Shrewsbury, as they awaited transportation. The Derby House Committee relied on Mackworth to safeguard the Welsh border adjacent to Shropshire, especially Montgomery Castle: *C.S.P.D. 1648-9,* 236-52.
39 David Underdown, *Pride's Purge. Politics in the Puritan Revolution* (Oxford, 1971), 361-98; Austin Woolrych, *Britain in Revolution,* 427-8; Lucy Hutchinson, *Memoirs of the Life of Colonel Hutchinson* (Everyman, 1995), 233; Auden, 'Shropshire Royalist Conspiracies', 109-10; Robertson, *Tyrannicide Brief,* 8, 124.
40 Barbara K. Lewalski, *The Life of John Milton* (Oxford, 2000), 230; Robertson, *Tyrannicide Brief,* 208; Theophilus Philopatrius [Thomas Paget], *A Religious Scrutiny* (1649). It is not

known if Paget and Milton were aware of each other, though Nathan Paget (son of Thomas) was the poet's friend. For *Eikon Basilike* see Sean Kelsey, 'The King's book', in Nicholas Tyacke (ed.), *The English Revolution c.1590-1720. Politics, Religion and Communities* (Manchester, 2007), 150-68.

Chapter 6

1 *C.S.P.D. Commonwealth*, vol. 1, 1649-50, 1-9; Ronald Hutton, *Charles II* (Oxford, 1989), 32-3; *O.D.N.B.*, Anne Fairfax, Thomas Fairfax; *The Poems of Thomas Third Lord Fairfax* ed. Edward Bliss (New Haven, 1909), 281-2. From 2 January 1650 the engagement to be faithful to the Commonwealth was imposed on all adult males.

2 Auden, 'Royalist Conspiracies', 112-5; *C.S.P.D. Commonwealth,* I, 231, 444-5, 503 (items 15,16).

3 *Reliq. Baxt.*, 64. For the controversy see J. T. Wallace, *Destiny His Choice: the Loyalism of Andrew* Marvell (Cambridge,1968), 43-68; Edward Vallance, 'Oaths, Casuistry and Equivocation: Anglican Responses to the Engagement Controversy', *Historical Journal* 44 (2001), 59-77.

4 Whitelocke, *Memorials of the English Affairs* (1732), 444; Paget, *Religious Scrutiny* (1650), 23-4. The prefix 'Saint' had generally been dropped at this time for churches and parishes.

5 *C.S.P.D. Commonwealth, 1650,* 20; W. R. Williams, *The History of the great Sessions in Wales 1542-1830* (Brecknock, 1899), 36-7; *Life of Adam Martindale*, Chetham Society, IV (1845), 92-8; *Autobiography of Henry Newcome,* I, Chetham Society, 26 (1852), 24-5.

6 *H.M.C. MSS of the Duke of Portland,* vol. III, 186-8; *C.S.P.D. Commonwealth,* vol. 2, 75; Auden, 'Royalist Conspiracies', 124.

7 Austin Woolrych, *Commonwealth to Protectorate* (London, 1982), 294.

8 Gough, *History of Myddle*, 269; Fisher, *A Love-Token for Mourners ... Unto which is added, An Antidote against the Fear of Death ...* (London, 1655), 183; Blake, *Vindiciae foederis* (1652). The entries in *O.D.N.B.* for Blake and Fisher do not have the correct details of their time in Shrewsbury although other information is useful.

9 Trevor Royle, *Civil War,* 553; Ronald Hutton, *Charles* II, chapters 3 and 4; Austin Woolrych, *England Without a King* (London, 1983), 11.

10 Auden, 'Royalist Conspiracies', 128-32; Hutton, *Charles II,* chapter 4.

11 G. Ormerod, *Tracts relating to Military Proceedings in Lancashire during the great Civil War*, Chetham Society, II (1844), 312-20; *O.D.N.B.,* James Stanley, seventh earl of Derby: after resting at Boscobel he went to Newport in Shropshire where he surrendered. After his death his estates were confiscated and some sold. Barry Coward concludes: 'It is difficult to envisage a more problematic legacy than the one he left his son [Charles Stanley].'

12 Austin Woolrych, 'Milton and Richard Heath', *Philological Quarterly* 53 (1974), 132-5; Lewalski, *Life of John Milton,* 252, 292; *O.D.N.B.,* Nathan Paget.

13 S.A. 6001/290, transcript of borough minutes (unpaginated): 12 Feb. 1651 -20 Feb. 1652.

14 *Calendar of the Correspondence of Richard Baxter*, ed. N. H. Keeble and G. F. Nuttall (Oxford, 1991), I, letter 93; S.A. 6001/290, 18 August, 16 December 1652; S.A. P257/2/1.

15 *Baxter Correspondence*, I, letters 93, 98, 243, 13; Gertrude Huehns, *Antinomianism in English History* (London, 1951), 37-8; *Reliq. Baxt.*, 56-7.

16 Newcome, *Autobiography*, I, 37-40; Christopher Hill, *The World Turned Upside Down* (Penguin, 1991), 208.

17 W.C. Braithwaite, 'The Westmorland and Swaledale Seekers in 1651', *Journal of the Friends' Historical Society* V (1908), 3-10 and *The Beginnings of Quakerism* (Cambridge, 1970), 58-

108; Joseph Smith, *A Catalogue of Friends' Books* I (London, 1867), 647; T. Auden, 'Early Quakerism in Shropshire', *T.S.A.S.* 4th ser., V , 303-4.

18 Christopher Durston, *Religion in Revolutionary England*, ed. Durston and Maltby, chapter 9.

19 *Baxter Correspondence,* I, letter 136; *Reliq. Baxt.*, 85; John T. Wilkinson, ed., *The Reformed Pastor (*London, 1950), appendix 1; N. H. Keeble, 'Richard Baxter's Preaching Ministry: its History and Texts', *Journal of Ecclesiastical History,* 35 (1984), 540-1.

20 Alexander Gordon, ed., *Cheshire Classis Minutes* (London, 1919), 104-5; Newcome, *Autobiography*, I, 46; *Life of Adam Martindale*, 112.

21 *Perfect Diurnal of the day*, 23 February 1652: quoted in Owen and Blakeway, I, 470.

22 David L. Smith, 'The Struggle for New Constitutional and Institutional Forms', in *Revolution and Restoration* ed. John Morrill (London, 1992), 19; Robert S. Paul, *The Lord Protector. Religion and Politics in the Life of Oliver Cromwell* (Grand Rapids, Mich., 1964), 280; *V.C.H. Shropshire*, III, 252.

23 Gough, *History of Myddle*, 160; B. Coulton, 'The Protector and the Preacher', *Cromwelliana*, ser. II, no. 2 (2005), 97-118; Woolrych, *Britain in Revolution*, 542.

24 Robert Paul, *The Lord Protector*, 294-5.

25 J.E. Auden, 'Ecclesiastical History of Shropshire', 283-4.

26 Ronald Hutton, *The British Republic 1649-1660* (Basingstoke, 1990), 62-3; Owen and Blakeway, I, 471. For Vavasor Powell's criticism of Cromwell see Coulton, 'The Protector and the Preacher'.

27 *Documents Illustrative of the History of the English Church,* 576-82.

28 J.E. Auden, 'Ecclesiastical History of Shropshire', 284-5.

29 *C.S.P.D. 1653-4,* 391; *V.C.H. Shropshire,* III, 253; W. C. Abbott, *The Writings and Speeches of Oliver Cromwell,* III (New York, 1945), 321, 558 (note). Cromwell's comment about Shrewsbury is quoted in *Diary of Thomas Burton* ed. J. T. Rutt (4 vols, London, 1828), I, xc-xci.

30 David Underdown, *Royalist Conspiracy in England 1649-1660* (New Haven, 1960), 51, 146-8; *C.S.P.D. 1655*, 255, 257; Auden, 'Royalist Conspiracies in Shropshire', 139-40.

31 Hutton, *British Republic*, 68; *V.C.H. Shropshire*, III, 252; *O.D.N.B.*, Berry; Sir James Berry and Stephen G. Lee, *A Cromwellian Major General* (Oxford, 1938), passim. For the regime as a whole see Christopher Durston, *Cromwell's Major-Generals: Godly Government during the English Revolution* (Manchester, 2001).

32 *Cromwellian Major General*, passim; F. T. Powicke, *A Life of the Reverend Richard Baxter* I (1924), 108; *Reliq. Baxt.,* 13, 57.

33 Coulton, 'Protector and the Preacher', 112; Swarthmore [sic] MSS, I, 1, 64, 179; III, 9.

34 Horton Davies, *Worship and Theology in England ... 1534-1690* (Grand Rapids and Cambridge, 1995), 492-6; Geraint H. Jenkins, *Protestant Dissenters in Wales 1639-1689* (Cardiff, 1992); Matthew Henry, 'Life of Mr Francis Tallents', *Two Funeral Sermons* (1709), 49. No Baptist group is identifiable in Shrewsbury at this time.

35 Baxter Correspondence, Dr Williams Library, MS 59, I, fos 253-6; Newcome, *Autobiography*, I, 48, 52, 55-8.

36 S.A. 2711/C/H/1 St Julian's parish book 1632-93, T. Auden, 'The Church and Parish of St Juliana in Salop', *T.S.A.S.*, X (1887), 188-91.

37 The correspondence is printed in the *Autobiography*, II, Chetham Society 27 (1853), 342-75.

38 For an unravelling of these events see B. Coulton, 'Cromwell and the "Readmission" of the Jews in England, 1656', *Cromwelliana* (2001), 21-38.

39 W.S. Samuel, 'The Strayings of Paul Isaiah in England, 1651-1656', *Transactions of the Jewish Historical Society of England* XVI (1952), 77-87; *Shropshire Parish Registers*, St Chad's, 262.
40 *Register of the Society of Friends, Shrewsbury, 1657-1834* (1903); *An Account of the Convincement, Exercises, Services, and Travels of... Richard Davies* (London, 6th ed., 1825), 31-2.
41 Auden, 'Parish of St Juliana', 35; Judith Maltby, 'Suffering and surviving: the civil wars, the Commonwealth, and the formation of "Anglicanism", 1642-60', *Religion in Revolutionary England*, chapter 7; *Baxter Correspondence*, I, 108-9; H. B. Porter, *Jeremy Taylor. Liturgist* (London, 1979); Robert Wilcher, 'Henry Vaughan and the Church', *Scintilla 2* (Usk Valley Vaughan Association, Usk, 1998), 90-104.
42 *C.S.P.D. 1658-9*, 166-7; S.A. 3365/2778, Prisoners in ward, 1658: I am grateful to Janice Cox for this last reference.
43 *V.C.H. Shropshire*, III, 253; Newcome, *Autobiography*, II, 103, 108-9; *Register, St Chad's*, xxiv.
44 Woolrych, *England without a King*, 45; *C.S.P.D. 1659-60*, 379
45 *O.D.N.B.* Hyde; *Documents Illustrative* ... 585-8;, *T.S.A.S.* 2nd ser., II, 144-7; S.A. 6001/290, borough assembly book, 11 May 1660: that Charles II be proclaimed.

Chapter 7

1 Herbert H. Rowen, *The Princes of Orange* (Cambridge, 1990), 110-30; N. H. Keeble, *The Restoration. England in the 1660s* (Oxford, 2002), 46; *O.D.N.B.* biographies of the royals.
2 *O.D.N.B.* for Andrew Newport and John Mordaunt; *HMC Fifth Report. Sutherland MSS*, 114; *T.S.A.S.* 3rd ser., 4, 141-4; S.A. 6000/17047, 17050, 17057; for Ottley, Owen and Blakeway, I, 478.
3 Keeble, *The Restoration*, 50-2; Tim Harris, *Restoration* (Penguin, 2006), 48-51.
4 *Documents Illustrative of the History of the English Church*, 588-94: Order for Savoy Conference.
5 *Sutherland MSS*, 154-8; Basil Duke Henning, *The House of Commons 1660-1690* (3 volumes, London, 1983). In October 1661 Andrew Newport was chosen at a by-election to represent Montgomeryshire where his friend and kinsman Lord Herbert was lord lieutenant.
6 Owen and Blakeway, *History*, I, 480; W. Phillips, 'The Lords-Lieutenant of Shropshire', *T.S.A.S.* 3rd ser., 4, 157-61; *O.D.N.B.* Vavasor Powell.
7 Joseph Besse, *An Abstract of the Sufferings of the People call'd Quakers etc.* (2 vols, London, 1738), I, 207-9 (Shropshire).
8 Phillips, 'The Lords-Lieutenant of Shropshire', 162-3; Hutton, *The Restoration*, 161.
9 'Shrewsbury MPs', *T.S.A.S.*, 4th ser., vol.12 (1929-30), 215-7 for Thomas Jones; S.A. 3365/2250 (Quarter Session rolls); Fisher, *Shrewsbury School*, 186; S.A. 6001/2338 (Tallents' sermon notes); S.A. 6001/290, 9 August, 12 September, 18 October 1662: borough minutes.
10 Hutton, *The Restoration*, 164; John Miller, *After the Civil Wars* (Harlow, 2000), 173.
11 A.G. Matthews, *Calamy revised: being a revision of Edmund Calamy's Account of the ministers ejected in 1600-2* (Oxford, 1988): entries on various ministers mentioned; *D.N.B.*, Hacket.
12 For the text of the Act see *Documents Illustrative of Church History*, 600-619; for the Prayer Book, Geoffrey Cuming, *The Godly Order* (Alcuin Club/SPCK, London, 1983). The Act related specifically to England, Wales and Berwick upon Tweed.
13 S.A. P257/13/3/2, fo. 212; *T.S.A.S.* 3rd ser., 4, 145-6; vol. 7, 120; *The Life and Times of Philip Henry* (London, 1848), 144; Matthew Henry, *Life of Francis Tallents* (London, 1709), 50.

14 Keeble, *The Restoration*, 118-9; Janice V. Cox (ed.), *The People of God. Shrewsbury Dissenters 1660-1699* (Keele, 2006), Introduction, xviii, lx-lxi.
15 Matthew Henry, *Life of Tallents*, 50; S.A. P257/B/3/2, fo. 212; Owen and Blakeway, *History*, II, 147-8, 218, 281-2, 350, 383; Auden, 'Church and Parish of St Juliana', 367; Kenneth Fincham and Nicholas Tyacke, *Altars Restored* (Oxford, 2007), 305-6.
16 Horton Davies, *Worship and Theology in England*, II, 386-9; Owen and Blakeway, *History*, 488-9.
17 *Diaries of Philip Henry*, ed. Matthew Henry Lee (1882), 135 and passim.
18 *Reliq. Baxt.*, 84, 77; Besse, *Sufferings*, II, 35-40; Hutton, *The Restoration*, 171.
19 Henry Gee, 'The Derwentdale Plot, 1663', *Transactions of the Royal Historical Society*, 3rd ser., 11, 124-42; Philip Henry, *Diaries*, 135; Phillips, 'Lords Lieutenant of Shropshire', 165-73; Owen and Blakeway, *Shrewsbury*, I, 485-6; *C.S.P.D. 1664-65*, 143-4.
20 *V.C.H. Staffordshire*, III, 61; Bodley, Tanner MSS, 45, fo, 13. Hacket was succeeded by the thoroughly unsatisfactory and largely absent Thomas Wood: *O.D.N.B.*
21 S.A. 6001/290, 18 October 1665.
22 Keeble, *The Restoration*, 120-1: for the text of the Five-mile Act see *Documents Illustrative*, 620-3; *Calamy Revised*, passim; Matthew Henry, *Life of Francis Tallents*, 51-6.
23 *Life and Times of Philip Henry*, 165; Coulton 'Thomas Hunt ... 1599-1669', *T.S.A.S.* 1999, 40.
24 Keeble, *The Restoration*, 121-2; *Documents Illustrative*, 623-32; Harris, *Restoration*, 77.
25 *C.S.P.D. 1663-64*, 672; James Parkes, 'Jewish-Christian Relations in England', in V. D. Lipman (ed.), *Three Centuries of Anglo-Jewish History* (Cambridge, 1961), 157.
26 Janice Cox, *Shrewsbury Dissenters*, Introduction, vii-ix. For problems with the Census elsewhere see John Spurr, *The Restoration Church of England* (New Haven and London, 1991), 199-200.
27 Matthew Henry, *Life of Francis Tallents*, 54-5; Cox, *The People of God*, xxi-xxii.
28 *Documents Illustrative*, 632-40; John Evelyn, *Diary* (Woodbridge, 1995), 196, 199; John Coffey, *Persecution and Toleration in Protestant England 1558-1689* (Harlow, 2000), 172-3.
29 Tim Harris, *Restoration*, 136-9; James and Ben Long, *The Plot Against Pepys* (London, 2007).
30 Matthew Henry, *Life of Francis Tallents*, 59-60.
31 John Miller, *The Stuarts* (Hambledon and London, 2004), 169-73: the political labels originated in insults, 'Whiggamores' being extreme Covenanters from south-west Scotland, 'Tories' being Irish bandits. See also Tim Harris, *The Restoration*, chapters 4 and 5. *O.D.N.B.* Thomas Merk.
32 Spurr, *Restoration Church*, 72; Philip Jenkins, 'Anti-Popery on the Welsh Marches in the Seventeenth Century', *Historical Journal*, 23 (1980), 275-93; T. B. Trappes-Lomax, 'Roman Catholicism in Montgomeryshire', *Montgomeryshire Collections*, 53 (1957-8), 17. The Jesuits encouraged cults such as that of Winifred and Eiluned of Brecon, with processions to their holy wells, as a means of reinforcing Catholic identity. Comparable cases occurred elsewhere in Europe: *Religion and superstition in Reformation Europe*, ed. Helen Parish and William Naphy (Manchester, 2002),14.
33 Owen and Blakeway, *History*, II, 216-8, 383; Francis Tallents, *A Short History of Schism; For the promoting of Christian Moderation and the Communion of Saints* (London, 1705), 103-12; *Life and Times of Philip Henry*, 190-1; G. Vane, 'Two Rectors of Whitchurch', *T.S.A.S.* 2nd ser., 12, 295-6: Fowler was restored to Whitchurch in 1667; the patron was the earl of Bridgewater. For the visitation reports, *C.S.P.D. 1682*, 362, 343.

34 John Miller, *The Stuarts*, 178; Tim Harris, *Revolution. The Great Crisis of the British Monarchy, 1685-1720* (Penguin, 2006), 40-1.
35 Owen and Blakeway, *History*, 493; Richard Gough, *History of Myddle*, 173-4.
36 *Documents Illustrative*, 641-4: Declaration of Indulgence, 1687; Owen and Blakeway, *History*, 495-6; Gough, *History of Myddle*, 235; 'Extracts from a MS Book at Sweeney Hall', *T.S.A.S.*, 4th ser., 7, 121-3: Sir Richard Allibone presided over the northern assizes in 1687, *O.D.N.B.*
37 Harris, *Revolution*, 269-307; 'MS at Sweeney Hall', 124; Owen and Blakeway, *History*, 499: they suggest that Lord Newport was the recipient but this is unlikely. *O.D.N.B.* Newport, More, Herbert, Harley. Sir Edward Harley, like his father, was a good friend of Tallents and Bryan – see the correspondence from the 1690s in *Congregational Historical Society*, 8 (1920-23) Newport House is now the Guildhall.
38 *Documents Illustrative of English Church History*, 645-64; Act of Settlement 1700, 664-70; John Coffey, *Persecution and Toleration in Protestant England*, 197-200; Nicholas Tyacke, *Aspects of English Protestantism c. 1530-1700* (Manchester, 2001), 77.
39 Janice Cox, *The People of God*, Introduction, x-xi.
40 *Life of Francis Tallents*, 57-8; *A Sermon ... by Thomas Dawes, B.D.* (1695); George Herbert, *The Complete English Works* (Everyman, 1995), 106-7, 195-254.

Index

Also from Logaston Press

St Laurence's Church, Ludlow. The parish church and people, 1199-2009
by David Lloyd, Margaret Clark and Chris Potter

This is in part a book about the physical church: its architecture, its furnishings and glass. But it is even more a book about people: those to whose lives the tombs and memorials in the church bear witness, and many others who have also played their parts in the history of St Laurence's.

The authors' careful research has uncovered the contributions of rectors, readers and other parish clergy, as well as many a tale (not all complimentary) of parishioners and visitors to the church. From the medieval Palmers Guild to the modern Team Ministry, they have traced the story of St Laurence's and its people. From the great harvest of information they have gathered, the authors have gleaned many insights, discerning trends in religious observance, changing attitudes to the clergy, and shifting views and allegiances among the clergy themselves. They also shed light on relations between the church and the townspeople of Ludlow, especially as represented by the Borough Corporation – all this against the dramatic backdrop of the history of the church in England through the centuries.

272 pages with 70 black and white and 25 colour illustrations
Paperback £12.95 (ISBN 978 1 906663 40 7)

The Shropshire Home Guard
by Bernard Lowry

The Home Guard, like its forerunner the Local Defence Volunteers, was formed in 1940 in response to the likely threat of an invasion of Britain that would involve German paratroop attacks aided by fifth columnists as had happened in Belgium and Holland. The Home Guard was a volunteer force that would defend its local area, territory well known to them, leaving the regular Army to concentrate on repelling the main thrust of any invasion. Shropshire was included in these plans, not least because it was feared that spies could be present anywhere in the country, and it was feared that the invasion might well come through Ireland directed towards the north Wales coast.

In its early days the force in Shropshire was poorly equipped in terms of both uniforms and weaponry, but as its role changed over the months, from keeping an eye out for parachutists to setting up road blocks, defending localities and forming more mobile units, the uniforms arrived and the weaponry improved. Towards the end of the war the Home Guard was equipped with machine guns and even lightly armoured cars.

The story of the Home Guard in Shropshire as told in this book is drawn from records held in Shropshire Archives and stories told by former members. It thus combines official documents and orders with personal accounts of what it was like to be a member —and what did and didn't happen in practice.

128 pages with 45 black and white illustrations
Paperback £10 (ISBN 978 1 906663 46 9)

Also from Logaston Press

Shropshire Almshouses
by Sylvia Watts

This book considers the nearly 40 surviving almshouses in the county, founded between the 12th and 20th centuries. Their history is often intriguing: the personalities of the founders, the sometimes diminished enthusiasm of his or her descendants when faced with repair bills, the greater or lesser efforts of Trustees to manage the buildings down the decades, the degree of social control to which the residents were subjected, and the ways which those residents found to evade the rules and regulations. The buildings themselves are often of architectural merit, and now add extra character to their surroundings. An Introduction surveys the architectural trends and also looks at the provision of almshouses across the county and how it compared with other parts of the UK, whilst the Gazetteer looks at each group of almshouses in detail, more so in some cases than in others due to the different survival rate of historical documents.

144 pages with 50 colour and 15 black and white illustrations
Paperback £12.95 (ISBN 978 1 906663 31 5)

The Folklore of Shropshire
by Roy Palmer

Shropshire's folklore is presented in a series of themed chapters that encompass landscape, buildings, beliefs, work, seasons, people, music and drama. In the eleven chapters the county's rich store of folklore unfolds in a way that allows you to dip into what most intrigues, or to read from start to finish. Here are stories of mark stones, stone circles, giants, tunnels, dragons, rivers, meres, pools, hills, church sites changed by the devil, vengeful spirits, bull and bear baiting, cockfighting, fairs, herbal remedies and those which involve peculiar activities, minstrels, histriones, waits, charmers and 'cunning folk', ghosts, witches, bountiful cows, of characters such as the early saints, Caratacus, Edric the Wild, Humphrey Kynaston, Jack Mytton and even recent folklore surrounding Hilda Murrell, of tales of the Civil War and of Hopton Quarter, of celebrations and customs surrounding times such as Easter, Christmas, All Souls' Eve, Ascension Day and Palm Sunday along with the likes of 'burning the mawkin', 'tin panning' and wife selling, of rhymes that link villages, ballads that tell of events in the county's past, of folk plays and mummers—to mention just some of what is included.

352 pages with over 250 photographs, drawings and samples of music
Paperback £12.95 (ISBN 978 1 904396 16 1)